W9-BCK-637

THE FREE PRESS

New York   London   Toronto   Sydney   Singapore

IN THE CLASSROOM

Dispatches from an Inner-City School That Works

MARK GERSON

THE FREE PRESS
A Division of Simon & Schuster Inc.
1230 Avenue of the Americas
New York, NY 10020

Designed by Carla Bolte

Manufactured in the United States of America

10 9 8 7 6 5 4 3 2 1

Library of Congress Cataloging-in-Publication Data

Gerson, Mark.
    In the classroom : dispatches from an inner-city school that works/
Mark Gerson.
        p.   cm.
    ISBN 0-684-82756-5
    1. St. Lukes's High School (Jersey City, N.J.)   2. Education,
Urban—New Jersey—Jersey City.   3. Catholic schools—New Jersey—
Jersey City.   4. Socially handicapped youth—Education (Secondary)—
New Jersey—Jersey City.   I. Title.
LD7501. J6785G47   1997
373.749'27—DC20   96-26333
                                                                CIP

For Rick, the best brother one could have

Author's note: All events recorded here are true. Quotations are closely adapted from actual conversations, and written material is quoted verbatim. Although a few events have been rearranged chronologically for thematic purposes, the circumstances of such events remain wholly factual. In order to protect the privacy of real people, I have changed names and created characters that are composites of the people I worked with in the 1994–95 school year.

Contents

....

Introduction

"I've seen the charm of Jersey City, but first let me remark, I've seen it from the Empire State solarium." The voice of Ella Fitzgerald filled my car as I approached the tollbooth at Exit 14C on the New Jersey Turnpike. Two great American landmarks rose to my right: the skyline of New York City, its skyscrapers poised to house a typical day of heavy commerce, and the Statue of Liberty, rising majestically from the still waters of the Hudson River and growing larger as I approached what might charitably be called her second home—Jersey City, New Jersey.

As Fitzgerald suggested, Jersey City is, and has always been, in the shadow of her great neighbor to the east. But longtime residents know that Jersey City has quite a history and identity apart from her wealthier cousin's. The federal government spent a good part of Prohibition trying to convict the flamboyant bootlegger Dutch Schultz, a man too smart for the government but apparently not smart enough for Jersey City's streets: he was gunned down on October 23, 1935, in a steak house. In that same year a 20-year-old singer who called himself "The Romancer" was making his debut on Jersey City station WAAT. The Romancer's relatives and friends in the area probably recognized the crooner as a local boy from the next town over, Hoboken. They probably recognized him as Francis Albert Sinatra. Since those days, Jersey City has gone from being a sometimes rough and sometimes sleepy adjunct to its eastern neighbor to representing an impoverished, often crumbling part of the nation known as the "inner city."

Jersey City is now the city that sends more politicians to jail than to Washington, and it leads the nation in one rarely discussed category: the percentage of public school teachers whose children attend private and parochial schools. It is also the city where I had my first job out of college—as a tenth-grade United States history teacher at St. Luke High School.

In the early spring of 1994—my senior year at Williams College—I was faced with the same question college seniors all over the country face: What should I do next year? Before that point, my friends and I had choices but never choices *about* choices. We had to choose a college, but the fact that we were going to go to college was never at issue. We had to decide what to do for the summer, but the fact that every summer ends in August limited the possibilities. In school we chose our courses, activities, and friends—but always from a clearly defined, limited, and preselected pool. Now, suddenly, we were thrust in the position of making a real decision, one that was not preordained and that could determine much about the course of our lives.

George Will once wrote that success begins not in knowing your destination but in knowing where to point your feet. Through their families, friends of their parents, professors, alumni, and the career office, graduates of schools like Williams are provided with three primary directions in which they can point their feet: some go to graduate school to obtain the Ph.D. degree they will need to become college professors; more go to professional schools, where they will study to become lawyers and doctors; and some go into business, which for Williams graduates generally means an investment bank or a management consulting firm. Of course, these avenues do not account for everyone, but they come pretty close.

I decided at some point to go to law school. A lot of the people I respect in a variety of fields have law degrees, so it seemed like the right thing to do. In January of 1994 I applied to two law schools, Harvard and Yale, and was happy to be accepted at both. One visit to Yale confirmed what I had already heard: it is a friendly place with no grades. I decided to go there.

Yale Law School has a generous deferral policy: once admitted, students can hold their spot while spending a couple of years working or obtaining a graduate degree. When this policy was explained to students who visited the campus in the spring, I became quite intrigued. I grew up in Short Hills, New Jersey, an affluent suburb of New York City in which nearly all adults have obtained the highest degree in their field from a top school. Success in Short Hills is so prevalent that children cannot help but grow up and think it perfectly ordinary. Not far from Short Hills, however, is a whole other world, a world in which people are terrorized by crime, saddled by poverty and without any of the sense of abundance that characterizes the part of America with which I was familiar. I wanted to learn all I could about this other place and perhaps help some kids as well. I decided to accept Yale's offer to take a sabbatical from the standard path of Short Hills residents and Williams graduates and to work in a different world.

I thought that I knew how to do this. During high school and college I had spent several summers working at a camp for poor, emotionally disturbed retarded children and adults from Irvington, Newark, East Orange, and Orange—all cities within ten miles of my home. As a teenage counselor I had had to deal with a young retarded woman whose mother had sold her into prostitution, an older retarded male with fresh belt marks implanted on his chest each week, countless children who would never know their fathers and whose only male acquaintances and relatives were in prison, or just out, numerous people who were made retarded by the drug or alcohol use of their mothers during pregnancy, and the vast numbers who would spend summer days cooped up in a hot apartment were it not for the breather the camp provided. And yet there was hope as well: the 6'8" camper who would stick by my side all day to carry twelve-year-old twins, both afflicted with cerebral palsy; the young man whose biggest concern after his grand mal epileptic seizures was that he not inconvenience his counselors or his mother; the twenty-year-old who would sing church hymns all day as he helped campers who were even less able than he was.

Intrigued by the possibility of spending more than a few months a year with the inner-city poor, I happened upon what I thought was the perfect opportunity: Governor Tom Kean's Alternative Route Program for New Jersey public schools. In this nationally heralded program, college graduates without education degrees could teach in a New Jersey public school while taking education courses at night and on Saturdays. The Alternative Route was a bold effort to bring dedicated and energetic people from various fields into the classroom, where they could share their expertise with schoolchildren. Thus, if Bill Clinton decided to teach high school history in New Jersey after leaving the presidency, the lack of an education degree would not stop him.

The requirements for participation in this program are minimal; all a prospective teacher needs is a college degree and a passing score on the National Teacher's Examinations. I returned from Williams to take this test, which I easily passed. The combination of my test score, my college grades, course work, recommendations, and my published articles amply demonstrated my competence to teach social studies and English.

I sent letters and resumes to the high schools and the boards of education in all eight urban districts within twenty miles of Short Hills. I stressed that I did not care about money; living at home, I would have no expenses, and I did not plan to accumulate any savings that year. I indicated that I would volunteer, if necessary, and would coach any teams or advise any activities for free as well. After a few weeks I had received a reply from only one district—Irvington; a woman called to say that she would start reading applications soon and would get back to me. During the next few weeks I waited for her return call and for responses from the other districts. I heard nothing. Five of my good friends from Williams, who shared an apartment, had sent job-seeking queries in November; by February their rather large basement was literally wallpapered with rejection letters. At the very least, I wanted to add to their decor.

I began to wonder if I was misreading the mores of the education profession. I asked a few people in New Jersey who had connections to inner-city schools if I was missing something. Surprisingly, they all answered yes. And they offered the same advice: Do you know somebody who is owed a favor by someone in charge of hiring at one of the schools? Unfortunately, my answer was no. In that case, they said, go to the board of education office in each city, hand-deliver a copy of your resume and letter of intent in person, and ask for a short interview. That I could do. So I drove from Williamstown to New Jersey and visited one office after another. No one in any office would speak with me, though the secretaries graciously accepted my letters and resumes. I returned to college to wait some more. Still I received no replies, until my mother called to say that a friend of a friend had put in a good word for me at one of the offices I had visited. This was exciting news at the time, but nothing came of it.

So I waited some more. Not even a response, let alone an interview. I still had hope, but I decided to broaden my search beyond public schools and into the Catholic system. I applied first to St. Augustine in Newark, one of the best known urban Catholic high schools in the state. My father, a clinical psychologist, was a good friend of the headmaster, Father Peter, and had done a lot of volunteer work for St. Augustine. We contacted Father Peter in April, and an interview was set up for the day after my father spoke with him.

The interview went beautifully. We spoke warmly about meeting years before and about my father and his partner, of whom Father Peter was a long-time friend. The meeting concluded with Father Peter saying that he had the perfect place for me: one of the history teachers was taking a sabbatical for a year and his position needed to be filled. Subsequent meetings with the chairmen of the history and English departments went very well; I shared a common interest in American intellectual history with the former and discussed how I would coach the mock trial team with the latter. I finished the day in the gym by watching a student–faculty basketball game being played to a packed crowd of screaming teachers, students, and administrators. I barely restrained myself from pointing out to Father Peter that the faculty team needed a point guard and that I could fill that role. Instead, I just watched, but I knew immediately that this was the place for me.

I sent Father Peter two letters within ten days to tell him how much I had enjoyed my day at St. Augustine and that I hoped to teach there in the fall. I received no reply, so I called. "Father Peter," his secretary said, "Mark Gerson is on the phone. Can you take it now, or do you want to call him back?"

"Mark Gerson?" he shouted from what was obviously another room.

"Yes."

"Tell him to stop being so Jewish and not to worry about it!"

"Mr. Gerson," the secretary said with a laugh, "Father Peter says that you should stop being so Jewish and not worry about it."

"Okay," I said, laughing as well, "tell him I won't worry about it." *This is a great sign,* I thought; *the job offer is imminent. "Not to worry about it" means that Father Peter will call me shortly. He commented on my religion to tell me that my being Jewish will not be an issue at St. Augustine. Surely, it's a lot easier to approach this issue casually than to say, "Welcome to the faculty. Your religion does not matter to us."*

But Father Peter's return call did not come, and I had to go to class. Afterward, I called my answering machine from a phone in the library, but there were no messages. Nor was there a message from Father Peter later that day or the next day or later that week. I placed a few more calls to Father Peter, but they too went unreturned. This was strange. My father then asked a mutual friend if she could find out what was going on with Father Peter.

Father Peter told her, "You know Ben Cohen. [Ben Cohen is the nationally renowned baseball coach at St. Augustine.] You know how he is. Well, he and Gerson have the same problem. They're both too Jewish."

I was not yet ready to give up on St. Augustine, but I figured that it would be best to begin looking elsewhere. So I sent out twenty-two letters—one to every Catholic high school in the nearby cities that was listed in a directory I found at the Seton Hall University library. Many of these schools responded but with the news that no job was available. Every Sunday morning I pored over the classified advertisements in the *Newark Star-Ledger*. I responded to a few ads each week for jobs in public schools, which are required by law to publicly advertise any openings. I received no responses. June passed, and July was doing the same when I ran across what seemed like a promising advertisement in the *Star-Ledger:* "History, English and Math teachers needed at St. Luke High School in Jersey City. Call 656-4127 and ask for Sister Theresa." Finally, what looked like a real possibility! I could actually talk with somebody!

I called at 9 A.M. the next morning, and the vice-principal, Paul Murphy, answered the phone. I told him that I was responding to the job offer.

"Okay, can you come in for an interview tomorrow?"

"An interview?"

"Yes, an interview. How's ten o'clock tomorrow?"

"Great!"

I left my house at 8 A.M. the next morning, giving myself a cushion against traffic delays or getting lost. I was in front of the school by 8:30, which gave me time to explore the neighborhood. The school was small as schools go, but still occupied the main spot on a short block. Another building was attached to the school; I figured it housed the Catholic clergy who taught at the school or worked in the church. It was urban all right. I did not spot a tree or a patch of grass, let alone what I considered the staples of extracurricular American high school life: a baseball diamond and a football field. Although the school was in what seemed to be a predominantly residential area in a run-down section of the city, there was not an errant wrapper, can, or piece of garbage anywhere near the building. A few people were milling around on the steps of homes and in the street, chatting amiably as the summer sun began to rise above the New York skyline. There were ten or so cars lining the block, ranging from a glistening BMW with tires that would have fit a monster truck to several beat-up American jalopies from the seventies.

I was early, so I drove around, exploring while keeping my bearings. The obvious economic linchpin of the area was a half mile away; the enormous Newport Mall was introduced by a large sign declaring it to be the product of a federal government enterprise zone. A half mile in the other direction was Liberty State Park, with its open fields off a waterfront, some light manufacturing, and the embarkation point to the Statue of Liberty and Ellis Island. In the few blocks I drove I noted discount department stores, liquor shops, government offices, a couple of diners, a McDonald's, a train station, and a public library. Most of the street signs and advertising posters in stores were in English and Spanish; some were exclusively in Spanish.

With forty-five minutes left before my interview, I parked in a lot across from the school and went down the street to find a place where I could get a Diet Coke and read the *New York Times*. I found a small coffee shop on the corner, its windows plastered with posters advertising cigarettes and ice cream, posters that were surely older than I. I walked inside, noticed a cat wandering around, and approached the counter, which had five or six stools in front of it. An elderly white woman sat behind the counter.

"Do you have the *New York Times*?" I asked.

"The *New York Times*? Usually, yes. But today, no! They drop the papers off in front of the door early in the morning. Today, some colored guy comes and takes them all and goes to sell them on the highway. I paid for them, and I got robbed again. Where are the police? Where are the goddamn police when you need them? The guy steals the papers once a week, at least. I report it every time. And what happens? Nothing. He comes back again. So do I have the *New York Times?* No. Do I have the *New York Post?* No. The *Daily News?* No. Usually, I get to sell them every day. And the *Village Voice* and the *Jersey Journal,* too. But today, nothing. Is there anything else you want?"

I drank my soda and talked with the woman. She ranted for a while but settled down, clearly enjoying the fact that she had company. Her children, I learned, had moved out long ago. The neighborhood they grew up in was no longer. Still, the old woman kept her small apartment and the coffee shop. I told her that I was going to try to teach at the school down the street, and she assured me, "It's a very good school, very religious."

After a half hour I thanked the storekeeper and walked back to the school. I passed through the gate and entered the front door. In front of me was the gym. I looked in and saw a couple of kids shooting baskets. They looked pretty good, but that I expected. What I did not expect was the size of the gym. It was at most three-fourths of regulation size. Two good strides and one could get from the half-court mark to the three-point line on either side. A newspaper article on a bulletin board in front of the gym praised the team. *But,* I wondered, *is this where they played?*

I continued down the hallway to a flight of stairs. I was greeted by a tall black girl who looked to be about fourteen or fifteen years old. "Hello," she said, smiling broadly. "Can I help you?"

"Sure. I am here for an interview. Can you show me where the office is?"

"For the high school?"

"Yes. Isn't this all a high school?"

"No. Now you're on the staircase leading to the elementary school."

We walked down the hall and up three flights of stairs. Posters with inspirational sayings from the Bible, Michael Jordan, and Martin Luther King lined the walls near the staircase. There were more of these posters on the third floor, but they were joined by a different kind of decoration: blown-up photographs of smiling students and teachers at graduation, in classrooms and science labs, and at basketball games. We stopped at an open room that was clearly the office and went inside.

A woman was sitting behind a metal desk on which neatly arranged papers and books were stacked. The office contained just enough room for the desk, a table, a small refrigerator, and teachers' mailboxes in a wooden holder. A first-generation fax machine and a phone rested on the desk, and a copy machine and a coffeepot were near the table. On the table was a platter of cookies, clearly available for anyone who passed through.

"Are you here for the interview?" the woman asked. She was a heavyset older woman, dressed in a beige blouse and a long blue skirt.

"Yes, I am. I am Mark Gerson."

"Well, if you would, please go next door to the library and fill out these forms. I'll come get you in a few minutes."

The library was small, with only enough room for four round tables and a desk in the back. One section was devoted solely to Catholic works. The random assortment of other works ranged from a history of boxing to Daniel Patrick Moynihan's 1973 collection of essays, *Coping*. Many of the books had the seal of another Catholic school on the inside, which had apparently donated much of its collection to St. Luke.

Ten minutes later, the woman returned to the library and led me down the hallway to another office, this one even smaller than the first. It contained only a metal desk, two chairs, and a filing cabinet. A single window overlooked the roof of an apartment building. The woman sat down behind the desk, offering me the chair in front of her. Her nameplate revealed that this was Sister Theresa, but where was her habit? As I found out later, sisters no longer wear their habits in school; they don't want to intimidate the students. Recovering from my surprise, I answered Sister Theresa's questions about my background: Where did I go to school? Did I have any teaching experience? What was it like at the camp I worked at? Sister Theresa seemed satisfied with our conversation and proceeded to tell me about the school: The 430 students came from forty-two different countries. More than half were on welfare. Some didn't speak English, few were white, and many were from broken homes.

"You know, Mark," she said, "the one thing you have to be careful of is that you can't feel sorry for these kids. They may have a hard life, but that makes it all the more important for them to do well in school and get in the habit of turning in their work on time. If they say, 'I couldn't do my homework because there was no room in my apartment to work,' you've got to reply, 'Then lock yourself in a bathroom next time.' These kids can't afford for us to tolerate any excuses."

"I know that, Sister. When I worked those four summers with retarded people at Camp Hope, we had to discipline the campers strictly. And they were retarded. Although they weren't doing any schoolwork, they only painted, swam, and played well when given structure."

"Right. Now, we can't pay competitive wages. Here, take a look at the wage scale." I would start at $15,600.

"That's fine."

"We have excellent benefits, so you won't need to worry about that. I'll check on your references and get back to you very shortly."

At 9 A.M. the next morning I received a call from Sister Theresa. Would I teach five sections of tenth-grade United States history?

Absolutely.

....
RACE

IT WAS THE FIRST DAY OF SCHOOL. I STOOD IN MY CLASSROOM—ROOM 306. It was the smallest classroom I had ever seen. If I had been asked to gauge it, I would have said that it was half as large as the smallest classroom in Millburn High School, the school I graduated from in 1990. The teacher's desk sat no more than a half foot in front of the first row of student desks. Thirty or so student desks were packed close together in three long rows stretching to the back wall. A few inches separated my desk from the blackboard, which covered most of the wall behind me. On one side of the blackboard was an American flag, its pole placed right next to a statue of Jesus on the cross. On the other side of the blackboard was a television set, supplied by Christopher Whittle's Channel One.

I glanced at my schedule and class lists. Of course, the names of students didn't mean anything to me at that point. The only useful information the list conveyed to me was the level of the class. I had all five sections of sophomore United States history, from the top class to the bottom. The classes were titled 10Y, 10E, 10L, 10O, and 10W, with the ability level corresponding to the placement of the letter in the word *yellow*; 10Y was the highest, 10W was the lowest, and the rest fell into place accordingly. My first-period class that day was 10O. Veteran teachers had explained to me that 10O was the class where the less intelligent overachievers meet the more intelligent underachievers. At least, I reasoned, it was a class of achievers.

Students from 10O streamed in at 8:45, milling around before taking their seats. I looked over my notes, going over again in my head the first lesson—why the lives and deeds of long-dead men are worth their careful study. As the bell rang, two stragglers wandered in, jawing at one another as they stopped to face each other in front of the room.

A tall, black, and athletically built boy stood face-to-face with a heavyset kid, clearly of Hispanic origin. "Tell your mother to return my underwear," the black kid insisted. "I fucked her once; what does she want to keep it for?"

"Yeah, nigger, tell *your* mother I'll give her panties back when she gives me back . . . my boxers . . . and shit."

2

"Fuck you, spic mother!"

As they moved ever closer to one another, I could see that my plan to explain to them why history was important would have to wait. "Cut it out right now, and sit down!" They chose to stare each other down instead. As I went between them, a large black girl in the back began to laugh hysterically. I shot her a look. (*Why is she rejoicing at the moment of a racial confrontation?* I wondered.) She understood that I couldn't address her by name because I didn't know it, but she got the point, anyway.

"Mr. Gerson, that you name? You be chillin'. Jamal and Luis are best friends." A good portion of the class broke up laughing along with the girl, whose hysterics intensified now that she had an audience.

Jamal cocked his arm and threw a punch at Luis—a friendly, fake punch that barely grazed the face of his classmate. "Man, it good to see you, yo. Have a good summer?"

"Real good, yo, real good. And this year is goin' to be buggin' too, man. I goin' to study real hard and make at least second honors every marking period. You ain't goin' to see no mo' Ds for this motherfucking spic."

"Same here, man, same here," Jamal concurred.

"Except you ain't a spic. You a nigger."

"And fucking proud of it, man."

Then Jamal and Luis sat quietly throughout the rest of the class, seemingly intent on fulfilling their summer resolutions.

I continued to come to work early that week, often chatting informally with students outside of homeroom before school began. Later in that week I ran into Walt. A 6'3" black student in 10Y, Walt had an excellent sense of humor feeding a charm that made him one of the most popular boys in the sophomore class. Gregarious and outgoing, he was the kind of person to whom others take an instinctive liking. On this particular day he was wearing a Tommy Hilfiger sweatshirt that was several sizes too big, baggy pants, Nike high-tops casually laced, and about eight gold chains around his neck. This outfit would have been unremarkable except that St. Luke students had to wear a uniform: a light blue knit shirt tucked into black polyester pants, no sneakers allowed. The color combination was selected because it could be worn comfortably by both sexes. The uniform policy, we were told during orientation, was to be strictly enforced. Anyone not in uniform was to be sent to the office and would not be allowed to attend class that day. Exceptions were made in special circumstances, as when pregnant girls needed to wear loose-fitting sweat pants. So it was not a borderline infraction when Walt arrived in his street clothes.

"Walt," I said, "I won't comment on your choice of clothing. But I am pretty sure it is not our new uniform. Where are your St. Luke's shirt and pants?"

"In my book bag, Mr. Gerson."

"Don't you think you ought to put them on?"

He looked at his watch. It was 8:12; homeroom would begin in three minutes.

"Yes, I better change now, Mr. Gerson. I got a few minutes, though."

"Why, Walt," I asked, now thoroughly mystified, "would you not wear your uniform to school? Why would you want to have to change clothes by 8:15?"

"I got to, man, I just got to." And with that he went off to the bathroom to change.

After Walt left I looked around. There were several other students scampering to the bathroom as well, all dressed like Walt and carrying bags that presumably contained their school uniforms. I did not know what they were up to, so I decided to find out by asking Walt's class.

"Help me out here," I said to the students in 10Y as the class began. "I saw a couple of you—and a few not in this class—come to school this morning dressed in sweatshirts, baggy pants, and lots of chains. Then these students changed into their uniforms before homeroom. So, I'm wondering, why doesn't everyone just come to school in their uniforms?"

Shanquilla Johnson raised her hand. Shanquilla was Walt's

counterpart among the girls. A 5'2" black girl who looked a couple of years older than her fifteen years, she was popular, outgoing, and very astute. From Day One it became apparent to me that she had an opinion on nearly every issue—from racism to my sports jacket—and would voice it forcefully and articulately. I called on her, though she probably would have spoken anyway.

"It's simple. The guys don't want to get beat up."

"Shanquilla, what do you mean?"

Walt cut in. "She right. If we wear our uniform to school, we goin' have to fight. But if we wear our regular clothes and then change, we okay. That's why the school don't make us wear our uniforms whenever we are in the building—only during school hours. 'Cause then we can change back right after school and go home or to work without fightin'."

I asked the class what they thought about having to change before homeroom in order to avoid a fight. But no one in this vibrant and opinionated class had anything to say at first. It seemed to be a normal fact of life for them, one not deserving of consideration or comment, much as changing for gym was for my high school classmates. After a moment, Charles raised his hand. A quiet and diligent student, Charles was always polite and well-mannered.

"Can I ask you a question, Mr. Gerson?"

"Of course, Charles."

"Why do white people copy our dress?"

"What do you mean?" I asked.

"I mean, you turn on the TV, and what do you see white people wearing? Tommy shirts, big pants that were—you probably didn't know, Mr. Gerson—invented by the brothers in jail. You know, they're not allowed to have belts in jail, so they got baggy pants. They kept wearing them on the outside, as did others, and now the whites be copyin' them."

"That's right," Walt added. "And what about all that rap music?" (The day before, Walt had come to class humming a rap lyric, a lyric so full of vulgarity that I was surprised he would sing it in mixed company. I told him and the other students who had walked in with him what I thought about the misogynist, racist, violent, and hedonistic messages in much of rap music.)

"Oh, yeah, what you be listenin' to, Mr. Gerson?" Shanquilla asked.

"The big four: Frank Sinatra, Ella Fitzgerald, Glenn Miller, and Duke Ellington."

"I ain't be listening to your grandma music," Shanquilla stated emphatically.

"You'll mature some day, Shanquilla, and see the truth," I said facetiously. "In the meantime, can you possibly defend that rap you listen to?"

I waited for a variation of the defense I had often heard from partisans among my acquaintances at Williams, namely, that rap expresses what goes on in the street and reflects the mood of the community. But no one defended rap music, on those grounds or any other. Shanquilla merely repeated that she thought the sound of the golden age of jazz and the big bands was corny.

"What about rap music, Walt?"

"You hate it, right?"

"Yes."

"Well, who do you think buys it? Brothers, yeah. But more whites buy it than blacks. You think we got enough brothers to make Dr. Dre and Slick Rick and all them the top sellin' singers in the U.S.A.? No way. It's whites. They listen to our music and go around singin' them lyrics. Then, when they want, they start dressin' like you, wearin' light blue polo shirts and tan slacks and listenin' to Frank. It ain't right." The others murmured in assent. "What do you got to say to that, Mr. Gerson?"

"Walt, do I wear baggy clothes or listen to rap? No, I listen to Frank, Ella, Glenn Miller, and the Duke."

Loud groans filled the room. Walt quieted his classmates down. "Yeah, you do, fine. But you ain't saying that whites don't buy most of the rap music. You people buyin' the rap music that you, Mr. Gerson, tell us we should throw away for Frank."

Shanquilla spoke up: "I mean, Mr. Gerson, how can *you* say rap is so bad when whites buy so much of it?"

At first this struck me as a non sequitur. I was clearly not a white person who dabbled in black culture by listening to rap, adopting ghetto lingo, and dressing in baggy clothes. So why did the fact that some whites do this invalidate my arguments against rap? Even if my students identified whites with that stereotype, I clearly did not qualify.

I learned more about this puzzling attitude in a conversation with Simon after the bombing in Oklahoma City, which happened during our spring break. Simon, a student of mixed race and ethnicity, was perhaps the brightest and best-informed student in 10E. His big problem was that he had a nasty habit of telling off teachers who inadvertently offended him. In the second week of school a math teacher made a mistake in grading Simon's quiz; Simon called him "a fucking idiot" and left the room, slamming the door on his way out. Two years before, he had been kicked out of public school for throwing a chair at a teacher who had said something to him that nobody even remembered any longer. I told Simon from Day One that I would not tolerate even a rude word from him, but since I was one of the teachers he liked right away, he caused me no trouble.

"Mr. Gerson, I bet you are real ashamed of what happened," Simon commented after the bombing.

"Certainly, Simon, I am deeply saddened by the incident. But ashamed? In order to feel shame, one must have responsibility, and I certainly have no responsibility for it."

He looked at me incredulously, as if I did not understand something completely obvious. "Mr. Gerson, Timothy McVeigh is *white*."

"Yes, and?"

"And you are white, too."

"Simon, are you suggesting that I have any connection with him because we are both white?"

"Well, you are both white, right?"

This powerful and prevalent idea, that white people share common bonds, was as foreign to me as any I would encounter all year. No matter how I protested, nothing I said could rid the students of the notion that whites identify with one another on the basis of race.

Jamal brought the issue up again as he approached me one day after class in the early fall. Despite his encounter with Luis on the first day of school, I had grown very fond of Jamal. Friendly, sharp, and witty, he was a young man whom everyone liked even though his behavior and work ethic left a lot to be desired. He was also the resident black-power activist in the sophomore class. Toward the end of one class in September, after I had apparently assigned too much homework for his liking, Jamal raised his fist in a black-power display of defiance. As tended to happen whenever Jamal did anything, many of his classmates, of various ethnicities, imitated him. "Jamal," I corrected him, "if you are going to be a good militant, do it right. Raise your left fist, not your right one." The class laughed, and they switched fists for a moment before we returned to work.

Jamal was definitely a militant with a sense of humor. He was laughing the hardest when Luis asked me to rewind the movie *Glory* to a specific scene between Denzel Washington and Morgan Freeman so that, Luis explained, "I can use that on Jamal." (After a fight, Freeman had called Washington "a smart-mouth, stupid ass, swamp-running nigger.")

Jamal gave as good as he got, and his frequent comments about whites were intended to be understood sarcastically. Jamal constantly balanced his radical and militant sympathies with his fundamentally pleasant, easygoing nature—not an easy task. Though he sometimes used the issue of race to further his own purposes, he could exaggerate its importance only so much: race was an enormous factor in his consciousness.

"Mr. Gerson," Jamal asked me after class that day, "is Mr. Murphy your brother?"

"What?" (Paul Murphy was the school's vice-principal. In his capacity as disciplinarian, he came to know Jamal quite well.)

"You know, Mr. Murphy. He yo' brother?"

"No, Jamal, he's not."

"Sure he ain't," Kenny responded. (Kenny was a follower of

Jamal's who often was not sure whether the latter's black-power proclamations were to be taken seriously. Kenny erred on the side of taking them seriously—so much so that Jamal, fortunately, often told him to cool down.) "Mr. Gerson, you just don't want to admit it because we gonna think that you got the job because Mr. Murphy is your brother. Don't worry. We ain't gonna be thinking that. I bet your real name is Murphy, and you just disguised it."

A couple of students looked on, waiting to see if the hypotheses of Jamal and Kenny were correct. I went over this in my mind: Paul Murphy is forty years old and looks like an Irish Catholic police officer (which is exactly what he was when he was not at school). I am twenty-two years old and Jewish, and look the part. "Kenny," I asked, "where did you get that idea from?"

"'Cause you look just like him."

"No, Kenny, I don't." We left it at that, my confusion unabated.

This strange situation would be elucidated weeks later in a conversation with Walt's parents. I was watching one of St. Luke's first basketball games of the year, in which we played one of Jersey City's public schools. They played us tough, and the game was tied at the half. We pulled ahead in the second half and were up by three with a few seconds left. One of the opposing players drove to the hoop with almost no time on the clock and was fouled. It was not a smart play for us. No doubt our coach had told the players, "No foul!" numerous times during the last time-out. If the kid hit the layup and the subsequent foul shot, the game would be sent into overtime. A disaster was averted, however, when the kid missed the layup.

He hit the first free throw. He shot the second one and charged the basket as soon as the ball left his hands. A potentially great move: if he missed the shot and could jump over our center and power forward, he could tap in his rebound and tie the game. But he wasn't going for the ball: He was running out of the gym, where there was apparently a St. Luke fan he wanted to beat up. Students from both schools stormed the court, and only the sizable presence of Jersey City police officers stopped what could have become a very ugly incident. The police cleared the gym slowly and methodically.

Waiting outside the school I introduced myself to Walt's parents, who were standing with him. Walt was on the junior varsity team, and he and his parents were waiting for the gym to reopen so that that game could begin. (As a result of the near fight, the police soon decided that it would be too dangerous to have the JV game, and it was canceled.) After Walt introduced us, Mr. Barnett said to me, "I bet your brother wished he could have been at this game."

I thought this was strange. My brother is a basketball fan, but as a sophomore at the University of Virginia, he would have no special interest in a Hudson County basketball game. But how did the Barnetts know I had a brother, let alone that he might be interested in a basketball game, or a fight? "Sure," I replied, "I guess he would."

"Being a cop and all, I bet he would have broken up the fight right away."

Then I realized that Mr. Barnett was talking about Paul Murphy. "Oh, Mr. Murphy is not my brother. All the students think so, and I just can't figure out why."

But I was determined to find out. Later I told this story to Paul, who knows Jersey City better than anyone I know. He was not surprised at the perception of Jamal and Kenny and of the Barnetts; as he put it, "The students think that all white people look alike."

"And the Barnetts?"

"Walt tells them we are brothers; how do they know otherwise?"

Rarely in any of my discussions with the students about race did categories other than white or black come up. This was strange if for no other reason than the fact that a good 40 percent or more of each of my five classes was Hispanic. In its peculiar American usage, and to my brighter students who had heard the term, *Hispanic* refers to people whose ancestors came from countries that were colonized by Spain. All of my students perceived two politically significant races in America—white and nonwhite—and at St. Luke Hispanics were welcome members of the Nonwhite race and were culturally dominated by blacks.

Early in the year I saw Jamal flirting after school with Monica, a Puerto Rican girl in my lowest class. The next day another student told me that Monica and Jamal were a couple. I did not say anything, of course, but thought, *Isn't there a contradiction here? Ordinarily, young men who express themselves with black-power salutes do not date very far outside their ethnic group.* After a while I realized that Jamal did not consider himself dating very far outside his ethnic group. That would have been the case if Monica had been white, but she was Puerto Rican and thus Non-White.

It might have been relatively harmless if the students had thought of the world as White and Non-White and left it at that. If the most egregious misrepresentation generated by such a belief had been the notion that Paul and I were brothers, so be it. But the White–Non-White dichotomy had important consequences in the way the students conceived of their identities. Again and again, from every class, came the comment that Whites look down on "minorities" in the cities, that Whites unite around their skin color and share an intense dislike, usually resembling condescension, toward Non-Whites.

Seeing themselves as the helpless victims of this uncontrollable force, my students responded accordingly. Maura was one of the best students I had. The star of the top section, she had an extraordinarily agile wit, a fervent intellectually curious mind, and an ability to conduct intelligent conversations in either English or Spanish, moving effortlessly between the two. She was half Puerto Rican and half Dominican, a mixture that in Jersey City results in far more street brawls than marriages.

In late September she began an early writing assignment by asking rhetorically, "Am I a racist?" "Absolutely!" was the next sentence. I tried to convince Maura and her classmates that there is no sense of common identity, let alone unity, among most whites and that most are not racist—but to no avail. Gathering evidence from a variety of sources—an unkind look, an unpleasant encounter, a television program—they were convinced of the near-universality of impenetrable white racism.

In a discussion in October, for example, Shanquilla commented that she knows that whites are racist because of what happened the previous year in a grocery store with her mother. "We went in to buy some food. And the white owner be followin' us around. We ain't stealin' nothin', but he just thought we would because we black."

"Shanquilla," I pleaded, "all whites aren't that way."

"Yeah, then why did he do it?"

"Shanquilla, it ain't just the whites who are doing that," Walt added. "I went into one of those groceries on the corner with my brother the other day, and the same thing happened to me. The owner, the guy who was following us, was Dominican."

"What do you make of that?" I asked him.

"I didn't like it. The guy was an asshole."

No one added anything, and the different interpretations of a similar circumstance were striking. Shanquilla used her experience to generalize about a race, and Walt, who had a similar experience, did not. There is nothing in their personalities, backgrounds, or temperaments that would generate this difference. Then why the discrepancy? I think it is because inner-city blacks know so many Hispanics. If the corner bodega owner distrusts black shoppers, his attitude must be considered along with the attitudes of one's Hispanic friends. When familiarity with another ethnic group is so high that its members are virtually invited into yours (under the unspoken category of nonwhite), what room is there for prejudice? But with so few whites in their world, and even fewer respectable whites, it was easy for my students to generalize from one bad experience with one person.

As the old saying goes, you can't beat a horse with no horse. With precious few functional whites in the inner city, my students had little opportunity for experiences that would have countered their views of racism and conspiracies, views that were based on isolated incidents. Given the quality of contact the students had with whites outside of school, it is hardly surprising that their racial attitudes were not more tolerant. The class discussion continued: Maura said that her mother becomes scared whenever whites enter the bodega where she works because no white person up to any good would be in that neighborhood. Carmen reported that the one white person in her neighborhood dumps her garbage in the street and will not let her child play with any of the black kids. And on and on.

Because my students did not live in integrated communities, it was hard to replace their bad notions with good ones, but whenever a rare opportunity to do that presented itself, they were always pleasantly surprised to have their strong suspicions contradicted. Jack, a recent Filipino immigrant in my top section, came to see me after school one day. He was, without a doubt, the hardest-working student in the school. "Mr. Gerson," he announced, "I was chosen for HOBY!"

"Really? Well, congratulations, Jack. That's wonderful."

It took me a second to realize what he was talking about—the Hugh O'Brien Youth Leadership Conference. New Jersey has a conference every year to which one high school sophomore from every school is sent. The students travel to a central location to hear speakers from the fields of politics, finance, and business and to meet each other. I was the representative from Millburn High School in 1987 and had a marvelous time. It was my first opportunity to meet peers whose backgrounds differed from my own. In conversations with sophomores from inner-city schools, from working-class Catholic schools, and from schools in farming communities, I was introduced to different worlds that existed in New Jersey. HOBY would be, I was convinced, as good an experience for Jack as it was for me. All Jack knew about America was what he saw at St. Luke. By meeting students from schools like Millburn, he would surely have the same eye-opening experience I had.

"But, Mr. Gerson," he explained, "I don't know if I should go."

"Jack, don't be silly! Of course you should go. I went and had a marvelous time."

"But I have to meet lots of new people. They may not like me."

"Jack, of course they'll like you. Everyone likes you."

His expression had not grown any less skeptical. "I don't know."

"Well, then, trust me on it. I went there."

"And I'll miss school. My grades may hurt for missing school."

"Jack, that I highly doubt. I can only speak for my class, so I'll tell you what. You go, and you can do an extra-credit paper on the weekend at HOBY for me."

"Really?" He perked up immediately.

I knew Jack would respond well to this added incentive, even though it really made no sense: he had already clearly sewn up an A in my class and had no use for extra credit. "Jack, just go. It will be a wonderful experience."

It was hardly a surprise to me when Jack came into my classroom at 7:30 A.M. on the Monday after the conference with the extra-credit paper.

"Jack, how did the conference go?"

"Great. Read this now, please. I want to know what you think." He handed me the paper.

Recently I went to the HOBY FOUNDATION LEADERSHIP SEMINAR which was a 3-day seminar. I was nervous for I didn't know anybody there so I was also really worried about this prejudice thing. I was worried that the people that I would meet are "valley girls" and whites whom are prejudiced. I was scared that they were going to be down on me because I'm Oriental. But when I got there I just acted normally and showed them that I am a person with class. I used good English and dressed properly due to occasion and I was treated as a normal person. There was no racism or prejudice. I made some very good friends.

I wrote, "A—Great job!" on the top of the paper, but I could not help feeling a little sad. If only others could experience the lesson Jack learned. It is one thing for a peer to be able to say to Jamal or Kenny, "How can you think that about whites? What about Mr. Gerson and Mr. Murphy?" It would be another thing for a peer to be able to say to Jamal, "How can you think that about whites? What about Mr. Gerson? Mr. Murphy? Dr. Harris? Mr. Fields, who always gives us free ice cream at the corner parlor? Mrs. Rossi? Officer O'Hare? Reverend Johnston? Our friends Jill, Pete, and Sarah?" Without a lot of examples to counter the "all Whites are racists" hypothesis, it was easy and understandable to dismiss the few white people they knew as being the exceptions. After all, it would have been easy for my students to conclude that a conspiracy of whites against blacks could go on without me, a couple of sisters, a few other white teachers, and the vice-principal of St. Luke High School.

I was pleased that the students never let my skin color interfere with expressing their opinions on the subject of race. Only once during the year did they moderate such expression, and it had nothing to do with me. I gave a writing assignment to 10Y related to a *New York Times* article on the O.J. Simpson case. A couple of students handed in their assignments as they entered the room, and I put them on my desk. When the class was seated, I walked around the room to collect the rest of the papers. I did not notice Walt, who was sitting at the front of the room and reading the papers that had been handed in a few minutes earlier. After I saw him doing so, I told him to stop immediately, and I gave him a detention for the next day. Walt's action, though, was not a transgression that could be handled through mere detention. I did not know what was in the papers he read, but I was aware of the fact that sometimes my students wrote things that were clearly not intended for public consumption. I thought it possible that Walt had come across material of the most personal kind, which could have consequences well beyond my class, but there was no way to find out without making the situation worse.

When the classroom discussion on the writing assignment began, Maura started to explain why she didn't like white people. "Hey," Walt interrupted. The class looked at him. "Cut it out. Some people in this room might get offended."

Maura started to reply. "Mr. Gerson doesn't get . . ."

"I ain't talkin' about Mr. Gerson." Walt shot a look at one of the two white students in the class, Henry, who was sitting in the back. Although Maura did not know why Walt was silencing her, she trusted his judgment and changed the tenor of her comment. I ended the class a few minutes early, and the students talked quietly as Walt approached my desk. "Read Henry's paper, Mr. Gerson."

"I will, Walt. Later, along with everyone else's."

"I think you should read it now."

I wouldn't normally have buckled to such a demand, but I wanted to know what he was responding to, especially if he planned on sharing the contents of the paper with his friends. Henry's paper went as follows:

I did not appreciate the way this article slandered the white community, with the comments of the people who were interviewed. Quite frankly it made me very upset.

I am sick and tired of the "Minorities" who constantly blame the white community, for the faults and mistakes that they make. I constantly hear "Minorities" who get into trouble say, "If I was white I wouldn't be here."

To me this article tries to say that Mr. Simpson is innocent simply because he is black.

In the article it states that the prosecution said to Ms. Rosa Lopez that right now she is living better than she ever has. The article turns that statement around and claims that this proves that white people think of "Minorities" as freeloaders.

This article puts down white people, in the same way "Minorities" claim white people put them down.

It's people like this who make society impossible for themselves and then blame it on the white community. They are racists and teach it to their kids. If this keeps up, the problem of racism will never end, it will just get worse and worse.

After I looked up from the paper, Walt said, "Mr. Gerson, I think Henry goin' to the other side."

"Walt, let's have this conversation in the hallway."

We left the room and I asked him, "What do you mean, the other side?"

"I think Henry's goin' racist."

"Walt," I responded sharply, "Absolutely not. Henry is not a racist, and you know him too well to even suggest such a thing. He is voicing a perfectly valid opinion, even if you disagree with it."

"He ain't right to think that."

"It is fine that he thinks that, just as it is fine that you don't. But keep in mind, Walt, how you feel being a minority in society."

"But Henry ain't a minority."

"Henry isn't a minority! C'mon, Walt, look around. How many other white people do you see in this room or, for that matter, in this city? And as you yourself noted, how about his views? Who is more of a minority here than Henry?"

The lunch bell sounded, and Walt shrugged his shoulders and walked out. I was very worried and felt that my carelessness with the papers could easily generate a racial incident. I decided to skip lunch and go to the cafeteria to see if this would be the case. Thankfully, lunchtime was uneventful, but I was concerned about the possibility of an after-school incident. I went outside at the conclusion of my last class and saw Walt and Henry huddled together on a nearby street corner. They did not see me casually pass by, and thoughts of what they could possibly be talking about hurtled through my head. Their conversation began to break up, and I heard Walt say to Henry, "Go back, get changed, and meet me at Hamilton Park in one-half hour, man." I froze for a moment, thinking, *I have to get to the park first to ward off the problem I caused.*

"You won't get a single point off me," I heard Henry call out as he walked away.

I felt relieved; that was a close one. In fact for the rest of the year, the racist comments against whites that used to fall so freely from the lips of many of the students were all but eliminated—but not because of anything I said. Before Walt publicly silenced Maura's racial comments that day, the students did not know that any of their friends could possibly take offense at racial comments directed at whites. They did not want to launch a rhetorical missile that would strike a friend.

Nonetheless, I owed Henry an apology for my carelessness and asked him to see me after class. I said to Henry, "I just want you to know that I am very sorry for not guarding the papers more carefully. It was my fault, and I hope you didn't suffer for it."

"Oh, don't worry, Mr. Gerson. No one said anything. But thanks for giving me an A+, though. That doesn't happen all the time."

"Henry, don't thank me—you deserved it. Your arguments were very well reasoned, and your paper was passionately argued and well written. Now, Henry, I am going to make a request that I want you to feel perfectly comfortable in declining if you should choose to do so. I think it would be very valuable for the class to hear your views. You present them so eloquently, and they are views that are not often heard at this school—though they are widely held in the rest of society."

He was silent for a moment. "I don't know, Mr. Gerson. I kind of just wanted you to hear my thoughts. You know."

"I know, Henry. I know that it is tough to have unpopular views and even tougher to voice them. I can't deny that. But keep in mind that I will back you up one hundred percent at all times. Think about it."

"Okay, Mr. Gerson, I will."

We did not have a follow-up discussion. Henry's continued reluctance to speak his mind told me his decision, and it was not one I wanted to pressure him to change. In his papers, which continued to be excellent, he had a forum to develop and express his ideas—even if I was his only audience.

With regard to St. Luke teachers and administrators, racial differences were sometimes a matter of curiosity but were rarely more than that. Race became an issue only when students thought they could use the race of a teacher to get out of work or to obtain higher grades. Many of my students understood that some whites can be easily manipulated by an accusation of racism. Thus, after I gave several black students a detention one day in late October, Kenny insisted, "You a racist."

I ignored his comment with a look. It was not the first time he had responded this way to a detention. "You know, Kenny, you figured me out. I wanted to find a job where I could deal with as many white people as possible, and I found it."

"He played you out!" Jamal shot back. Others started to tease Kenny as well; his scam failed and he was caught. At the end of class Kenny came to see me. "I know you ain't a racist. I just wanted to waste some time. You know, the stuff you were teaching was boring."

Kenny was hardly the only student to charge me with racism. In every class, students would respond to a bad grade or a detention by claiming that I was a racist. They knew that some whites are terrorized by that charge, no matter how unfounded it is. Many students continued to level this charge against me even after they knew it wouldn't work. We had fun with it.

Carmen, always a good student, nonetheless had a penchant for talking and chewing gum in class. She could be caught fully turned around in her chair and gabbing with someone behind her—and she would still deny that she had been talking in class. I gave her the nickname "the Kevin McHale of 10Y," after the Boston Celtics' great who had a long and illustrious career during which—judging by his reaction when he was whistled for a violation—he never committed a foul. Even though Carmen may not have been black (she was the product of, by her admittedly conservative estimate, at least a half dozen ethnicities), she called me a racist several times after receiving a detention. On the day before our break in October I caught Carmen with a double violation: talking to her neighbor and passing him gum. "Detention for Kevin McHale!"

"No way! Mr. Gerson, I didn't do nothin'!"

"No whining at the ref."

"Why did you do give me a detention?" She had not heeded my last instruction.

"Because . . ." I said, thinking for a moment, "because I am a racist." The class broke into laughter, with Carmen joining in.

Because the students trusted the few whites they knew, irreverent comments about race seemed just fine. This was nothing like the atmosphere at Williams, where discussions about race were best conducted in hushed tones and followed by obsequious glances begging for approval from all those present. At St. Luke, from the very start, race was treated as a fact of life, not the third rail of political discussion. The year before I taught at St. Luke, my department chair, Sam Morgan, had given Walt a ride home from school one day. As they entered Walt's neighborhood, Mr. Morgan had become frightened, apparently because there was a gang of youths approaching his car and they did not look friendly.

"Walt," he said, "you got to get me out of here."

Walt, slightly amused, replied, "But I haven't even got home yet. But don't worry, you're almost there. And you know the way back, Mr. Morgan."

"Stop fucking around! You got to get me out of here. You got to get me to . . . to the white section!"

Walt said, "Okay, Mr. Morgan," directed him to the white section, and walked the couple of blocks to his house.

Walt told me the story without any rancor or offense. Mr. Morgan, as Walt and everyone else clearly knew, was not a racist. He was well liked and respected by students of all ethnicities and races. He was simply reacting out of fear—a fear that Walt understood. There was trust between Walt and Mr. Morgan, and the specter of racism was conspicuously absent.

I was banking on this reservoir of trust in October, when I

started to wage a crusade that I had been planning since mid-September, for Standard English. By the second week of school I knew which phrases I would prohibit first: "We be going"; "I ain't goin' to do nothing"; and "Word is bon" and its corollary, "Word up." The latter two expressions meant "That's the truth!" They were used to punctuate a powerful point. For example, if one student said, "I ain't doing no work for that teacher," another might reply, "Word is bon!" Or "Word?" could mean "Really?," I said, "Burr, the sitting vice-president of the United States, killed Hamilton, the former Secretary of the Treasury, in a duel," I might hear, "Word?" Another common expression was, "Yo," pronounced with a long stress on the vowel so that it sometimes sounded like "Yuh-oh-oh." Sentences were ended with this word, which served no discernible communicative purpose. For example: "What's the homework, yo?"

Some of the students cursed regularly in class but meant no offense. For instance, after making a good point in a discussion with Carmen, Walt turned to her and exclaimed, "My shit is sweet!" I had to explain why that was inappropriate. New rules were imposed by early October: Verbs must be used and conjugated, double negatives are forbidden, slang expressions are banned, and cursing is a cardinal sin. I knew that abiding by these rules would require significant effort, considering that the students regularly violated them without even knowing that they were doing so.

I realized that my crusade for Standard English would have to be approached carefully and that entertaining my students' objections might compromise my authority, and I knew that arguing with fifteen-year-olds does not do much for one's dignity. But serious change was needed here—change that could not be accomplished by my activity alone. The only question was, how to approach my campaign for Standard English.

Pure power could work in a sense: I could simply give the students detentions for using nonstandard English. But would the students leave the detention thinking that Standard English is an idiosyncrasy of their corny white teacher? Maybe. They sure would not leave the

detention convinced that their way of communication must be inex-
orably altered. I would have to convince them that changing their way
of communication was in their best interest. I could set an example
and correct them when they speak incorrectly, but long-term success
depends on what happens when I am not around.

Noting that several of the students had said they wanted to be
lawyers, I started my crusade by telling them that an attorney or
witness who once slipped into nonstandard English would have
the team laughed out of the courtroom. "Can you picture O.J.
taking the stand," I asked my students, "and saying, "I ain't be
killin' nobody!'" None could, but they said it was irrelevant because they could turn nonstandard English on and off. "No, you
can't," I maintained. "Look how you talk in class."

Then my students began to defend nonstandard English by
using relativist clichés, such as "You speak one way, and we
speak another. Why is yours better?" And so on. I pointed out
that they had referred to "proper" and "improper" English in our
discussion several times. "Aren't *proper* and *improper* synonyms
for right and wrong?" I asked. They were eventually convinced,
and they agreed to make a concerted effort to speak Standard
English in class. I tried to tell them that they should adopt these
new speaking habits out of class as well, considering that language is not clothing! You cannot simply slip into something
more comfortable when the company leaves. "Mr. Gerson," Walt
responded to one such entreaty, "that just ain't goin' happen."
Several other students let me know that Walt was right. I had no
way to enforce my rules of language outside of class, and they
were not going to change on their own. *Oh well,* I sighed, *I sup-*
pose it is just a limitation that I will have to accept.

After our discussion most of the students began taking pains
to catch themselves before using nonstandard English in my
class. At times they sounded plodding. Maura suggested that her
classmates sounded retarded. "There is hardly any shame in
this," I replied. "Actually, what sounds plodding is, in this instance, the melody of real progress." I pointed out that if Thomas
Jefferson counted to ten before he spoke to ensure that he would

not embarrass himself, it was certainly permissible for students at St. Luke to count to five or six before speaking.

My strongest weapon in my crusade for Standard English was the fact that I liked many of the students' locutions and incorporated them in my teaching. The brighter classes could, even if just to humor me, switch to Standard English with relative success. The slowest class, 10W, had the hardest time with Standard English; they could not adapt to this new form of language and had more difficulty than my other classes in understanding why it was important. In November, about a month after I started my crusade in their class, Shaneka turned to LaToya in the middle of class, said something, and laughed. Shaneka and LaToya were easily distracted; my goal with them was to stop them from talking in class. They needed to learn to be polite and could not be allowed to disrupt their classmates, many of whom really wanted to learn. "Okay," I declared, "detention for you today, Shaneka."

"But, Mr. Gerson, I didn't say nothin'! I wasn't talking."

"Shaneka, I didn't say *anything*. And, yes, you did. You were talking to LaToya. I saw it—it was obvious."

"All I be doin' was asking her a question!"

"Shaneka, I have yet to see anyone ask a question without talking."

"Yo, Shaneka, he played you out!" their classmate Rodney shrieked. The whole class joined in: "Mr. Gerson played you out, Shaneka!"

"Playing out" was a big thing for my students. This term, like pornography, has no exact definition, but one knows it when one sees it. The closest one can come in capturing this important concept is what *Mad* magazine used to call a snappy answer to a stupid question. Playing out was easy to do. Even for those who were usually on the receiving end (like me). For instance, when Eunicia in 10W, who always asked if she could use the bathroom, asked to go for the third time in a week, I nodded my head and said, "Absolutely, Eunicia, you can go in twenty-five minutes," which was when, the students immediately recognized, the class would end. Eunicia smiled and I added, without missing a beat,

"Eunicia, I played you out." The class roared, Eunicia especially. "You got it right," Shaneka told me confidently. "You used *playing out* right."

The term *playing out* was descriptive, but it's not as good as *bugging*. If I was worried about my students cheating, not doing homework, or talking in class and if I let them know it in no uncertain terms, they would say, "Mr. Gerson, you *is* bugging." This term was used when someone overreacted or responded in an especially creative way to a common problem. Shaneka often spent class time asleep, and I would continually try to wake her up. It rarely worked. So one morning I went beside her desk and began to sing "Rock-a-Bye Baby." The class laughed, and Eunicia approvingly announced, "Mr. Gerson, you be bugging!"

"No, Eunicia," I firmly declared, "I am not bugging. When I *bug*, you will know it."

I would have begun my crusade for Standard English when I first noted it—on Day One—but I had to gain my students' trust first. The administration warned the teachers to be extrasensitive regarding race, for fear that one errant remark could spark an explosive situation. The point was well-taken. From the beginning of the year it was obvious to me that everything was reduced to race. In September Shanquilla announced to the class that Oreo cookies should not be sold in the cafeteria anymore.

"Why not, Shanquilla? You think the students at St. Luke need to lose weight?"

"No. Those Oreos are racist. My teacher last year told me."

"And why did he say they are racist?"

"Because it is two blacks crushing the white. It is meant for whites to be scared of blacks. That's why whites take the Oreos apart, so they can eat a black without eating a white. Ever see a white person eating the white part?"

"That's the most ridiculous thing I ever heard, Shanquilla. What teacher told you that? He should be fired."

"You don't know him. It was in public school."

Shanquilla was not kidding. Nor was she alone. If a teacher wore a white shirt or a dark shirt, that had racial significance, as did whether a teacher used a black pen or a blue pen. There was no predicting what could trigger a racial thought, and the administration advised the teachers to be very careful. Although the school's administrators worried that an errant comment or misunderstood remark would accidentally light the ever ready racial powder keg, no such racial incident occurred at St. Luke. However, the public school a mile down the street, Ferris High School, was the scene of a racial conflagration that caught the attention of the national media. The incident started with the following dialogue:

Black student to Puerto Rican student: You are only good at baseball because you are Puerto Rican.

Puerto Rican student to black student: You are only good at basketball because you are black.

Black student to Mrs. Montgomery: You must be good at golf and tennis, because that is all that whites are good at.

Mrs. Montgomery to black student: The only reason why there are so many blacks on the Ferris track and field team is because blacks had to run away from their masters during slavery.

The students walked out in anger. The next day was crucial: their anger could have either dissipated into forgiveness or solidified into hate. It was the latter. After school 150 or so students went to a planned protest that included speeches and chanting. One of the teachers at St. Luke, Jill Riley, was the wife of a Ferris teacher. She was particularly worried about the Montgomery situation, which could rapidly escalate if the politically active ministers and/or Al Sharpton became involved. However, a lucky confluence of events prevented such an escalation: the ministers were busy protesting a nearby high school; they were upset that the administration of the school was insufficiently black. And Al Sharpton? He was busy hunger-striking against Governor Pataki's budget cuts in New York.

If Mrs. Montgomery had apologized, there is little doubt that the matter would have dissipated immediately. Teenagers have short memories and are quick to forgive. But Mrs. Montgomery refused to apologize for anything, and the matter faded into the summer unresolved. I wish the teachers' unions knew when to purge the poison from their ranks. For then the superintendent of schools, Frank Sinatra (that is his name, no kidding; imagine living in Hudson County, New Jersey—the birthplace of The Voice—with that name), would have been allowed to fire Mrs. Montgomery. She was completely wrong, for several reasons: First, a discussion of race has no place in a math class. Second, when talking about race, it is crucial not to appeal to the basest beliefs of the students; they are fully aware of their lowest common denominator and bitterly resent teachers pandering to it.[1] Third, her argument is completely unfounded. Even the slowest students can recognize ignorance and stupidity, and what is more ignorant or stupid than asserting that running from slave masters has anything to do with genes or implying that a generation or two can alter the genetic composition of a race?

My students reacted with a detached curiosity to the Montgomery case. They supported the student walkout, and some went to the rally, but in the same way that I support the New Jersey Nets and go to their games. There was no passion, no sense of comradeship, no sense of let's do that here. Of course, this was little comfort. Once discontent is in the air and the possibility of youthful rebellion is fertile, the energies of youth become a loaded pistol in the hands of a professional manipulator like Al

---

[1]Incidentally, this is one reason why young teachers have to be especially careful. Young teachers often want to identify with the students. They believe that identifying with the students means talking like them, developing an interest in the subjects that interest them, listening to their music, etc. But kids emphatically don't want this. They have enough peers and friends; they don't need another. When a teacher tries to identify with students, the students often think the teacher is vaguely absurd, and they lose all respect for the teacher. Students want their teachers to be the men and women they want to become, not one of the kids. Young teachers must realize that keeping their distance from students makes students more likely to come after school, wanting to talk about serious personal problems. If after the first month of school I had been asked to predict which four students would approach me with their deepest problems, I would have guessed wrong on each one.

Sharpton or Louis Farrakhan. Sharpton, though, is probably not the best example here because my students thought that he was absurd. But Farrakhan and the memory of Malcolm X are different. None of my students were active supporters of the Nationalists or particularly cared about the details of their message. Their support was political in the crudest sense: Farrakhan and Malcolm X were both symbols of defiance and presented a way for others to deal with their own confusion. Whenever Farrakhan came up in our discussion of current events, several black students would invariably raise their hands and crisply say, "Yeah, Farrakhan!" I explained, or tried to explain, that Farrakhan was an evil man, one who not only was virulently racist but had expressed sympathy for Adolf Hitler. Perhaps *explain* is not the right word here because I had nothing to offer that my students did not already know and had virtually no opinions on this matter they did not share—at some level. Nonetheless, Farrakhan fascinated my students more than anyone else, with the possible exception of Malcolm X.

In April, when the year was winding down and the end of the curriculum became evident, Walt said, "Mr. Gerson, I know why we don't study Malcolm X in this class."

"Walt," I replied, "as I have told you many times, we don't study Malcolm X because he was not born before 1865. This class goes up through the Civil War. I am sure that you will cover him next year or senior year when you take Contemporary American History."

"That's not it. We ain't study Malcolm because he said that all Jews were goldsmiths and that the term *jewelry* comes from the Jews, who control all the jewels in the world."

"Walt!" Shanquilla interjected immediately. "That was before Malcolm's trip to Mecca when he stopped hatin' Jews." She looked straight at Walt, almost staring him down. "Don't you be slandering Malcolm!"

In a subsequent writing assignment I gave my students on a historical figure who influenced them, Shanquilla explained her interest in Malcolm X:

My ideas come from me reading and seeing the movie *Malcolm X*. My motto is BY ANY MEANS NECESSARY. That's how I love. Some young people get their ideas from rap songs and people that really don't watch what they say. Some older people don't see that the young people take things the wrong way. It's like the Bible, so many people interpret it in so many different ways. That's why there is so many different religions. Adults need to teach children respect so that children's ideas may be better than what they are now. It's not right for young men to walk around calling young lady's tricks, hoes, booty, bitches, and other things that they mothers didn't name them. Malcolm was against all that.

My students' aversion to anti-Semitism did not stop Walt, Shanquilla, or any of the other students from supporting Farrakhan or Malcolm X. The students who admired Farrakhan did not do so out of bitterness toward Jews or anyone else. Simply, Farrakhan offered them a firm anchor in an otherwise inchoate world. My students had a vague sense that there are conspiracies designed to keep the black man down—a conspiracy by the Los Angeles Police Department to frame O.J. Simpson, a conspiracy by the government to give immigrants the jobs that blacks should have, a conspiracy by the white man to flood black neighborhoods with liquor stores and drugs, and a conspiracy to ensure that black neighborhoods remain dangerous. Once someone was able to provide an alternative to students' suspicions and fears—a refuge from the frightening, unjust world they could not understand or control—his powers of manipulation became nearly limitless. Farrakhan offered my students that alternative.

Farrakhan was hardly the only way for my conflicted students to channel their confusion. During a discussion of current events, Jermeine brought up something she had heard on a talk show the day before. Jermeine was a good student in 10E; when she put her mind to it, she did very well.

"I was watching this show, yo, and this black lady was on saying that she wanted reparations."

"Jermeine, why don't you explain to the class what reparations are?"

"She said that she wanted the United States government to pay every black person a million dollars to compensate them for having ancestors who were enslaved."

Simon replied, "It's like saying, 'Oh, slavery has hurt me so much. It will feel all better if you give me a million dollars.'"

"Well," said Jermeine, "maybe."

"Jermeine," I asked, "what do you think?"

"One million dollars is too much money. Definitely too much."

"How much is right?"

"I don't know."

"Let's put it this way. If the government said that it was going to give X amount of dollars to blacks for having ancestors who were enslaved and if you could fill in the X, would you do it?"

"I don't know. I mean, I wasn't a slave or anything."

"Then why the hesitation?"

"Yeah," Simon said, "why don't you think the woman is crazy?"

"I know what to do," their classmate Carlos volunteered. "Give all the blacks a bucket of fried chicken and grits, and they'll all be happy!"

The class roared, and Jermeine had a retort for Carlos: "Can't do that, Mr. Gerson. Then we'll have to give all the Puerto Ricans tacos and beans."

"Okay, Jermeine, you got him back. Now, seriously. Take Simon's question. Why don't you think that woman was crazy?"

"Maybe she is. But I see where she's coming from. She knows what is missing."

"What's that?"

"Recognition. We need more recognition."

One possible source of recognition—the one most frequently tried in American institutions—came to the fore in the fall. None of the students had ever heard of affirmative action before this year, and I did not intend to bring it up. But in November all of the history teachers disseminated questionnaires from a college placement group. The survey was clearly trying to assess the students' interests and academic backgrounds. The questions solicited information about intended majors, grade point averages, and even hobbies; they were answered quietly and without incident until the students reached the end of the survey, where the students were asked to identify their race. In every class, the students were appalled. Someone in each section asked, amid echoes of support from the class, "What does my race have to do with anything?" Is this survey racist? My students know.

"No, the survey is not racist," I replied. "You raise good questions about whether race should ever be an issue with something like this, but those questions are for another day. Fill in your race for now."

"Forget it," Jamal came back.

"Look. They want to know your race because they want to help you if you are black or Hispanic. You may not want to be helped on account of your race, and, believe me, I can certainly appreciate that. But this can help you get scholarship money."

"Mr. Gerson," Luis responded, "how can you tell us to respond to such racism?"

"This is bullshit," Jamal proclaimed. "I ain't helpin' no racist."

"Jamal," I pleaded, "it will help you."

"I don't need no help from no one who thinks the black man need help." With that, he ripped up the survey and was joined by several of his classmates.

Only a handful of students among all of my classes filled out that part of the form; many more were offended that I told them to do so. I had mixed feelings about asking them to do this and was only slightly encouraged when I remembered that the libertarian economist Milton Friedman accepts Social Security. However, the students did not share this view; they refused on principle to accept anything from an enterprise they considered morally sullied. They sensed hypocrisy in those who distributed the questionnaire and in me for encouraging them to complete it, and they responded accordingly.

The issue of affirmative action did not come up again—except for one instance: After class one day Maura and I were talking at my desk. "Mr. Gerson," she said, cutting off our conversation for a moment and pointing to a magazine lying facedown, "what is that you are reading?"

"It's the *New Republic*," I said, flipping it over.

"Affirmative Action by Class," she said, reading the title of the lead story on the cover. "Isn't affirmative action what those college forms were about? I remember you sayin' something like that."

"Yes, you're right."

"What is affirmative action by class?" The next period was about to begin, so I asked her to come after school so we could discuss the issue in depth. She agreed to come, and after the final bell sounded we went to the library.

That afternoon I presented the issue as dispassionately as possible, and Maura voiced opposition, as she had earlier in the year. But the idea of affirmative action by class interested her, and she asked if she could write an extra-credit paper on the article. Of course I said yes. And this is what she wrote:

Affirmative action states that preferences in education and public contracting should be based on race. A new idea has been suggested, which states that all of the above should be based on class, not race.

When applying for a job or school, wouldn't you want to be chosen because you are qualified for the position and not because of what racial background you are from? Being given a job because of your race/color is very degrading. This can also bring about conflicts between people. Let me enlighten you on what is meant by these "conflicts" that can be brought about.

You are at the workplace and you get into an argument with one of your co-workers. In the middle of this argument your co-worker says, "You got this job only because of your race." Wouldn't one feel like less of a person? Like you really didn't earn the job? Like you just got lucky because you turned out to be the race of their preference?

You know you are qualified for the job because you are experienced and have the skills but how are you to prove to yourself and others that you are truly deserving of the job if you were chosen out of pity because of your racial background? Situations like this one can and would make things worse than they already are.

Class. Judging someone's ability to do work according to one's class is also the wrong way to go about choosing. Your economic standards have nothing to do with performance at school or at the job.

In all, one should not be judged by race nor class because this has nothing to do with one's ability to perform. One should be judged on how well one can do a job or how well one did on an exam like the SAT.

We have to face the fact that racial and social class discrimination continues to afflict our society. That's one problem with the world today. Everything revolves around your racial, economical backgrounds and who you know instead of who you are as an individual person and your ability to do something right or wrong.

Hopefully, people and the government as a whole will realize that your background in a racial or economical way has nothing to do with how well you do in school, perform at the workplace or anywhere else.

"Maura," I said after I had read her essay, "there is nothing that I can add. Perfect." She slapped me five and took the paper to show her friends, who were waiting outside the classroom.

RELIGION

I always looked for prominent ideas in American history that the students could see at work in their own lives. In late October I assigned a rather freewheeling writing assignment asking the students to identify examples of individualism they saw in contemporary Jersey City. I expected the students to respond in the way my friends and I did in high school, that is, with platitudes about the need to develop one's own personal identity, the dangers of conforming to society, and the importance of carving out personal space where one can identify one's own desires and pursue one's own goals. But this prediction of mine ranks right up there with the *Chicago Tribune's* forecast of the 1948 presidential election. Typical responses were the following:

> "Religion, family and hope for the future help me to live with others in society. Religion influences my life a whole lot. Religion brings hope and expectations for me in life. Knowing that Jesus is coming again is what keeps me going every single day in this lifetime. Religion also brings out the best in me." [Maura]

> "This was supposed to be the land of the free, but in those days it seemed as if it was the land of the ignorant. If everyone would turn to religion we would see it through God's eyes, the way we should see it. We would see a very special gift and that gift is the ability to see equality when we look at each other." [Carmen]

> "A factor like religion helps me to be able to live well in my society. If we didn't have religion people would not stand for there morals and respect they want. Instead they would fight, and bring out war." [Charles]

Grace, the most serious and most highly disciplined student in the sophomore class, wrote, "I do not accept any other religion other than the Christian culture but I am not prejudiced toward them." Grace came to see me before school one morning with her friend Jermeine. "Happy Easter, Mr. Gerson!" Grace proclaimed.

"Thank you, Grace, you . . ."

"Grace!" Jermeine cut her off. "Mr. Gerson is Jewish. He don't celebrate Easter!"

Grace looked horrified. "Mr. Gerson, I forgot. I'm so sorry."

"Grace," I assured her, laughing lightly, "don't worry about it."

As soon as I decided to teach in a Catholic school, I knew that I would be in a position I had never before experienced: I would be the only Jew. And if I hadn't thought about it before, Father Peter would have certainly reminded me. Like most American Jews, I had always been aware that I was a member of a "minority group," though that fact never seemed as real to me as the statistic that confirmed it. I had never lived in an environment that did not seem predominantly Jewish, even if demographics denied my impression. Whether I was growing up in a community of upper-middle-class doctors, lawyers, and executives in Short Hills or being educated with the sons and daughters of these people at Williams College, there was never a shortage of Jews. It is, after all, hard to feel like an outsider when even the gentiles curse in Yiddish.

After being hired at St. Luke, I was vexed over how to deal with the Jewish question. The issue had not come up in the interview. This could, I surmised, mean one of two things: that Sister Theresa knew I was Jewish and didn't care or that she thought I was Catholic. I hoped for the former but had even greater hopes that the issue would never arise.

That greater hope evaporated as soon as I looked at the school schedule shortly after being hired in July. The first day of school was Rosh Hashanah, the Jewish New Year: I would have to take the day off. "There is not," I mused to a friend at the time, "a worse way to raise this issue I was hoping would remain dormant." She thought it was pretty funny and congratulated me on being the first teacher in the history of the diocese to take off the first day of school on account of a High Holy Day. But, I decided, looking on the bright side, that at least Rosh Hashanah presented a way to pose the Jewish question once and for all, before the school year began. If when I said that I would have to miss the first day, Sister Theresa said that there was a misunderstanding and that St. Luke could only hire Catholic teachers, I would resign gracefully and go to Yale in the fall.

I did not call Sister Theresa that morning. I wanted to seek out advice on how to handle the situation, how best to present what was really a very simple problem—or perhaps not a problem at all. People were sympathetic, but everyone said it would be better to make the dreaded call sooner rather than later. I continued to put off until, finally, I did what had to be done.

"Hello, this is Mark Gerson," I said to Mr. Murphy, who answered the phone when I finally called. "Is Sister Theresa in?"

"One minute, Mark. I'll find her."

As one moment piled onto another, my nervous state increased with ever-louder heartbeats. Finally, Sister Theresa picked up the phone: "Yes, Mark, what can I do for you?"

"Well, you see, Sister Theresa, I have this problem. The first day of school is . . . I see . . . it is on, you know . . . a holiday."

"A holiday? What holiday?"

"You know, it is . . . well, it's Rosh Hashanah." There was a moment's silence, time enough for a deep breath before continuing. "And I can't work on Rosh Hashanah. I just wanted to let you know that I would have to miss that day, and to be sure it was all right. I understand if it's not."

"OK, Mark, that's no problem."

"Really?"

"No, not at all. I'll see you in a month at orientation."

"Okay, thank you very much." The Jewish question was answered.

I was hoping it would stay that way. The only faculty religious activity that I could see on the school schedule was a mass to be held after an orientation session. This would be no big deal: I had been to plenty of masses before for funerals and confirmations. This mass, however, was unlike any of the others I had been to in large churches; this one would be a tiny mass in a small room with my soon-to-be-colleagues who did not know I was Jewish. While it was highly improbable that anyone could look to see if I knew the prayers, there would, I thought, be one moment when my Judaism (or at least my non-Catholicism) would become quite evident: during Communion, when the Catholics would stand in line to receive the wafer from the priest or nun at the front of the room.

The mass was small and cozy, with twenty-five or so teachers and administrators sitting in folding chairs in the cafeteria. A priest standing in front of us led the mass. After about a half hour, he delivered a short homily that I thought signified the end of the service—as sermons generally do in synagogue. So, I figured, the Jewish question would not be confronted because, for some reason, this service would have no Communion. But no such luck. After the homily, the rest of the people in the room began to line up before the priest—and it was no secret why. As everyone surrounding me stood up and walked past to stand on line, I quickly scanned the room looking for someone else—perhaps another Jew, maybe even a Protestant—whose nonparticipation in the service would make me feel less alone. That was not to be. So I just sat there, alone in the middle of a row in the middle of the room. Here, for the first time in my life, the world was, if for just a moment and in an entirely painless manner, teaching me a lesson that has been painfully evident to almost every other generation of Jews: we are different from Gentiles, not just in our culinary tastes, choice of slang, or holiday celebrations but in indelible ways not of our choosing.

Right after the service, a teacher sitting next to me, Sister Patricia, introduced herself and commented, with a curious voice and an open expression, "I didn't see you take Communion." "I didn't, Sister—I'm Jewish."

"Oh, really!" she exclaimed. "I grew up around Jews. They were so smart, so hardworking, have such good food. It will be so nice to have you around." To the few other teachers who either noticed my lack of participation in the service or overheard my conversation with Sister Patricia, my Jewishness was, at most, an item of mild curiosity. And so I learned that my religion was certainly not an issue at St. Luke—and that continued to be the case for the rest of the year.

Most of the faculty had met Jews before but few had ever been in close contact with any before I came to St. Luke. Incidents recalling this fact happened all the time. For example, I was the one called on to explain that Hanukkah is really a minor holiday (in America, it is really a Jewish Christmas), what matzoth tastes like (cardboard), why Jews don't drink (I don't know), why Jews are so pro-choice (a political rather than religious phenomenon), and why rabbis are not celibate (having children used to be a precondition for prospective rabbis; in fact, marital sex on the Sabbath is a *mitzvah* or "good deed"). And so on.

Far more important than being the only Jew on the faculty was being the only Jew most of the students had ever met. As I found out, the faculty's curiosity about my Jewishness was nothing compared to that of my students. In the second week of school I was in the middle of a lecture on Christopher Columbus when Shanquilla raised her hand.

"Are you Jewish, Mr. Gerson?"

"Yes, Shanquilla. Why do you ask now, in the middle of a lesson on Columbus?"

"Because you look Jewish."

Shanquilla, like most of my students, was greatly interested in my Jewishness—just as I would have been greatly interested in Martians if one taught my sophomore history class. There is no doubt that I would have drawn a vast array of conclusions about Martians on the basis of meeting one, as I realized my students would do about Jews on the basis of knowing me. In the middle of a discussion on the Mexican War, Shaneka in 10W raised her hand.

"Mr. Gerson," Shaneka asked, "Why don't Jews watch TV?"

"Shaneka, where did that come from?"

"You said that we can ask questions. So that's my question."

"Fair enough. Some Jews watch TV, some don't. Who told you that we don't?"

"Well, you don't watch TV."

After Shaneka's question, I felt a special sense of responsibility when teaching my classes. For better or for worse, a whole range of stereotypes and beliefs about Jews would be confirmed or contradicted by my behavior.

Shortly after I explained that some Jews watch TV, Carmen raised her hand and asked, "Mr. Gerson, why are all Jews racist?" I was glad that she was so honest, and I responded that her impression was false. I made a reference to the involvement of Jews in the civil rights movement, describing how Jews and blacks worked together to eliminate segregation. I told the students about Schwerner and Goodman, two young Jewish men who were killed fighting for civil rights, and explained that many other Jews had sacrificed a great deal as well. They listened politely before Carmen interjected an opinion: "Mr. Gerson, that civil rights movement was a long time ago. I don't see what that has to do with anything today."

Okay, so I did not seem to be transforming their attitudes. But I did not expect to, for prejudice cannot be eliminated by talking; only persistent examples to the contrary can conquer a stereotype. But it is not as though the students harbored an array of anti-Semitic stereotypes that I needed to expend much effort contravening.

Jamal surprised me in the hall one day around lunchtime and said, "Mr. Gerson, what is your ethnicity?"

"Jewish."

"Oh," he responded, "so that's why you read so much." He nodded to himself and walked away.

The day after our discussion of Jews in the civil rights movement Shanquilla came up to me during my free period. "Mr. Gerson, are you a member of the ADL or the JDL?"

"Neither."

"Really, Mr. Gerson, which one are you a member of?"

"Shanquilla," I stressed, "I am not lying to you. I am not in either group."

"Why not?"

"Members of the JDL, if there still are any, are militants who like to blow things up. I think they blew each other up, or at least tried to. And I have political disagreements with the ADL. Why do you ask?"

"I thought all Jews had to be members of either group."

"No, both are strictly optional."

"What do those groups do?"

"I don't think the JDL does much of anything anymore now that its leader, Meir Kahane, was killed. And the ADL fights anti-Semitism. Sort of like the NAACP."

"My cousin asked me if I knew any Jews. I said, 'Yes, I have a Jewish teacher.' He told me to ask whether you belonged to the ADL or the JDL."

"What does your cousin do?"

"Nothing. He's unemployed."

"I mean, why would he be concerned about the ADL and the JDL?"

"I don't know. He didn't hear about it at work."

"Apparently."

Many of the students found Judaism fascinating. I am not sure exactly why. Perhaps it wasn't Judaism per se but just the fact that a member of a mysterious and important religion was available to answer questions about his faith. Indeed, there were few things my students found more interesting and meaningful than religion, from both a personal and a sociological perspective. This became especially clear on a sunny Friday before the Christmas break; the sun's rays were coming through the window and were all but pulling the students outside. I saw the longtime guidance counselor, Nathan Siderville, after a poorly behaved first-period class. "Today," I commented to him, looking out the window, "is going to be a behavioral nightmare."

"Don't worry about it."

"Nathan, look at the weather. And Christmas break is only a few days away."

"Granted. But we have mass in an hour."

Although that sounded like a non sequitur, I knew Nathan well enough to trust his predictions about the students. So I just nodded and went on my way. In church with the students an hour later, I knew that my instinct to trust Nathan was correct. Paul Murphy looked relaxed, a powerful signal because he was always vigilantly looking for students who were misbehaving. But there were none. There was complete silence from students of every faith and every temperament—the Catholics, the Protestants, the Muslims, the quiet kids and the wild ones, the popular kids and the loners. They all sat in the pews without so much as looking at the person sitting next to them. No student even used the service as an opportunity to steal some sleep. I did not think this could last, and waited for someone to be disruptive. Given that I could not partake in a mass, I would be in a good position to find and discipline troublemakers. The opportunity for the students to misbehave arose during Communion, when the Catholic kids lined up before sisters administering the blessing.

Because most the students were not Catholic, they remained seated. While many teachers and administrators were taking or administering communion, I walked up and down the rows of seats to ensure that none of the non-Catholic kids took advantage of this time to talk to or hit his neighbor. As I paced throughout the aisles, I first eyed the students I would have suspected, but I spotted no rule-breakers. The students sat there, some glancing at the Bible and the prayerbook in front of them, others quietly watching the religious ritual in the center aisle. Classes resumed ten minutes later. I now had 10L, the worst-behaved class. I had several writing assignments planned to occupy them in the likely event that they decided to let loose after being so calm in church. This proved unnecessary; whatever led them to behave impeccably in church was still with them in the classroom, and the two classes that came after 10L that day were the same. No one discussed the service or even religion; some inarticulate force in the church led them to behave the best way and learn the most they did all year. Indeed, every one of the best classes I taught all year came after a mass.

I wished we had more masses, but we had only four or five throughout the year. The sisters did not want to take the students from class, and kept the masses we did have short for that reason as well. These services generally revolved around one particular theme, not a specifically Catholic one. There was the mass of reconciliation, where the students were encouraged to come closer to loved ones from whom they had grown apart. That service was the only one with confession—and the students were invited to speak with the priest regardless of their faith, as they would with a counselor. However, the only kids to do so were the best-behaved Catholics. I looked at Jack (the HOBY winner), for instance, and wondered what in the world he could be confessing.

Easter is the most serious Catholic holiday, and the least Americanized. The Easter service at St. Luke was held on a Wednesday, which was also a half-day leading into the holiday that would start with Holy Thursday and extend through the following week. There were only two events scheduled for that day: the service and the student-faculty volleyball game. To move things along, the service was not to be held in the church, as usual, but in homeroom.

This was an appropriate venue considering that there were prayers every morning in homeroom. They usually consisted of a student reading over the loudspeaker a passage from an inspirational figure like Jesus or Martin Luther King followed by the Lord's Prayer, after which the Catholic kids crossed themselves. Although I never crossed myself, I doubt that the students noticed; they probably thought I was Catholic on the basis of the anger I displayed on the one or two occasions when a student didn't stand for prayers or talked during them.

So, how would this Easter service work? Excusing myself from this service would be far more obvious than not saying the few words in the Lord's Prayer before most of the students were fully awake. I expected Sister Theresa to pull me from homeroom on a pretext, but she apparently had more important things to worry about. One of the girls in homeroom, Rosala, asked me with a knowing smile if she could lead the service. Rosala was Maura's sister—and Maura had probably told her that I was Jewish and could not lead a Catholic service.

It did not take much to note early on that the extent of the religious orthodoxy at St. Luke did not extend far beyond the masses and the posters throughout the school, which featured slogans like, "God Rules: Always Has, Always Will! End of Discussion," with citations from Psalms 66:7, 145:13 and Revelations 1:18. I asked the religion teacher, a devout Catholic, Martha Jones, about this around Thanksgiving.

She replied simply, "You hear a lot about God at St. Luke, right?"

"Sure."

"Whenever we talk about God, we are teaching theology."

In her own classes Martha allowed discussions of theology and religion to run free. During one of my free periods in December she asked me to watch her class while she made a phone call in the office. I was so impressed by the high level of interaction and maturity of the students that I asked Martha if I could come every Wednesday during first period (when I was free). Martha said sure, and thus I not only gained insight into the religious beliefs of the kids but also watched a master teacher practice her craft.

Though the students knew that Mrs. Jones was a devout Catholic, they were encouraged—though they probably needed no encouragement—to speak as they really thought on a variety of subjects. The subject of the first class I observed was death. At first I thought there were surely many other topics a religion department could address that would be more appropriate for high school kids. But after sitting in on a couple of classes, I knew just why the subject of death was being taught. One girl's brother took three bullets in the head, another's mother had been stabbed, another had a father who died of AIDS, and another lost her mother to cancer. It is a cliché to say that death is a part of life, but that fact is a burning reality for St. Luke students. Their intimate contact with premature, violent death shaped them; what most teenagers would find shocking in a movie is a normal thread in the fabric of inner-city life. And it almost goes without saying that such a fact of life is as instrumental in forming their views of American society and their place in it as it is in forming their views of God and His place in their lives.

Most St. Luke students believed in God, a universal God whose blessing is not monopolized by a particular religious faith. It was not that the students demonstrated religious tolerance, for tolerance implies a begrudging acceptance. Though many students believed that they practiced the one true faith, they were always respectful of and eager to learn about the different services their classmates attended on Sunday. And St. Luke students surely did not practice the bourgeois maxim that one's religious faith should not be discussed in public. It was debated as fervently as anything else and with as much civility. In one discussion in the religion class one of the students volunteered that though she respected her Catholic friends and teachers, she could never, under any circumstances, become a Catholic.

"Why?" a Catholic classmate asked.

"Because of the pope."

"What's wrong with the pope?"

"I believe that all people are equal, and the pope thinks he's better than everyone else."

"Well, not exactly," Mrs. Jones responded.

"Close enough. And that is why I would never be a Catholic. There are a lot of starving people in the world, and the pope has a lot of money. Especially in gold. The whole Vatican is gold."

"No doubt," Mrs. Jones interjected, "but most of the Vatican was built a long, long time ago. And the Church does a lot for poor people."

"If it really cared about the poor, the Church would sell its gold and give the money to the poor."

Catholic school administrators in inner cities everywhere surely know that most of their students are not Catholic. And converting non-Catholic students is not an immediate goal, if it is a goal at all. Nevertheless, the Church continues to equip its schools with the financial and personal resources that allow them to succeed under the most negative conditions. I often wondered how the Church hierarchy reacts to the lack of theology taught at inner-city Catholic schools. How does the Church feel about devoting all of these resources—not only money but also the lives of sisters and priests—to children who will, truth be told, never become Catholic? I did not know the answer to that question, and looked forward to a conference in nearby Bayonne, where we would be addressed by Michael Herring of the National Catholic Education Association. Before his speech he passed out a packet to the teachers assembled before him. The prologue to the literature Herring distributed read as follows: "Catholic schools are deeply rooted in the life of the church, the body of Jesus Christ, who is the source of all life. Catholic schools draw their life's breath from their roots in the Catholic community and they, in turn, breathe new life into the Church."

Other key points reflected the same theme:

- The Catholic school is an integral part of the Church's mission to proclaim the Gospel, build faith communities, celebrate through worship, and serve others.
- The Catholic school is an evangelizing, educational community.
- Catholic schools are called to be catalysts for social change based on Gospel values.
- We challenge our faculty, staff, students and families to witness to their belief in Jesus Christ.
- We commit ourselves to teach an integrated curriculum rooted in Gospel values and Catholic teachings.

Herring was well aware that his mission was serving many non-Catholic students and employing many non-Catholic teachers. He pointed out that there are more non-Catholics than clergy teaching in Catholic schools nationwide. The role of the non-Catholic teacher, he explained, is to help instill in the students Catholic values—which are no different from Protestant or Jewish values.

After Herring's speech, I had lunch with Nathan Siderville. Nathan was the school guidance counselor and was familiar to the teachers for a reason other than his widely acknowledged kindness and generosity of spirit.

"Nathan," I remarked, "one thing that has struck me is how

much the Church gives to non-Catholic kids it has no intention or possibility of ever converting. So many clergy and lay faithful are devoting their lives to St. Luke when relatively few of the kids are Catholic—and when so many are devout Protestants or Muslims. St. Luke doesn't even make the slightest effort to convert the kids; religion classes don't even teach Catholic theology."

"Why do you think that is?"

"I don't know. I think the school runs on the spirit of Catholicism and the attendant ethic of service."

"Mark, I am not denying anything you have said. You are partially right. But the greater truth is that the Church can and should do so much more."

"More?" I asked. "If it were not for the Church, these kids would not get nearly the education they are receiving now."

"First, the Church—the diocese—only takes care of health insurance. Oh, and it indemnifies us so that one lawsuit can't put us out of business. But you're from Short Hills, and I am sure that you had Catholic friends who went to wealthy parishes—St. Rose's, isn't that the one in Short Hills? Parishes like that could give a lot more to urban parishes but choose not to."

"Nathan, one can always do more. But the pay scale here caps at twenty-five thousand dollars. And the clergy make more sacrifices than I can even fathom to the Church—or, more specifically, to kids, many of whom are not Catholic and in all honesty will never become Catholic."

Like Nathan, most of the teachers with whom I discussed religion questioned major aspects or teachings of the Catholic Church. While they disagreed strongly with the pope on some of the more controversial issues of the day—abortion and homosexuality, to name two—there was something far greater than politics, something far more meaningful than anything they could vote for or against, that was pulling them to the Church. The teachers, young and old, taught at St. Luke for very little money and advised the youth group and the Catholic singing and drama groups for nothing. They had been devoting their lives to the Church and had no plans to stop. Their politics and their faith did not always coincide, but they had little trouble separating the two when necessary.

The lack of orthodoxy at St. Luke was not, though, an indication of the role religion played in the school. Faith in God—a strong, resilient faith in a compassionate, just God—was the animating principle that drove both teachers and students. Prayer in homeroom was never recited by rote; it worked because the students who prayed felt it and wanted to thank the Lord before the day began. It was God who provided the ultimate inspiration, who supplied many students who suffered under grinding poverty with confidence that their hard work and good behavior would, perhaps in a way they could not now foresee, be redeemed.

But what God? For the students and the faculty, it really did not matter what religion one used to access God. Though many students believed that their faith was the Truth, they were always respectful of and eager to learn about the different ways in which their classmates worshipped God. This came through in conversations, in church, and in teaching. During a lesson on the Great Awakening, Jermeine, a Baptist, raised her hand.

"Yes?"

"Yo, is Catholic a Protestant sect?"

"No, Jermeine. Actually, Catholicism is what they were protesting against; hence the root of the word *Protestant*."

"Well, I ain't see what they be protesting about. We all in this Catholic school."

The others agreed. When I tried to explain the differences between Catholicism and Protestantism, the students were briefly interested but ultimately unconcerned. This sentiment was universal among the students in all my classes. When I quoted President Eisenhower—"Our government makes no sense unless it is founded in a deeply felt religious faith—and I don't care what it is"—they identified immediately.

I taught far more religious history than originally planned because it never ceased to captivate the imagination of my students, and it would invariably lead in fascinating and productive directions that I could never predict. Perhaps the idea that enchanted the students most was one I casually mentioned in the midst of teaching a unit on religion in the colonies; when a student asked if there had been any nonbelievers in colonial times, I replied that there were probably not many and that they had probably all internalized Pascal's Wager.

"What's that?" Shanquilla asked.

"It goes like this. No one can be absolutely 100 percent sure that there is a God and a heaven and hell. So look at it this way: Say you live your life obeying God's law and positioning yourself to get into heaven, and it turns out that there is a heaven. You're happy. What if there is no heaven or hell? Well, then you haven't lost anything; you've lived a good life. Now let's say that you bet that there is no God and no heaven or hell, that you blaspheme the Lord, and that you don't care what the Bible says. If you are right, you don't gain or lose anything. But if you are wrong and there *is* a heaven and hell, you are in big trouble. So it is safe to bet that what religion says is true; you don't have a thing to lose if you wager that."

"Pascal's theory ain't gonna work," Walt asserted.

"Why not?"

"'Cuz God knows whether you really believe in him or are just bullshittin'. And he ain't gonna be fooled if you fake it."

"That's right," Shanquilla came back. "If Santa knows whether you be naughty or nice, God knows whether you believe in him for real or not."

On the mid-term exam, almost everyone in 10Y chose "Pascal's Wager" as one of the seven of ten terms to identify. They all got it right, some adding spirited comments agreeing either with Pascal or with Walt's challenge.

When I planned our unit on the Puritans around Christmas time, I decided to give a straight account of how religious freedom led to political freedom and what both mean for contemporary American society. But the students were not satisfied; in nearly every class they wanted to know exactly what the religious beliefs of the Puritans were. And these questions were posed specifically. For example, Walt asked a question that was reiterated in one form or another in all of my classes: "What did the Puritans believe about heaven and hell, and how did that differ from the beliefs of other Christians?"

"Well," I explained, "the Puritans believed in unconditional election. That meant that God determined before you were born whether you were going to heaven or hell."

Maura seemed confused. "Then why did people behave? Because they thought it was right to behave?"

"Partially that. But Puritan communities were extraordinarily tight, and people were very concerned with what others thought of them. So, if Shanquilla prospers in business and is a kind and generous person, you will think that she is one of the elect, that she is one of those chosen by God before birth to go to heaven. But if she is lazy and mean, you will think that she is destined for hell."

"But why would Shanquilla care if someone thought she was going to heaven? If she was happy, then who cares if somebody ain't like her?" Walt demanded.

"Walt, your reasoning makes some sense—from today's vantage point. For better or for worse, we now live in a rights-oriented culture based in large part on the primacy of the individual. In other words, we are sometimes just concerned with satisfying ourselves without a care as to what others think or whether our actions are right or good. But that was not true for most of American history, and Puritan societies are an especially striking example of another way of living. Puritans could not have been happy if others didn't like them. Their happiness was dependent on their being safely embedded in a web of associations revolving around their church and each other."

"C'mon, Walt," Charles said. "You change out of your uniform when you come to school in the morning because you care what others think of you. And you dress in the best clothes because you want the girls to think you are phat. And you don't get why the Puritans cared if people thought they were going to

Hell? Some people care that others think they dress dope, other people care if others think they be goin' to Heaven. Everybody cares what others think about them in some way."

Walt, who like everyone else respected Charles, thought for a moment before nodding in agreement.

All the students could understand this, for they actively considered religion to be a quintessentially communal activity, something to be shared proudly and practiced joyously with others. I prepared my lecture on the Second Great Awakening—when Americans gathered in Missouri in 1800 in the midst of a wild religious frenzy—by reading the textbook (if I had learned about it in school, it had not made much of an impression on me). My students, however, identified completely, and what I expected to be a rather shallow lesson was anything but. Concluding the lecture, I asked, "What do you make of the fact that these grown men were writhing on the ground, literally barking, in the midst of this religious experience?"

"They be 'catchin' the Holy Ghost'!" Shanquilla exclaimed.

"They ain't barking! The Lord is barking through them," Carmen added. Some in the class contributed a chorus of "amens" as others assented by nodding.

On the final exam most of the students selected the essay question dealing with the Second Great Awakening, though they had what I considered to be several easier choices.

For the unit on the Civil War I showed the movie *Glory*, the story of the 54th Union Regiment, a black regiment commanded by a patrician white officer. I was sure the students would like the movie, considering that it is an utterly absorbing story featuring two of their favorite actors (Denzel Washington and Morgan Freeman). Given that *Glory* contains many of the racial themes that engaged them so much in daily intercourse, I expected conversations about race and lessons about history to result from the movie. I was sure that the scene between Matthew Broderick (the patrician officer) and Denzel Washington (a former slave and enlisted man)—in which Washington refuses Broderick's offer to become an officer out of doubt that a Union victory would have much to offer a black man—would speak to the students' interest. They responded to this scene when I played it twice, but it was not what really captured their imaginations.

The scene that entranced the students was before the great battle at the end of the film. The soldiers of the 54th worship in a Christian service in which, through song and the recitation of scripture, they speak of their love of Jesus, their faith in one another through Christ, and their confidence that God will see them through the battle, whether they survive or not. In every class the black students sang along with the soldiers in prayer and requested that I rewind the scene over and over again. I did, of course, and allowed several of the students to spend the class after the movie reenacting the testimonials that the black soldiers gave to Jesus. Walt, Charles, and several others even rented the movie and viewed it at home so that they could memorize their favorite speeches from that scene. Shanquilla and several others asked me for books and movies that would explain how that period in American history had inspired such faith and love of God.

In a discussion of how this scene from the movie mirrored their own church experiences, I asked my students, "Why do some religions worship by rising and sitting at appointed times while others demonstrate great emotion during prayer?"

Shanquilla raised her hand. "It ain't religion. It's race. The whites can't do anything except sit down and stand up while we blacks know how to *feel* religion."

"Why do you think that whites worship one way and blacks another?"

"'Cause," Shanquilla replied, "the whites don't *loooove* the Lord enough!" The blacks in the class whooped and the non-blacks sat in amused silence.

A few days later Walt offered something of an explanation as to why whites have a problem loving the Lord. "Jesus was black," he informed the class.

"No, he was not. Jesus was probably Mediterranean, swarthy. Like he had a good tan," I said.

"No. He was black. You obviously haven't read Revelations."

"Yes, I have. But I didn't see anything there about Jesus being black."

Carmen chipped in, "Mr. Gerson, it is in Revelations, chapter one, verses fourteen to fifteen."

"That's right," Walt added, "Revelations, chapter one, verses fourteen to fifteen."

"Okay, you two. Come by after school, and we'll go to the library and check out a Bible."

"Do we get extra credit if we right?"

"No."

They came to the library anyway, and we checked Revelation 1:14–15: "His head and his hair were white as white wool, white as snow; his eyes were like a flame of fire, his feet were like burnished bronze, refined as in a furnace."

"See, he was black. His feet were burnished bronze."

"Sorry, that's the tan I talked about. I don't know too many black guys that have hair white as white wool, white as snow—unless they have gray hair, and Jesus died too young for that."

"That's the racist version of line fourteen."

"What are you talking about? Its the Oxford Bible. It's not racist at all."

Walt volunteered, "Well, I'll bring in my Bible with the proof tomorrow." Tomorrow, at least in that sense, never came.

Walt may not have offered proof that Jesus was black, but found plenty of other Biblical passages that sparked his interest. I came to a class a minute late one day to overhear a heated discussion between Walt and Carmen. Walt said, "Man, this shit is dope! The best porno I ever saw!"

Walt did not know I was around, so I ignored the curse and told him to put away the book, take out his notebook, and get ready for class.

"Mr. Gerson, you got to see this! I'm going to memorize this and say it to my girl."

"Walt, two things. First, I am not going to look at pornography. Second, I would not recommend reciting pornography to your girlfriend. It's not very romantic. I would recommend Frank Sinatra or Johnny Mathis, or if you don't want that, some poetry instead. You know the Bible pretty well, you can find some love poetry there."

"But, Mr. Gerson, I read it for Sister Peter's class!"

"Walt, I do not think that Sister Peter assigned pornography in her religion class."

"Mr. Gerson, it's in the Bible!" Walt showed me the passage to which he was referring, from Song of Songs, 7:6–9:

You are stately as a palm tree,
and your breasts are like its
    clusters.
I say I will climb the palm tree
and lay hold of its branches.
Oh, may your breasts be like clusters of the vine,
and the scent of your breath like
    apples
and your kisses like the best wine
that goes down smoothly,
gliding over lips and teeth.

....

DISCIPLINE

"GENIUS," GEORGE ELIOT WROTE IN *DANIEL DERONDA*, "AT FIRST IS LITTLE more than a great capacity for receiving discipline." The same is true for ordinary academic success; a good school must have students who are disciplined in the way they behave and the way they work. It is obvious that high disciplinary hurdles—fights, drugs, an environment where students can get beaten up for wearing their school uniforms to school—will choke the learning process. And it is only a bit less obvious that students cannot learn in a classroom where talking in class, passing notes, sleeping, and more subtle manifestations of disrespect for the teacher are tolerated. In other words, before learning can begin, there needs to be discipline. And before there can be discipline, there needs to be a capacity for receiving it.

How can this capacity be acquired? At St. Luke, in one of two ways: The first was through fear—fear of being sent to Mr. Murphy, fear of having one's parent called in, fear of being kicked out of school. As soon as the fear is lifted—if students know that they can get away with wrongdoing—discipline is gone. A far more lasting source of effective discipline is trust. When students trust their teachers and administrators and are confident that strictly enforced rules advance a valuable learning process, discipline becomes natural, even the norm.

The acquisition of trust is a gradual process that escapes easy articulation. Trust is a sharp instrument. The students who came to trust me and their other teachers did so one by one, for unique reasons and in different ways. Basketball helped me acquire the trust of several students right at the beginning. Early on I told the students that I would sponsor after-school games of pickup basketball in which I would play. I stressed that everyone was welcome to participate but they had best be aware that my team would win and that I could whip any one of them in one-on-one if so challenged.

I set the first game two weeks in advance so that the students could get psyched about it and brag about how they would destroy me. And boast they did. "You ain't got no game, Mr. Gerson. You be playin' with those white boys in Short Hills who don't run to the hoop when a black man steps on the court; they run home to Mommy and Daddy," Jamal said.

"All right, tough guy," I replied. "We'll see next Tuesday."

Tuesday came, and we all changed in the locker room, which was really a small and narrow hallway with benches. There were no showers; players apparently had to clean up when they got home. After changing, we climbed a few steps to the gym. A few guys had balls they were shooting. When they saw me, the trash talking started: "Mr. Gerson ain't got nothin'!" "White boy can't even shoot!" And so on. It was so merciless that I wondered if my own team would try to show me up as well. After a few minutes I said that we had had enough warming up and should get started. We shot for teams: the first five to hit a foul shot were on one team, the next five were on the other, and whoever missed sat out the first game. My team took the ball out two minutes later.

As soon as the game started, I immediately saw my students playing a style of basketball I detested.[1] I like a controlled, passing team game, but that was not what was being played here. My students would grab a rebound and race the length of the court only to miss on a wild, though sometimes acrobatic, drive to the hoop. I hit a couple of threes early on, but they were unimpressed. Shooting in playground ball is *déclassé*; one is supposed to beat his man off the dribble and go strong to the hoop for a layup or, preferably, a slam dunk. Fine. Walt had decided to guard me and took full advantage of this opportunity: "Mr. Gerson, you ain't got nothin'. You can't beat me worth shit. You ain't got nothin'. Go back and play with the white boys."

I was growing rather annoyed at Walt's rudeness, but I could not give him a detention in this circumstance. Instead, I grabbed a defensive rebound and dribbled down the court, stopping only

---

[1]The basketball coach later explained to me that there are two types of players in the city: those who have been disciplined by team structure and those whose game has been conditioned by the playground. There is not necessarily a difference in ability, but those who are trained in a structured basketball program are much better players, for they play a graceful, beautiful game that their undisciplined agemates do not.

to tell Walt that I would fake right at the top of the key, cross over, and pass him on my way to the hoop. He grunted an indication that he did not take me seriously. So I approached the top of the key, dribbling with my left. I made a quick move to the right, and Walt went with it. Just as quickly I went back to the left and drove to the hoop for an easy layup.

Walt was obviously embarrassed as his teammates began to shout that he had been beaten by a white boy. Walt said that he was going to get me the same way. That would be impossible, I knew. Walt wore the scarlet letter of the undisciplined player: he dribbled too high. Every time the ball bounced off his fingers and onto the floor, it sent the same signal that a slumbering bank guard must have sent to Willie Sutton. After I scored on the layup, Walt took the ball up the floor, meeting me midway between half-court and the three-point arc. He was dribbling with his right hand and tried an acceleration move to his left. I stuck out my left hand and knocked the ball loose, recovering it in the next move. Jamal, who was on my team, saw what I was doing a play ahead and took off, streaking down the court. One bounce pass later, Jamal slammed the ball home for an uncontested dunk.

When word circulated that "Mr. Gerson got game," I had passed the first test necessary to begin earning the trust of many of my students. Having successfully challenged them at their game, I could not be dismissed easily—on the court, in the classroom, or out of school altogether. I continued to use basketball as a way to continually accumulate trust. Throughout the fall, I instituted a game that a well-behaved class could play at the end of the period: stump Mr. Gerson on the NBA. The rules were simple: If any student could stump me on a question relating to the NBA and I could not stump him back, the student would earn an A on the next test. But if any detentions were given during the class, there would be no game. This strategy was effective, for students often told a classmate whose conduct might have canceled the game to behave.

The students came in with obscure questions I could not answer: for example, they would ask me how many points Patrick

Ewing scored on a particular game in 1989. But their sense of basketball history was poor; no one knew, for instance, that Oscar Robertson went to the University of Cincinnati or that Wilt Chamberlain played his first professional ball with the Harlem Globetrotters. So no one ever won the contest, but this was not for lack of trying—the students asked fathers and uncles and any other knowledgeable adults about basketball history, hoping to be prepared for my question. But basketball is a broad subject, and I was secure in assuming that I could stump them by asking "Who was selected over Bill Russell in the 1959 NBA draft?" or "Who is the only Jewish player in the NBA?" Sihugo Green and Danny Schayes did not have many fans among the sophomores of St. Luke.

Two of my students, Walt and Jamal, played junior varsity basketball and loved the NBA as much as I do! So before the season started, I lent them my copy of John McPhee's *A Sense of Where You Are*, the classic book about Bill Bradley's senior season at Princeton. We knew about Senator Bradley from our discussions of current events, so Walt and Jamal were able to place the subject of the book in perspective. I instructed them to read the book carefully and to study how Bradley—perhaps the greatest college player of all time—developed his game. As McPhee exquisitely demonstrates, Bradley excelled by virtue of being the quintessentially disciplined player; he used an impeccable command of the game's fundamentals to dominate his far more athletic opponents. The test of Walt's and Jamal's understanding of McPhee's point was given on the court.

After school one day during the middle of the season Walt, Jamal, and I went to the gym, and I told them to shoot like Bradley. They looked in the book to refresh their memory and knew exactly what to do. Jamal went first. He took a few quick dribbles, bouncing the last one hard off the floor. Then he slammed his foot against the floor and went up for a jump shot. (The hard dribble helps the player jump higher, and the foot slamming prevents drifting on the jump.) Swish! Walt went next, and he met with the same result. We kept practicing until I was convinced they had it right.

By now Walt and Jamal trusted me; they would have let me teach them anything from jump shooting to proper grammar. Though each of them tried to maintain a tough guy attitude in different ways, the process of trust had begun early in the year and was cemented by basketball. But this was not the case with all students. After the Christmas break, a new student from South America, Rosa, entered my freshman homeroom. She spoke not a word of English. I saw her wandering around the third floor after lunch looking lost and terrified. She had her schedule with her but it was in English and she could not make sense of it. This problem was easy enough to solve. I turned to a Spanish-speaking sophomore who was nearby. "Anna, help that girl over there. She is new and does not speak any English. Her name is Rosa and she is lost." One short conversation in Spanish later, the problem was solved. Later that day I gave a quiz to Anna's class. Anna finished early and came to my desk. "Mr. Gerson, if I get a B, I'll really get an A, right?"

Confused, I responded, "No, Anna, if you earn a B, you'll get a B. What are you talking about?"

"Don't I get extra credit for helping that girl?"

"What girl, Anna?"

"The girl who was lost. You asked me to help her understand her schedule, remember?"

"Anna," I said, understanding what she was talking about, "Sit down."

This incident stayed with me all day. Anna and I had not been close; she often slept or talked through class, did little homework, and never came to see me outside of class. I talked with her repeatedly about her school performance and called her home, but nothing could rid her of the notion that the goal of school was to graduate having done as little work as possible. Though I was initially surprised by its apparent callousness, her demand for a reward for performing the simplest human kindness was really not so odd. Anna thought of me as nothing more than a service provider and expected compensation for any expenditure of effort on her part. Without trust, everything had to be accounted for.

Jersey City has a major problem with truancy. The very word *truant* sounds to me like something out of a 1950s comic book, but the reality is as present as ever. Moreover, given what truant kids do when they are not in school nowadays, the truancy problem is probably a lot worse than ever. The May 31, 1995, issue of the *Jersey Journal* ran a banner headline—"Jersey City's Big Hooky Problem"—and reported that the attendance rate at seven schools, including the four major public high schools, fell below the mandated 85 percent. Lincoln High School plunged below 80 percent, and Snyder sank below 75 percent. In response, the district started a program, Project REACT, offering crisis intervention assistance, alternative education, placements, and other services. The flagship organization of Project REACT was the Truancy Task Force, which was inactive for an entire month because one of its members was arrested for attempting to distribute heroin near Ferris High School and an elementary school. Critics charged that the Truancy Task Force, which employed only ten attendance officers to roam the city looking for kids who belonged in school, was undermanned. A major political fight ensued, with one faction seeking an enhanced task force and an opposing group claiming that the district's limited resources could be better allocated elsewhere. No doubt this same fight continued as people debated Superintendent Frank Sinatra's latest tactic—a computerized system that triggered calls to an absent student's home.

I received a firsthand lesson in public school truancy midway through the first semester, when Karl entered the sophomore class and was placed in 10W. On his first day in my class I did not know where he came from, but I was immediately impressed by his knowledge of American history. We were discussing pre-Revolutionary America, and he was familiar with all of the relevant events—from the Hat Act, Molasses Act, and Navigation Act to the Boston Massacre and that city's Tea Party. Moreover, he had an alert and engaged expression on his face, a welcome sign in any classroom. Karl clearly did not belong in the bottom section, and I detained him for a few moments after class.

"Karl, welcome to St. Luke. Did you just move from out of town?"

"Oh no, I've lived in Jersey City all my life."

"Then how did you wind up here in February?"

"I started the year at Dickinson High School and ran into some problems there so that I had to leave."

"What kind of problems?"

"I never went to class. I would go in the morning, sign in during homeroom, and then take off for the rest of the day."

"And how did you get found out?"

"My English teacher discovered that I hadn't been in class for a month. So she called Sister Theresa, and here I am."

"You know that kind of behavior will not be tolerated here. For one, all of your teachers are going to know if you are not in class. If you are not on the absence list, I and all of your other teachers will be in Mr. Murphy's office faster than you can say C-U-T. And the attendance list is flawless. It is taken every day during homeroom and first period. So you can't come in during homeroom and then take off. You'll be found out."

"That's fine. That's why I'm here. I don't want to cut, but I will if given the chance. St. Luke will keep me from myself, I guess."

My God, I thought, *this kid speaks the Queen's English.* "I hope so," I told him.

"Can I make a slightly different point, though, Mr. Gerson?"

"Sure."

"I can't learn here."

"Why not?"

"It's just that this class I am in is too slow. I know everything the teachers teach, and, between you and me, I'm much smarter than the others here."

I had a hunch he was right. The slow section was quite slow, and Karl was sharp, alert, perceptive, knowledgeable, and well-spoken. Nonetheless, I did not want Karl to know that he did not belong in the bottom section. The administration deserved the benefit of the doubt against a transfer student effectively forced out of his last school for cutting.

"Karl," I responded, "Sister Theresa put you in this section for a reason."

He cut me off. "A bad reason, apparently."

"Karl, G. K. Chesterton once said that you shouldn't try to knock something down unless you know why it was put up. And you don't know why it was put up. You can always ask her, though. Moreover, there can always be changes at the end of the year. In the meantime, it is important that you work hard and not get any ideas about cutting. And just keep it to yourself about being too smart for this class."

"That's a good quote. Can you tell me again? I want to get it down," Karl said, taking out his notebook. "And, Mr. Gerson, one more thing. Who is G. K. Chesterton?"

Later in the week I had Karl's class for seventh period, the last of the day. He didn't show up for class, which was especially troublesome because his name was not on the absentee sheet. Five minutes into the period, right after the class settled down, I gave the students an assignment so that I could go to Paul Murphy and check on Karl. Just as I was about to leave the classroom, Karl walked in.

"Karl, where have you been? You better have a good answer, so think quick."

"I'm not late, Mr. Gerson," he said, handing me a note from the office, "I was in Mr. Murphy's office. He called me there because my sixth-period teacher said that I left the class and did not return. What happened was that I went to the bathroom, with permission, and then the bell rang. So I came here directly."

By the end of the week I saw that my and Karl's initial impressions were correct—he was way too smart for 10W. I became more and more impressed with his maturity, powers of reasoning, base of knowledge, and a burning curiosity to learn and to engage his mind. He didn't just deserve to move up; Karl was clearly suited for the top section. So I asked the guidance counselor, Nathan Siderville, if Karl could be transferred.

"I know he is very smart, Mark. Karl does deserve to be with the top kids. But, unfortunately, that's not possible," Nathan replied.

"Why not?"

"Because he has to go to the trailer with the others in that section for remedial science. We don't know for sure because Dickinson lost his records, but apparently he did not take science. That is what he says, and tests we gave him point to a deficiency in science. I have tried to move around his schedule in every way possible to put him with the top section, but it just doesn't work. He'll move next year, though, for sure."

I saw Karl the next day on his way to the trailer, where some students went for remedial instruction. "Karl," I asked, "why didn't you take science last year?"

"They don't let the dumb kids take science. Instead, we take shop."

"But you're not dumb."

"No, but I cut class all the time. So they thought I was dumb, and my science grades weren't good. I was failing, so they put me in shop."

"Did you pass shop?"

"No one fails shop."

Why did St. Luke succeed so much more with truancy and discipline than the nearby public schools? We, of course, had students who played hooky, but we never had a problem catching them. If a student missed a day, he or she had to bring in a note from a parent. And the disciplinarian, Mr. Murphy, was a vigilant man with expertise at detecting student forgery (he knew the handwriting of most of the students and had seen enough notes to know which phrases parents use in absence notes and which they do not). St. Luke students playing hooky were bound to be caught. Jermeine decided to celebrate Christmas a bit early with a two-day vacation at the Newport Mall. On the second day, Mr. Murphy called home to see how she was feeling, and that was that. She was given an in-school suspension for three days, which meant that she had to spend the better part of a week in a lonely office writing hundreds of times how sorry she was. Jermeine failed the tests, quizzes, and exercises given those days as well and was told that less than perfect behavior for the duration of the year would be punished by expulsion. She was not absent once for the rest of the year, nor did she receive detention.

A major reason for St. Luke's success with truants or, more appropriately, would-be truants was the size of the school. A student with a hundred classmates is bound to be missed a lot more quickly than one with a thousand classmates. Furthermore, the disciplinarian in a small school will know each student by name and will know every problem student very well. Because each problem student is responding to different demons, only a disciplinarian who knows everything important about the student will succeed in reforming him or her. Through no fault of their own, disciplinarians in large schools simply have too large a caseload to do more than enforce the rules, in most cases. Small schools are able to help students in more subtle, more important ways as well.

An institution is much better able to help a child when its processes are lubricated by trust, which follows when people know, like, and respect one another. It is difficult to acquire that kind of trust in an institution much bigger than St. Luke. But even there such trust was far from universal and sometimes had disastrous consequences. There were the small problems, like Anna's expectation of reward for helping Rosa, and larger ones, like physical violence. I was not surprised that there was a good amount of fighting at St. Luke; what did strike me, though, was that most of the fights were between girls. Before I began teaching, I barely realized that girls could fight, and the idea of them doing so struck me as something midway between disgusting and ridiculous. But at St. Luke girl fights were common (as they were, a Jersey City police officer informed me, throughout the city). At St. Luke the fights usually broke out when one girl spread a rumor (which may or may not have been true) about another girl. The latter would then confront the former by asking something like "Did you say my mother is a whore?"

Things weren't always easy to resolve. A few years before I arrived at St. Luke a senior, Nancy, got into a fight with a girl from another school outside the building after school hours. No one was seriously hurt, but that did not stop Nancy from suing the school after graduation. Nancy claimed that she had informed an administrator that she was going to be attacked after school; which, by all accounts, did not happen. In the lawsuit against St. Luke, Nancy's attorney claimed that her injury had impeded her ability to engage in sexual activity. School had to be canceled the day of the trial because several teachers and all the administrators had to be in court with the lawyers retained by the archdiocese. They sat through a day of jury selection and half of the next day. Then the case was abruptly postponed: the defendant went into labor right after the morning session concluded.

Fights, I learned, were a normal part of the social tapestry of the inner city. The students reported seeing fights all the time and occasionally taking part in them. Many had friends and relatives who had been injured in fights, and some even reported deaths. In the early spring I asked 10Y why there were so many fights. Shanquilla answered, supplying three reasons: mothers, sisters, and girlfriends.

Shanquilla's answer proved predictive when the next day her classmate Maura burst into my room during lunch. "Ah, Maura," I said, "I am just so touched that you are so excited to learn history that you come running to class twenty minutes before your section meets. Well, sit down and we'll talk about John Brown's raid on Harpers Ferry."

"What?" She thought for a quick moment. "Mr. Gerson, there's a fight outside!"

I bolted down the stairs and outside, but two other teachers had already broken up the fight. This one, between two senior boys, had started to get vicious; it was a good thing the teachers got there in time. There would have been broken faces if the fight had continued. A few minutes later, after the pugilists and onlookers had calmed down a bit, it became clear what these students were fighting over: one had accused the other of "looking at" his girlfriend.

Such brawls were entirely alien to my own experience, where no one really cared if another guy looked at his girlfriend. This is not to say that my friends and I lacked pride or honor, but we dealt with our sense of honor differently than did St. Luke students. Without saying a word, let alone making a plan or agreeing to a pact, we constructed a social code to avoid violence. For one thing, there were very few, if any, cases of cheating on girlfriends among my friends and acquaintances in high school and college. Consequently, we knew that a "look" would not progress to action. When it came down to it, my friends and I trusted our girlfriends and, just as importantly, trusted each other. Again without talking about it, we invented new ways to protect our honor without fighting. For one, a new girlfriend immediately became a sister to all of the friends of her boyfriend. She offered these friends advice on romantic matters, listened with compassion when their hearts were broken, and acted as a willing intermediary to smooth their often clumsy pursuits of the fair sex. What she did not become was an object of sexual desire herself, even after a breakup; this aspect of the code reflected the truth that serious relationships have residual effects that remain at the nerve center of a man's vulnerability and sense of honor. Romantic relationships do not die quick deaths; they ease into their slumber, and not always gently. And we made sure never to do anything to disturb that often troubled beast. This code jealously guarded our honor and pride, protecting us from violence. In short, we rationalized ways to insulate ourselves from our irrational inclinations, and our approach seemed to work.

Even if our code had broken down, we probably would have considered the consequences of fighting. St. Luke kids did not think that way; the aforementioned pugilists were seniors in high school, only a few months from graduating. And here they were, fighting over an accusation that one had "looked" at the other's girlfriend. Everyone at St. Luke knew that fighting could result in expulsion, but because one young man felt that his honor had been violated, he had to fight. No consequences, no rational ordering of priorities, no verbal diplomacy, could ever get in the way of that. Not even the fact that his girlfriend was pregnant, making his need to secure a high school diploma all the more urgent. He saw no choice but to fight, and the young woman involved perceived the situation in the same way.

The school dance in early December was a big deal. Several students spent an entire Friday decorating the cafeteria, setting up the sound system, ordering the food, and doing everything else necessary to make the evening possible. Sister Peter called a meeting for several of the first-year teachers to tell us what to expect and to assign responsibilities. Sister Peter was a well-loved sister, pious, compassionate, experienced (she was in her seventies), and demanding of her students. She always had a kind word and a warm smile for other sisters, lay teachers, students, and strangers, and her younger colleagues. She is the nicest and most concerned person I have ever known. Sister Peter had no illusions about how kids behave, and told us the rules we were to enforce at the dance: All students were to be searched for illicit substances, and those who left, for whatever reason, could not return (so no one at the dance could get high or drunk). Then she came to the subject of dancing. "Their dancing might get a little explicit," she told us, "but there is nothing we can do about it—until it resembles foreplay. Then stop it."

"Sister Peter!" Will Donaldson, the young English teacher, exclaimed.

"What, Will? You don't know what that is?"

There was quite a lot of dancing as foreplay, but that did not bother me as much as the rap music did. For one thing, it was terrible. Moreover, it was so loud that any attempt at conversation was futile. This was not peculiar to the inner city, I knew; I had been to plenty of parties at college and elsewhere where it seemed as though part of the fun was in trying to be heard over the worst possible music. I lobbied with the student disc jockey for at least one Big Band song (I even promised her an A on a test) but to no avail. With that option foiled, I asked the police officer who was serving as the security guard to shoot the stereo system. He sympathized but resisted. It was not my night.

I escaped the scene at times by standing with the police officer outside the school gates, ostensibly to tell him whom he should not admit (only St. Mary students were invited) but really because I could not stand the music. Another officer approached us and asked me, "You teach here?"

"Yes, why?

"You know those three kids on the corner?"

I looked and saw Walt, Jamal, and Kenny. "Sure, I know them."

"They're smoking pot."

"What?"

"I just told you, guy. They're smoking pot."

I approached them rapidly. Jamal and Kenny scampered away, but Walt remained. He reeked of the sweet smell of marijuana. I asked him what he and his friends had been smoking.

"A cigarette. Just a cigarette, Mr. Gerson. I'm sorry and won't do it again."

"Don't bullshit me! How fucking dumb do you think I am?" I stared at him for a moment.

"People don't pass cigarettes around," I continued. "You were smoking pot, which makes you not only a criminal but a liar as well."

"Okay, Mr. Gerson, I am sorry. Real sorry. I promise never to do it again."

"You know, after all your parents do for you, after all your teachers do for you, you go ahead and just fuck things up by acting like an idiot." My voice was growing progressively louder, and Walt's panic level corresponded.

"Mr. Gerson, I am sorry. Really." He looked at the policemen across the street. "I am not going to be arrested, am I? I don't want to be locked up."

"I don't know. I would say there is a good chance you will be spending some time in prison tonight. Not as much time as your friends who ran away but some time. After all, you broke the law and lied about it."

"Oh, God, Mr. Gerson, I can't go to jail! I can't be locked up. Please don't let the cop do it. Please. Please. I am very sorry. I can't go to jail."

"Sorry, Walt, nothing I can do about it. Better go over to those gates like a man and take whatever punishment the police officer gives you like a man."

"Oh, Mr. Gerson, please—"

"Move!"

Walt slowly walked across the street. The two policemen searched him, finding nothing. They did not expect to find anything; they were just searching him for the same reason I was refusing to allay his fears of jail. Walt went into the dance and spent the next few hours with a dazed look of fear contorting his face. He kept approaching me and asking if he would be locked up after the dance. I replied that I didn't know but that he deserved to be locked up regardless of whether he escaped the punishment or not. He asked me to ensure that he would not spend the night in jail. I assured him that I did not have that power and would not exercise it even if I did.

After coming down from his high, Walt realized that he was not going to be arrested, but he began to fear something else, something even more terrifying, something in my power to control. "Mr. Gerson, please don't tell my father," he pleaded.

"Walt, you have got to be crazy. Why do you keep thinking I'm your friend here? My first call on Monday morning is to your father, and I will tell him the whole story."

"Please, Mr. Gerson, don't tell him. He'll . . . he'll . . . he won't be happy."

"Walt," I responded, walking away, "whatever your father does to you, you deserve."

"Mr. Gerson," he pleaded, "is there anything I can do to make you not tell my pops?"

I thought for a moment. "Yes, Walt, there is."

"What? Anything!"

"You tell him yourself."

"Aw, c'mon, Mr. Gerson."

"Walt, either you do or I do. And let me give you a hint. Your father would probably rather hear it from you. So if you don't want me to call him on Monday during homeroom, bring in a note before homeroom from your father acknowledging that you told him."

Walt asked to have until Tuesday, explaining that his mother was away and he wanted to tell his parents together. I said that was reasonable enough. In the meantime, I told Sister Theresa and Paul Murphy about the three sophomores. They were not surprised and said that many of the kids probably came high or drunk. But they promised to handle the situation on Monday, using all necessary force.

The first person I saw when I arrived at school on Monday morning was Walt. I was in no mood for our early morning chats, and neither was he.

"Mr. Gerson, I have the note." I was impressed; it was not due until Tuesday.

"Let me have it."

11/13/94

Mr. Gerson:

This note is to let you know that Walt informed myself and his father of what happened. Needless to say, we were disappointed and upset by his inability to make a responsible decision.

We would like to take this time to thank you for your interest in Walt. He speaks very highly of you.

On this and several other occasions we have talked to Walt but as children grow up we understand the peer pressures. I am sure this will not happen again. Walt realizes he made a bad decision and we will not tolerate any of his nonsense. Thank you again.

—Mr. and Mrs. W. Barnett

I read it over quickly. "Your mother came home early?"

He nodded. "Mr. Gerson, I just want to tell you again how sorry I am for what I did and how I let you down after all you have done for me. And I am sorry that I let down my parents, too."

"Time will tell if you speak the truth or are bullshitting, Walt. Just get ready to take your punishment from Sister Theresa this morning."

"Mr. Gerson, I have a problem with that."

"Oh, you do, Walt? And what might that problem be?"

"Jamal and Kenny said I should lie to Sister Theresa. They are going to lie, and it would hurt them a lot if I told the truth. So I don't know what to do. I'm confused."

"Well, let me clarify things for you, Walt. Whether you, Jamal, or Kenny lies, I am going to tell Sister Theresa the truth. And I have a feeling—call me crazy—that she is going to believe me over you. And I have an even stronger feeling that she is going to be much, much madder at you if you lie than if you come clean. But you can still lie, if you wish. Lie, I mean, to Jamal and Kenny. Tell Jamal and Kenny, if you must, that you told Sister Theresa that you guys were smelling roses on the corner, and that is why your breath smelled sweet."

"I guess I got to try something like that, Mr. Gerson."

"Guess so."

During the beginning of first period, the three boys were called to the office. I had second period free, so I asked Paul Murphy what happened. By that point, he had called the boys' parents and informed them of the punishment: the boys were removed from the sports teams and suspended from school until they submitted to a drug test. I thought that was an excellent punishment.[1]

---

[1] All three went for drug tests, and all three tests came back negative. I immediately thought that the boys must have taken Golden Seals, an over-the-counter pill that masks marijuana in drug tests. Paul Murphy said that the kids would not have known to use that. Even if they had known about this pill, they would not have had time to take it between the declaration of the suspension and the drug test. And they would not have thought to use it over the weekend; they did not expect to be tested. Because they tested negative, they were reinstated on their sports teams.

Walt saw me on the stairs and asked if he would be kicked out of school. He was as worried now as he had been two nights before about being locked up. I told him no but that I thought his place on the junior varsity basketball team was in jeopardy. Also, if he did it again, I guaranteed him that he would be expelled. He assured me that would not be an issue.

Twenty minutes later Paul came to the library, where I was grading papers, and asked me to come into his office to meet the Barnetts. I followed. Mr. Barnett was just as I remembered him from the basketball game early in the year—a large and powerful man who exuded authority. His wife, who had obviously been weeping moments before, was by his side. Walt stood beside them, looking very frightened.

"Mr. Gerson, let me say what an honor and a pleasure it is to meet you, you who have been so good to our son," Walt's father boomed.

"Yes, yes," Mrs. Barnett joined in, emotions bubbling rapidly to the surface, "Thank you from the bottom of our hearts."

"Well," I said, recovering from this unexpected reaction, "It has been my pleasure to teach Walt."

"Mr. Gerson," Walt piped, "it has been great being in your cla——"

"Shut the hell up!" his father yelled, pounding Paul Murphy's desk.

Mr. Barnett continued. "Mr. Gerson, as you probably know, Walt is suspended, put on probation, and may not be allowed to play basketball. That is fine with us, just fine with us. He has to concentrate completely on his schoolwork, and can afford no distractions. None. And I am adding to the punishment: Walt will never be allowed out of the house except to go to school."

"That is our usual policy," his wife added

"Yes it is, and I don't know why I let it lapse. Walt wanted to go to the dance, and I said that was fine. But then I let him go to Jamal's house first. That was my big mistake."

"Mr. Barnett, there was nothing you could do about that. A boy can go to his friend's house without doing drugs," I said.

"No, no, it was my fault. Walt did the drugs, right? So it was my fault. Now, you listen here, Mr. Gerson. If Walt ever messes up in school, if he does anything, you have our permission to do anything you want to him. He must obey you as though you were his third parent. Two is apparently not enough for this boy. If he ever slips up, if he ever steps out of line even one centimeter, call me immediately. Interrupt me at work—never worry about anything like that. It may be impossible to believe it now, but this boy is going to be something. And whatever we have to do to protect him from himself, we'll do. Right?"

"Absolutely."

Mr. Barnett's request for constant involvement was a sure signal that Walt would be all right and was repeated a couple times more throughout the year. I had the pleasure of meeting other parents who also took their child's education and school behavior seriously. Two weeks after midterms, I was giving a test to 10O. I announced that it was time to hand it in, and within a minute the students had passed their papers forward. Except for Rafael Emiriez, a student who was sound asleep. "Rafael," I commanded, "get up *now!*" He did not arise. "Rafael," I shouted, "rise and shine! It's a brand new morning, and you are invited to greet the beautiful day!" The class laughed, and Rafael's head jerked up.

"Man, what the fuck is your problem?"

"Rafael," I responded, reversing my tone 180 degrees, "I don't have a problem. But you do. Go to Mr. Murphy's office *now*. He'll deal with you now, and I'll deal with you after class."

"I ain't goin' nowhere."

"First, Rafael, let's phrase this right. You should have said, 'I am not going anywhere.' And second, yes, you are—*now!*"

He did not move.

"Okay, Rafael, have it your way. I'll go get Mr. Murphy and see if he can convince you to move your sleepy self out of this classroom."

"Aw, shit," he said, getting up and leaving the classroom. He went to the vice-principal's office and received two general detentions. Rafael's behavior continued to degenerate for the next few weeks. His homework was spotty (when he turned it in), and he rarely paid attention. At my request, Mr. Murphy called in Rafael's stepfather, Mr. Baylor; an hour later he called me into his office.

"Mr. Gerson, this is Mr. Baylor," Mr. Murphy said, introducing me to a 6'8" black man in a business suit. Rafael was shuffling nervously in a chair behind him.

"Mr. Gerson," Rafael's stepfather began, "I just want to apologize. My wife and I have great admiration for what you teachers are doing and are deeply ashamed of how Rafael interrupted your class. And so is Rafael. Right, Rafael?"

"Yes, sir."

"We want to make it up to you, and we are going to do that by ensuring that Rafael is a model student. I will come in here every Friday to meet with you, Mr. Murphy, and maybe some other teachers to track Rafael's progress. Take my card, and call me at work or home or beep me if Rafael messes up even a little. Again, let me say how sorry I am and that it will not, I promise you, happen again."

I don't know what Mr. Baylor said or did at home, but Rafael's behavior improved dramatically and his grades started picking up as well. After Rafael aced his second test in a row, I pulled him aside after class.

"What's up, Mr. Gerson?"

"Rafael," I said, "let me just tell you that your work has improved dramatically, and I am proud of you."

"You ought to tell that to my stepfather."

"What?"

"You ought to call my stepfather and tell him. You tell him when I am bad, so why not when I am good?"

"Fair enough, Rafael. I am going to do just that. I have his numbers, and I'll call him right now."

I called Mr. Baylor and got his answering machine. I hung up, called again at the end of the day, and got the answering machine again. So I left a message: "Mr. Baylor, this is Mr. Gerson at

St. Luke. I just want to tell you how well Rafael has been doing, both in terms of his behavior and his academic performance. He is really making us all proud. If you want to talk about it, give me a call anytime."

I did not hear from him, but Rafael came in on Monday (I had called on a Friday) and showed me a bag. "Man, Mr. Gerson, nice job. After you called and said all those things, my stepfather took me shopping and got me all these new threads. Look at this stuff!" I saw Tommy Hilfiger shirts, Nike sneakers, and other assorted attire.

"Very nice, Rafael. You earned it."

"And you, too, Mr. Gerson. Let me tell you what. Wait a couple of weeks, call back and tell my stepfather how I have been improving even more, so much that you think I be ready to go to Harvard. Then he'll take me shoppin', you give me your size shoes, and I'll sneak in a pair of Air Jordans in your size."

"Sorry, Rafael, I can't be bribed. I admire your ingenuity, though. And forget about Harvard. It is overrated. Williams and Yale are much better."

"All right, Mr. Gerson. I'll catch you later."

"Rafael," I called out, "one more thing."

"What's that?"

"Your stepfather would never believe that you are ready to go to Yale if you say, 'I be ready to go to Yale.' Try, 'I am ready to go to Yale.' You have to conjugate verbs at Yale."

"I'll keep that in mind, Mr. Gerson. No matter where I be goin' to college," he said with a laugh. "I played you out, Mr. Gerson."

"Yes, you did."

I never spoke to Mr. Baylor again—except on back-to-school night, when we exchanged a few pleasantries. My conversation with Mr. Baylor that night might have gone on longer, but there was a tall black policeman waiting patiently to speak to me.

"Mr. Gerson?" the officer said as soon as Mr. Baylor was momentarily distracted.

"Yes?"

"I am LaToya Harrison's father."

"Hello, Mr. Harrison. It is a pleasure to meet you."

"I want to speak to you after the presentations. I understand my daughter got detention two weeks ago."

I thought for a moment. LaToya . . . detention? Oh, yes. Two weeks earlier, LaToya's class could not settle down after gym. Shaneka had put her head down, and I told her to wake up.

"It's my neck bone, and I'll do what I want with it!" Shaneka exclaimed.

The tone of the class was set. I walked around the room, checking the homework. When I reached LaToya's desk, I asked her, "LaToya, where is your homework?"

"It's here, Mr. Gerson."

"Where?"

"Here . . . I don't know. It's on Eunicia's desk. Eunicia, where is it?"

"I ain't got none of your damn homework."

"LaToya," I said, "it was nice of you to lend Eunicia your homework to copy, but at least get it back by the time class starts. I will have to mark it as not being done."

"Dammit! I can't take it no more. I ain't want to be in this class no more! Shit!"

"LaToya, please leave the room now," I demanded, surprised at her outburst. She went to the vice-principal's office. Mr. Murphy asked why she was kicked out of class, and she responded, "I just couldn't take the pressure no more!" LaToya was issued a detention. When she came to class the next day, she behaved perfectly.

Now LaToya's father was standing before me wanting to discuss an episode I had practically forgotten about. I told Mr. Harrison that it was a single incident, one out of character for his daughter, who was normally a pleasure to have in class. "I would consider this a very serious incident, Mr. Gerson," he replied. "I would like to discuss it during the open session." (The beginning of the night was for introductions from Sister Theresa, Paul Murphy, and Nathan Siderville and for a prayer from the St. Luke parish priest.)

Mr. Harrison came back to see me at the end of those speeches and continued, "Mr. Gerson, I just want to let you know how sorry I am about my daughter's conduct. You teachers work so hard for so little pay and don't deserve that from anyone. LaToya will never act that way again. I have grounded her for a month. If she does it again, please call me at home or at work. I will ground her for two months if she does it again. This behavior will stop right away. And let me apologize again."

Mrs. Harrison then came up to me and apologized as well. "Mr. Gerson," she asked, "did LaToya apologize?"

I thought quickly and lied: "Oh yes, Mrs. Harrison. Profusely."

LaToya's parents then turned to leave. They were just about out the door when Mr. Harrison turned back. "Mr. Gerson, one more thing."

"Yes?"

He handed me a card. "Here are my numbers. Actually, let me write my beeper number on that." He took the card back for a moment. "Remember, Mr. Gerson. You are to contact me at any time if LaToya misbehaves."

"I will, sir. Thank you for your help."

The vast majority of the discipline problems were like the one for which LaToya was sent to Mr. Murphy, that is, talking in class, passing notes, being rude, not doing homework, and so on. However, while few of the discipline problems were major, these minor problems disrupted class and impeded learning significantly. Innocuous as it may sound, talking in class is a big deal. Students who talk in class are not listening, and they make it difficult for a teacher to communicate a lesson to those students who want to learn. When two students begin to exchange notes, several others inevitably join in, and the interruption escalates as the notes demand verbal elaboration. There can be no learning in such an atmosphere. Moreover, since the subject of such a student discussion is invariably more interesting to the students than the one on which the teacher is lecturing the class is not easily brought back to order.

Realizing how such "minor" incidents could easily destroy an entire class period, I had to develop strategies to deal with each common type of misbehavior. Stopping note passing was easy and essential to maintaining classroom discipline. I would confiscate the notes and read them aloud, offering my commentary along the way. This punishment was harsh but necessary—and certainly not inevitable. If students did not want their notes read aloud, all they had to do was not pass them. The content of these notes often was sufficiently embarrassing to convince would-be note passers to forsake their trade in my class. I realized this right at the beginning, when I took the following note from Luis and read it aloud, with accompanying commentary (which is reproduced in the footnotes):

Dear Elvie,

What up, baby? [1] I'm chillin' here missing you like crazy.[2] Damn baby why don't you call me no more?[3] I see you in school and you don't speak to me.[4] Man why you doing this to me?[5] Man you drove me crazy every time I see you.[6] Girl I wanna tear you up.[7] Man, and I no you got my beeper # if you don't my # is 219-1472.[8] But baby call me I miss you so much.[9]

P.S. Don't diss me baby, I need you badly.[10]

—Luis[11]

---

[1]"Luis, you need a contraction here. *What's up?* is proper."

[2]"Needs a transition word. Perhaps *because I'm* between *here* and *missing*. Better yet, rearrange the whole sentence. Perhaps *I am chilling here because I miss you like crazy*."

[3]"Luis! What have I taught you about proper English this year? The forbidden usage—double negatives—scream out throughout this sentence. And the curse is superfluous. This sentence should be transformed to *Baby, why don't you call me anymore?*"

[4]"Good!"

[5]"Big problems here. First, it is not a good idea to woo a girl by calling her *man. Baby*, as in the third sentence, is better though still not perfect at this stage in the relationship. *Darling* is much better. Second, this sentence needs a verb: *Why are you doing this to me?* is right."

[6]"Again, the mistake with the *man* usage. Moreover, your tenses must be consistent. Therefore, change *drove* to *drive*."

[7]"This sentence should go. *Girl* is better than *man*, but no girl wants to be torn up."

[8]"Again, *man*. And *no* should be *know*. Also, separate into two sentences. Perhaps *Darling, I know you have my beeper number. And if you have misplaced it, my number is 219-1472*."

[9]"Again, this is a run-on sentence that should be broken in two."

[10]"Repetitive. A bit too grasping when coupled with the *I miss you so much*, clause in the closing sentence of the main body of the work. The *P.S.* can go altogether. And if, Luis, you insist on keeping it, include it after the salutation."

[11]"Use a better salutation. If *love* is too strong, *yours truly* would suffice. But given that this note is pretty forward, I think *love* would be appropriate.

This made for effective discipline, although there were some notes I confiscated that I could not read aloud. One I collected from Shanquilla and did not read aloud was:

> Shenia called me last night and said that her and Rasheed had a physical fight and she was cryin and shit now see this shit startin already he goona swear he own her and you know she ain't haven that.
>
> —w/b
>
> P.S. Oh, it was because she wouldn't let him have his beeper back.

In addition to reading the note aloud when it was appropriate, I gave detention to all note passers. I did the same with those who talked in class, and the detentions cut down on some of the bad behavior (though it by no means eliminated it). But after giving a few detentions, I realized that they can be a waste of time: no one learns anything by writing *I promise never, never, never to talk in class again* fifty times.

I could not abandon the disciplinary action of detention, so I decided to make it educational by teaching something important that did not fit into the conventional curriculum. In and out of class I spent a good deal of time trying to convince my students that their favorite kind of music—"gangsta rap"—was awful. "You should," I constantly implored them, "listen to the Big Bands and jazz vocals. If you want to isolate one artist, then choose the best, choose the Chairman of the Board—Frank Sinatra." Frank Sinatra, they scoffed. Many had not heard of Sinatra, and others knew of him only through their grandparents. But every student who knew him had the same reaction regarding The Voice: "He is corny."

"Okay," I said in the first class in which my love of Sinatra came up. "Let's see how corny Frank Sinatra is. If you talk in class, you will get detention. And at detention you will have to listen to Frank Sinatra and write thirty, forty, or fifty times, or however many times I tell you, something like, "When I get home, I'm going to listen to the Chairman of the Board," or "Ol'

Blue Eyes is much better than Ice T." I brought in a CD player and lots of Sinatra compact discs—everything from the "V" *Discs* to the *Columbia Collection* to *Sinatra in Paris* to the *Dorsey Sessions* to *Duets II*, when it was released in December. Realizing that there was a perverse incentive at play here, this was done with some hesitation. Was I using Sinatra as punishment? Yes, I was, and I didn't like it one bit. But there was no other way to get the students to listen to Sinatra, and I knew it would make detentions livelier, anyway.

At first when the students came to detention, most hated it. But I lectured them in detention on the need to open their minds to the wonder of American popular standards, the musical accompaniment of true love and enchanting romance. Gradually, they began to come around. Not completely, of course, but I took it as a good sign when some of the detention regulars began to request specific songs. And it was even more promising when some of the students came to the detention room just to listen to Frank while they did their homework or talked quietly with their friends. In November I stepped out of the detention room for a moment and returned to find Shaneka doing something with my CD player, which was supposed to be playing Sinatra. "Shaneka, what are you doing?" I asked. I was sure that she was—as others had done—substituting a rap tape for my Sinatra CD when I was not looking.

"I'm playing the best song again. I want to get it down just right."

"What's that, Shaneka?" I said, testing her.

"The Saturday night song. You know, 'Saturday Night Is the Loneliest Night of the Week.'"

Jamal explained, "She's not kidding, Mr. Gerson. We be hearin' that same song over and over because Shaneka keeps findin' it."

"Ain't notin' wrong with that, Mr. Gerson, right?" Shaneka asked. "I just want to be sayin' that, 'I don't mind Sunday night at all, because that's the night friends come to call. But Saturday night . . .'"

"Shaneka!" Jamal yelled to her. "It's bad enough that we got to be hearin' Frank singin' it. We ain't got to hear you!"

Jamal, another regular, also had a favorite, but it was not on the *Columbia Collection* that Shaneka favored. He liked "The Lady Is a Tramp," sung with Luther Vandross on the *Duets II* disc. The students knew of Vandross and liked him; Vandross's endorsement of Sinatra almost made it acceptable to the students to enjoy the Voice. So I played that song often, bringing Sinatra into the good graces of more and more students.

I did not want the good kids—those who never got detention—to have to suffer through a year without Sinatra, so I needed to devise something for them. In December I gave a couple of good kids detention for nothing, but the absurdity of stripping the punishment out of detention became obvious right away. Since I needed to become a bit more inventive, I implemented the following policy: Any student could come to Sinatra detention voluntarily, without having to write anything, and would get extra credit on the next test for doing so. (This was a big hit among all the students toward the end of every marking period.) I kept going: "If you want even more extra credit," I promised, "you can do something else." Then I explained that every Saturday morning on New York station 1560AM, disc jockey Jonathan Schwartz presents a marvelous array of Sinatra's songs with informative commentary. (Jonathan Schwartz is so perfectly suited for his job that one cannot imagine him doing anything else. The passion he had for Sinatra had long inspired me, and I hoped it would rub off on my students as well. I felt that if they could just hear the reverence in Schwartz's voice as he softly pronounced *Sinatra*, lusciously drawing out the three syllables in a hushed tone of reverence, then they, too, would come to love the Chairman of the Board). So, I instructed my students, "If you listen to Schwartz's program and simply write down the songs you hear, you'll get a point on the next test for every five songs you bring in. You can't just list Sinatra songs, because I'll have listened to Schwartz myself and will know if you are lying." Henry set the record by bringing in seventy songs the day after Thanksgiving break. He had listened to Schwartz's whole program on Saturday as well as several weekday *Sinatra in the Afternoon* sessions. I gladly awarded him the fourteen points he had earned.

Jamal's uncle was also a Sinatra fan, so I was excited at the news Jamal, rushing into my homeroom one Monday morning in the spring, delivered: "Mr. Gerson, there's a new movie coming out about Frank Sinatra's life!"

"Really? What?"

"It's starring Eddie Murphy, and it's called 'Ol' Blue Eyes Is Black.'"

"He played you out!" Shanquilla yelled.

Inspired by Jamal's joke, I told my students they could get extra credit for watching one of Frank's movies (and there are a lot of great ones): *On the Town; Anchors Aweigh; The Man with the Golden Arm, From Here to Eternity; The Manchurian Candidate;* and the greatest musical film of all time, *High Society.* None took me up on it, but a breakthrough seemed imminent in March, when Walt reported that he had seen a Sinatra movie over the weekend. "Great!" I said, quite excited, "Which one? *The Tender Trap? The Manchurian Candidate? High Society?*"

"'Frank Likes It Raw.'"

He had played me out, but I gave him a Frank Sinatra detention. We were even.

By learning about Sinatra, the students were also learning local history, considering that Ol' Blue Eyes was born and reared in Hoboken, the town right next to Jersey City. Several of the students knew someone who knew someone who knew Sinatra or had some other connection. When we were discussing the party system and electoral politics in November, Simon said that his boss had run for city council. Simon, however, did not know the party of his boss and was now curious.

"Well, Simon," I offered, "let's figure it out. What does he believe in?" Although I did not expect to figure out this man's party affiliation (if for no other reason than the fact that New Jersey local politics is decidedly nonideological and whatever political philosophy exists on this level is distilled into slogans with which everyone agrees), I reasoned that if, by some chance, Simon's boss verbalized his ideology, it would be a good way to teach the class the difference between the two parties.

"His whole campaign was on one issue. That was it," Simon said.

So there is a chance, I thought. *Single-issue candidates are usually ideological and thus can be used to illustrate parties.* "What was his issue?" I asked.

"He wanted to build a Sinatra museum in Hoboken."

"I hate to admit it, Simon, but I can't identify his party on the basis of that. But I'd sure vote for that guy."

"Wasn't Frank a Republican?" Jermeine asked.

"At various points in his life, he was a Democrat," I replied. "At other times a Republican. He was a friend of Kennedy, a friend of Reagan. He could be either party. You see, Jermeine, people of all political persuasions love Sinatra."

The students jeered, and we returned to the material at hand. But Simon's boss's crusade did not go away. In the spring the *New York Times* covered a debate over whether to locate the Sinatra museum in Hoboken or in a more glitzy city like Las Vegas. It remains undecided; I sure hope it ends up in Hoboken. That is where his roots are, and I have a memento to prove it: Simon gave me a photograph of Sinatra at age fourteen, singing on a Hoboken street corner.

Though only a few students left my class actually liking Sinatra (and wanting to hear more of him), many more left with more tolerance for this greatest of all popular singers. If nothing else, Sinatra served as a vehicle for cultural awareness. Shaneka came to me in March and proclaimed, "Mr. Gerson, Mel Torme is better than Sinatra."

"What? No, no, no, you are wrong. For God's sake, Shaneka, not even Torme would claim that. But, in any event, it's terrific that you know Torme. Where do you know him from?" I figured that she saw me reading Torme's memoirs, *My Singing Teachers.*

"He was on *Night Court.*"

Even though some of the students began to tolerate Sinatra that did not take away from the fact that it was still detention. And detention was still punishment, of course, and punishment was something the students took very seriously. They did not object to punishment per se, not even harsh punishment, when they knew they deserved it. There was never much argument on this. If a student broke a serious rule, he would accept the punishment without much trouble. And if he gave trouble when I imposed a punishment, his classmates would invariably tell him to shut up. But what is a serious rule? It was, I learned early on, one that is enforced with relentless consistency.

Every institution has too many rules to be enforced and everyone in a position of authority has to practice some form of prosecutorial discretion. From the beginning of the school year I decided that the rule against gum chewing was one I would not enforce. This rule was broken primarily by quiet, well-behaved girls, and it never disrupted a class, hindered the academic performance of a student, or contributed to a deterioration of classroom air. *If gum chewing is a problem*, I figured, *let the student take it up with his dentist.*

Jamal had a bad week toward the end of January. On Mondays I taught his class right after lunch, generally the worst time to teach any class. In the early morning the troublemakers were not sufficiently awake to practice their craft. But in the last period of the day the students were so excited to get out of school that they more or less humored their teachers by behaving. But in the middle of the day, no way. Each class had one or two students who anchored the class in any direction they chose. Jamal was the anchor of 10O, and on this particular Monday he decided that it would be best if the class spent the period talking, pelting each other with paper, and chanting rap lyrics. I disagreed, but not even the threat of a Sinatra detention could stop Jamal that day. In any event, the period was all but ruined, and the students had to make up much of the material for homework. Since I had Jamal's class first on Tuesdays, the early hour limited his ability to ruin the period even if he were so inclined. On the day after that Monday in January when he led the class in misbehaving, I asked him for his homework assignment—questions based on readings in the textbook. "I just didn't want to do it," he explained. On Wednesday he hid a rap magazine in his book for much of the period before I caught him. The next day he came in chewing gum. That did it.

"Jamal, you have been in for Frank all week, and you will get more now. Fifty Franks for you today after school for chewing gum!"

"Chewing gum!" He looked indignant. "Chewing gum! Man, I ain't do *nothin'*."

"Jamal, it's 'I didn't do *anything*.' And yes you did. You chewed gum; you know it is against the rules."

"You didn't what?"

Jamal looked at me, nonplussed, before deciding that perhaps I didn't hear him clearly. "*I ain't be doin' nothin'!*"

"Jamal, it's 'I didn't do anything, Mr. Gerson.' If you insist on being insolent, then at least do it using proper English. And you had three grammatical errors in that last sentence."

"Man . . ."

"Jamal, say it properly, or you will get twice the number of Franks."

The class was tittering with laughter. Usually, Jamal would go along with this and say "I didn't do anything," after some gentle prodding. But not this time.

That afternoon the students in detention listened to *Frank Sinatra: The Live Duets 1943–1957*. Frank had sung "As Time Goes By" (with Bing Crosby) and "Birth of the Blues" (with Louis Armstrong) when it became obvious to me that Jamal had been serious about not coming for detention. This was not good. Getting detention was bad, but cutting it was much worse. If he had come to my detention, Jamal would have listened to terrific World War II–era music for fifteen minutes before going home. Now, at the very least, he would have two general detentions, where he would write a three-line sentence on his behavior fifty times; if he forgot that he needed to print (as opposed to using script), he would have to start over. At a minimum, he would be detained for two hours—all the while earning a seat on the bad side of Mr. Murphy. If that seat was already occupied, Mr. Murphy might call his grandmother or could even suspend him. Why did Jamal, a street-smart young man with an intuitive understanding of human nature, want to deal with all of this when he could be free of the whole business after fifteen minutes of Sinatra?

This sounds easy, but there was a complication—the *f* word invoked by Jamal: *fair*. At the time I thought that students who responded as Jamal did—and there were many of them—were demonstrating an inability to sacrifice now in order to prevent much greater loss in the future. But I later came to realize that Jamal was operating from an important principle, not an irrational miscalculation. It was through Jamal's classmate Kenny Stevens—who was always in trouble—that I began to understand what motivated Jamal that day.

"Kenny, talking again? Okay, in for Frank this afternoon."

"I ain't be doin' *nothin!*"

"No, Kenny, you did *something*. Quite simply, you spoke when you were not permitted to do so; it is called talking in class."

"But I ain't be the only one talkin'."

"Kenny, I'll see you after school. We have no more time for this."

"Jamal and Luis be talkin' too, and you ain't do nothin' to them."

"Kenny, why are you trying to get your friends in trouble?"

"Because I got in trouble for the same thing he did, and they ain't get caught."

"Even if what you are saying is true, how does his being punished help you?"

Silence.

This happened so often in so many classes that I decreed another rule: the Kenny Stevens rule. The rule was the same as the governing principle of officiating in playground basketball: No blood, no foul. Or, as I put it: No autopsy, no foul. I did not want to hear one student telling on another unless it was to explain to me why I had to call the ambulance.

Before I started teaching, I never would have imagined this rule to be necessary; I had assumed that the kids would abide by the universal unwritten rule against snitching, against causing trouble for a friend. Not at St. Luke. Whenever Kenny violated the eponymous rule (which was often), none of his friends became upset with him. Kenny was merely following the code they all followed: If one person is punished for violating a rule, everyone who is violating that rule must then be punished in the same way. Of course, this policy was unfeasible for me to honor. For one thing, it was impossible to catch everybody who chewed gum or talked in class, and there were some people whom I would not want to punish, anyway. So I announced that punishment in my class would be determined by the "principle of selective incarceration." I explained that although I preferred to punish all violations, I could not possibly catch everyone who violated a rule. "Bad acts are to be punished because they are bad," I told my students, "even if equally bad acts unfortunately pass without notice. If you don't like the punishment, don't commit the offense." The students never became happy with this system, though they did grasp its logic.

But my rule—even when I enforced it with more detentions—did not begin to solve the problem that drove Jamal away from Sinatra and to general detention that day. This notion of fairness—the idea that fairness is manifested by making sure that all who transgress get in trouble—was too deeply ingrained for any edict I decreed to have any effect. The students continued to violate the Kenny Stevens rule with impunity, even though they knew they would receive a greater punishment for doing so. By pointing out that another student deserved detention as well, they were doing justice, and that was all that counted. No student ever complained about the severity of a punishment he felt was deserved. But if a student did not believe he deserved it—if, for instance, someone else got away with a similar offense—then any punishment was considered excessive. The penalty itself did not matter. Justice did, and justice was synonymous with fairness. If the punishment was fair, it did not matter to my students how strict it was; they did not complain. If the punishment was unfair, it did not matter how lenient it was; complaints were accusatory, vociferous, and invariably led to greater punishments.

Justice, for my students, was the same thing as fairness and fairness required treating everyone the same at all times. This made teaching very complicated. I would never let Kenny spend ten minutes of class doing anything except the work at hand. He had enough trouble obeying rules; given leniency, he'd abuse it. Charles in 10Y, on the other hand, had the good sense and maturity to negotiate through the rules effectively. If I had seen both of them reading magazines in class, I would have assumed that Charles would put his away in a minute and would not make a habit of it; I would also have felt it best not to embarrass him. With Kenny, no way. But if Kenny were penalized for doing something he knew Charles was getting away with, Kenny would have been furious.

Throughout the year I wrestled with this predicament. Two staples of American education are the beliefs that all students are different and all students are equal. On the one hand, every pupil is special, a valued individual deserving of targeted personal attention. At the same time, all pupils should be treated the same way. This contradiction makes things very difficult. Consider, for instance, the charge often leveled at teachers: showing favoritism. How could a teacher not like Shanquilla, a hardworking, polite, friendly, engaged, and curious student, better than many of her peers? If teachers are supposed to respond to individual pupils as different and special, they will like some more than others and will inevitably show favoritism in one form or another. Even though favorite students are invariably those who work harder, care more, and trust the teacher with difficult personal problems, that is no excuse. But favoritism is not "fair."

This culture of fairness could easily self-destruct, if it were not tempered by something greater. Fortunately, Paul Murphy knew how to convince the students to put "fairness" in perspective. I was in his office when he called in Jamal to discuss cutting my detention. Jamal's name was called over the loudspeaker, and he arrived moments later. He waited at the door while Mr. Murphy was berating another student. Finally, it was Jamal's turn. His feet were shuffling, and he looked uncomfortable and awkward—certainly not the way this ordinarily graceful young man looked on the basketball court. He knew that he would not drive by anybody here.

"Jamal, you cut Mr. Gerson's detention."

"I . . . you got to . . ."

"I got to what?" Mr. Murphy's voice had risen. "I got to what? Only one question here is important: did you cut his detention or not?"

"Yeh."

"What is your problem, Jamal? What is your problem? You are not dumb. You know that you will get in big trouble for cutting a detention. So why do you do it? Jamal, this is not the first time I have had to see you this year. You want me to call your grandmother?" Silence. Jamal looked at the floor.

I said, "You want me to call your grandmother?"

"No."

"Do you know how hard she has to work to send you here?" Again, silence. "Whenever I have spoken to her, Jamal, she is at work. She must work seventy hours a week. Is that right, about seventy hours a week?"

"Yeh."

"Your grandmother works seventy hours a week to pay your tuition so you can tell Mr. Gerson, 'I ain't comin' to no detention'?"

"No."

"You know how many people want your seat in Mr. Gerson's classroom?"

He looked down. Every St. Luke student knew of many friends and neighbors who would transfer to St. Luke in a heartbeat if a space opened up.

"You know how many?"

"A lot."

"That's right. A lot. You want one of them to get it? Because we can kick you right out of here and into public school. Want that?"

"No."

"I didn't think so. Remember, Jamal, it is a privilege to be at St. Luke. You are being given a gift—by your grandmother, who works so hard to pay your tuition, and by us, who let you in here despite all of your disciplinary violations. I am going to be watching your every move, as are Mr. Gerson and your other teachers. You mess up once, you know the consequences." Jamal nodded.

"Here, write line number four on this sheet fifty times." The line was really four lines. Jamal just nodded, took the paper, and left.

When I got back to my classroom to administer the Sinatra detention for that day, I was greeted by Rosalita. She was one of the best students in 10Y, but I was a bit concerned to see her. In early October Rosalita had given me a note saying that someone in her class was anorexic. She wouldn't tell me who, so I suspected her. I asked her a few days later, and she said I was correct. Throughout the month, we took long walks before and after school to discuss her family situation and her eating problems. On my recommendation she had started counseling, and it seemed to be going very well. On a test in January, she included this note,

Dear Mr. Gerson,

How are you doing? I am fine. I never get a chance to tell you thanks for sending me to the counselor. Even though he scares me I find that I have a better self-esteem. Though I still have to handle certain problems I thank you from the bottom of my heart.

Love always,

Rosalita Sanchez

P.S. My aunt loves you cause you love Frank Sinatra.

"It is not about me," she assured me. "It is about Charles."

"Charles. What about Charles?"

"Charles," she said, waiting for a few moments, "took a lot of pills last night."

"Do you mean . . ."

"I mean he tried to kill himself. And he took so much he almost did it. I'm not a doctor or nothin', but he took too many pills."

"Oh God."

"And he told me."

"What did you tell him?"

"I told him that he ought to get help. He said he knew, but would only talk to you. But you know Charles, Mr. Gerson, he's too shy, so he wouldn't come on his own. I told him I would tell you first."

"Rosalita, you're an angel. I'll get him now."

"Want me to come?"

"No, Charles and I better handle this alone. We'll get you later if it's appropriate."

I sought out Charles during lunch. "Charles," I said catching up to him after ten minutes of looking, "why don't you have lunch with me in my room today?"

"Well, okay, Mr. Gerson." We walked up the stairs, making small talk and knowing that our conversation would immediately become extremely serious as soon as my classroom door shut behind us, guaranteeing privacy.

"Charles," I said as soon as we were safely in my room, "I know what happened. Rosalita told me."

I waited for his response, but he didn't say anything. Instead, he began to cry softly. I put my arm around him, pulling him close to me. He began to cry even harder. "Charles," I said softly. "Charles, really, we have got to continue this after school. Twenty-five students will enter this room in about two minutes, and they shouldn't see you like this." He composed himself after about a minute and said that he would come back after school.

When Charles returned to my room after the last period of the day, he had calmed down considerably. His speech was still broken by a teary cadence, but he made his points nevertheless. Charles had no father and lived with his mother and three younger siblings. His older brother, Bill, to whom he was very close, had been shot to death the year before. Bill, who was not involved in anything criminal, had been shot in a dispute over a woman outside his apartment. After Bill's death his mother had experienced wild mood swings and spent most of her time in depression. Responsibility for the three younger children—ages six, nine, and ten—fell to Charles, who was simply overwhelmed. After discussing his situation for about an hour, Charles concluded with a demand: "Mr. Gerson, maybe I should have said this when we started talking. But you can't tell my mother."

"Okay, Charles, I won't."

"And you can't tell anyone else, either."

"Charles, I think it would be really helpful if you let me speak to Mr. Murphy or Mr. Siderville. Both like you a lot and are as concerned as I am about you. They would help you and would help me to help you as well."

"Mr. Gerson, please. I don't want you to tell anyone. Just between me and you. I wouldn't have told you if it could not be kept a secret."

At first I agreed not to tell anyone. It was good that Charles had at least been able to confide in me. But I wanted backup; I was required by law to obtain it. Teachers must report suicide attempts, both to ensure that the child receives proper mental health treatment and to protect themselves. If, God forbid, Charles had subsequently harmed himself and a friend of his then said, "Mr. Gerson knew that Charles was thinking about it, and Mr. Gerson didn't tell anybody"—well, the ensuing nightmare is apparent enough. When I first heard this rule, I thought it was rather cold but I then realized that it was, in our litigious climate, essential and would not harm any child.

"Charles," I said, "I would greatly appreciate you letting me talk to Mr. Siderville and Mr. Murphy. I will swear them to secrecy, and we won't do a thing without telling you."

"No, Mr. Gerson," he demanded, "Like I said before, I don't want you to tell anyone."

"Charles, look now. You trusted me to help you, and I want to do just that. Now let me. Mr. Siderville and Mr. Murphy can help you get counseling, permanent counseling, even lasting through the summer. Of course, you will be able to see me and talk to me whenever you want. You have my home number, and I encourage you to keep using it. But I won't be around all the time and I may be unreachable by phone for a couple of days for some reason during the summer. You trusted me to help you, and you have to let me do what I know is best."[1]

Charles reluctantly assented, and I told Paul Murphy. I had told Nathan Siderville the day before, without Charles's permission. I had few qualms about breaking my word with Charles because I trusted Nathan Siderville completely. He was a kind, compassionate, and competent man who would know how to help Charles—and how to help me help Charles. As I expected, Nathan told me to keep on seeing Charles and to come to him for advice whenever I wanted. What Charles told me would remain in confidence until the boy was ready to speak to someone else. At that point we would refer Charles to a counselor (as we had done with Rosalita), and I would continue to be available to him as well. I gave Charles my phone number (as I had done with Rosalita). I told Nathan Siderville that I had done this, and he said it was fine. Rosalita had never abused having my number, and I did not think Charles would, either. I was right. We spoke several times over the Christmas break, and Charles agreed to see a counselor when school resumed in January.

---

[1] We were warned in the beginning of the year not to give any of the students our home telephone numbers. It sounded reasonable enough, until several of the students came to me with very serious problems that were not confined to the school. I gave these students my number and told them that they could call at any hour of the day or night. No one abused the privilege. These students did not share my number—or even the fact that they had it—with their classmates. I did not receive one crank call all year, and no one called just to chat. I trusted the students with my number, they trusted me with their problems, and it worked out very well.

HISTORY

RIGHT AFTER I WAS HIRED IN JULY TO TEACH UNITED STATES HISTORY I, Sister Theresa introduced me to my department chair, Sam Morgan. A tall, friendly-looking young man, he was clearly eager to make the new addition to his staff feel right at home. "It's great to have you here. You have never taught history at a school like this before?"

"No."

"Well, that's fine. Just keep this in mind: the students do not see history as relevant to their lives. They don't know what some guy who died a hundred years ago has to do with them. Many don't know why they are studying it to begin with, and when they don't know why they are studying something, they won't study it. Perhaps the biggest challenge of your teaching is convincing them why they should learn."

"Do you have any advice on how to do that?"

"Hard to say. I haven't taught the current sophomores. Students react to every teacher differently. You'll have to see what works for you."

I saw his point. I was very fond of a lot of teachers in my years as a student—each for a unique reason. "Okay. I'm responsible for covering everything up through the Civil War, right?"

"Right. You are responsible for covering 1492 to 1865, including the Civil War, obviously. What you cover in those four hundred years, how you do it, is up to you. You know all of the big events: Columbus, the Declaration, the Revolution, the Puritans, the Pilgrims, the various wars, and so on. You choose what you want to stress and how you want to introduce the material. Sometimes you will want to lecture, sometimes show a film, sometimes role-play, whatever. Plan ahead, but not too far; you will have to gauge the interest and ability level of the students in order to determine what to stress and how. As for textbooks, they are in the history closet."

"What is the history closet?"

"Just a closet with textbooks, filmstrips, and other teaching devices. C'mon, we'll go."

We walked, and Sam opened a door at the end of the hallway.

It was the size of a walk-in closet, with textbooks stacked several feet into the air. Other books, filmstrips, and assorted material rested on shelves behind the books.

"There are four books available for the sophomores. In about one minute you can figure out which one your lowest class should have. All right, I'll give it away—it's the beige one." I looked at it for a few moments and could tell right away that he was right. Each chapter was only a few pages long, and the sentences were short and full of simple boldfaced words (like **revolution**).

"And you'll want to give your second-lowest class the same one, and give the blue Boorstin books to 10E and 10L. As for 10Y, we got new books in last year. I don't know if you are familiar with them, but they are called *A People and a Nation: A History of the United States: Volume I: To 1877* by Mary Beth Norton and five colleagues. They're challenging, but you might want to give them a try. If not, there are probably enough of *The American Pageant* books to go around. The only problem with them is the condition." He was right; about half of them were missing covers, and many seemed to be without chunks of pages.

When I returned home, I opened a Norton book to a random page (p. 322) and found myself reading about birth control in the 1830s. I hadn't planned to teach about antebellum birth control, not least because I didn't know a thing about it. But the text explained: "The birth-control methods women themselves controlled—douching, the rhythm method, abstinence, and abortion—were the ones that were increasing in popularity." Abortion as birth control? I surely did not look at abortion that way, and I highly doubted that Sister Theresa did, either. And I had never heard of douching as a method of birth control.

Perusing the rest of the book, I saw that this passage was no anomaly. In numerous chapters there were bold-lettered sections devoted to women's rights (which made reference to "male tyranny against women"), the role of women (repeated in different chapters), working women, etc. Moreover, the book included large pictures of Judith Sargent ("the first notable American feminist theorist"), Mary Read and Anne Bonney

(British pirates), and Rebecca Lukens, who apparently took control of the family steel company after her husband and father died. I went through the book carefully and found no picture of Jonathan Edwards, the extraordinary preacher and leader of the Great Awakening, one of the most important religious figures in American history.

"Hey, Mark. Did you look at the books for 10Y?" Sam asked me the next day.

"Yes, and if it's okay with you, I'm going to use *The American Pageant,* poor condition and all. I can't use the new one."

He looked down for a minute. "Mark, the school spent a lot of money on the Norton books last year. You can use the old ones, which are really old and falling apart, if you want, but these new ones were expensive."

"I'm sure, but who bought them?"

"The last department chair."

"Did he know what was in them? Look at this." I showed him a couple of the passages I had marked.

"Well," he replied, "She was into the women's stuff, and I guess that's why she ordered the book."

"Abortion as birth control?"

"Yeah." He took a deep breath. "Well then, maybe it is a good idea to use the *Pageant* books."

The potential book problem was averted, but textbooks would not matter if I could not solve the "relevance" problem of which Sam spoke. How would I handle it? The temptation existed to use the old adage applied to church and baseball— "Many go, few understand." But that wouldn't work; my job was to teach everyone, not just the happy few. So I considered explaining to my students directly why history was, in fact, relevant. How, though, to do this? I considered quoting Santayana to the effect that those who do not know the past are condemned to repeat it. But students probably could not imagine themselves in the position of repeating a mistake of, say, John Quincy Adams.

But was relevance really what the students craved? Everyone

is captivated by all kinds of things that are not relevant. Professional basketball is irrelevant; how does a victory of the Bulls over the Rockets affect our lives in any way that could be called relevant? *But, I mused, if these kids are going to be anything like my friends and I were, they will care a great deal about the outcome of a Bulls–Rockets game and will come to school excited about how Michael Jordan slams the ball down on Hakeem Olajuwon en route to a forty-point, fifteen-assist night. Of course, not a thing in their future will be different if Olajuwon trashes Jordan instead or even if the Rockets lose all eighty-two of their games. Why is it different about history? For one, basketball is not boring and history can be. It is exciting to see Jordan slam on Olajuwon, it is exciting to see Jordan bring his team to victory and put himself in the MVP running, it is exciting to see Jordan deftly handling reporters in the postgame press conference. But how about the fact that the Puritans came to the United States from England in 1607 for religious freedom? In the abstract, that is boring, and fifteen-year-olds can't be blamed for not wanting to learn all about it. So the only workable idea seemed to be: Come clean on Day One that history is often taught in a boring way, and I'll sharply distinguish this class from others the students have despised.*

That was the plan, anyway. Sam had warned me that the class with the largest "relevance problem" would be 10W. So, after calling roll on the first day in their class, I asked my planned question: "How many of you like history?" Among the fifteen students from 10W who were sitting in front of me, there were no raised hands. This I didn't expect. I was sure there would be six or seven students who would say they loved history—if for no other reason than to show me They Cared. But no, these kids did not need to be told to be completely honest.

"No one?" I asked. "No one likes history?"

A girl in the front row with a rather skeptical look on her face responded, "Look, man, you asked us to tell the truth, and there you go. No one likes history."

I glanced down at my roll list. "Shaneka—that's your name, right?"

"Yeah."

"And, Shaneka," I added, "I bet I know why no one likes history."

"Because," a student behind her piped, "it ain't matter what no dead guy a hundred years ago said to another dead guy."

"Let's explore that," I offered. "That might be it. But you may also have disliked history because you have found it boring. You have probably learned history as a collection of names, dates, and places. Columbus discovered America in 1492, James Madison was the fourth president, the Battle of Hastings was in 1066."

Shaneka was quick to respond: "History is just math except you ain't solve nothin'."

I pondered that for a moment. "Excellent analogy, Shaneka. But keep in mind, you have learned history in only one way in the past. And that's not the way we are going to study it. In this class you will only be responsible for two or three exact dates; you are okay if you come close on the rest. So if you tell me that the Constitutional Convention was in 1786 when it was really in 1787, you are okay."

"So what is we goin' have to know?"

"I want you to know what people thought; how they acted toward one another; what they loved, hated, and craved. That is the history I am interested in." They looked confused, so I elaborated. "What is the root of the word *history?*"

"*His?*" volunteered Shenia in the back.

"Good try, Shenia, but not exactly."

"*Story,*" she responded.

"Exactly. History is not the sum of dates, names, and places but, rather, a collection of fascinating stories. Most of what we discuss is in the form of stories—about ourselves, our friends, our families—and history should be looked at the same way. Historical figures have the same loves, hates, fears, foibles, passions, worries, and ambitions as we do. The personal lives of historical figures were every bit as spirited as are ours, and the personal lives of long-dead men intersected with their public personas just as ours do."

"Aw, this ain't no different, Teach," LaToya countered.

"What do you mean?"

"So, we ain't have to know no 1492. But we'll have to know the name of George Franklin or Washington or whatever's wives and kids."

"And slaves," Eunicia offered.

"Nope," I reassured them. "That's not it. Think about what you find interesting in your life. What is there?"

"Who is having sex with who, who shot who, crimes," a female student from the back offered.

"Right on. That is the kind of history we will be studying."

"We ain't going to be studying about no sex here," Shenia responded.

"Of course we are. Yours is not the first generation to invent sex; people have been having sex for a long time, and it has always been an important part of their lives. There is no sexless history; sex has always been a cause of, or at least a factor in, great events and in the actions of great people. There will be a lot of sex in this class."

The class roared. I thought of what I had said and caught my unintentional double entendre. "Or, should I say, we will study a lot about people's sex lives." We moved on.

Throughout the year I tried to live up to my word and to teach in the form of stories as much as possible. It didn't always work. In the first week of school we started with Columbus. I thought the story of how Columbus spent six years in Spain before convincing Isabella and Ferdinand to bankroll his voyage would be interesting to my students, but I was wrong. I was not fifteen minutes into my first lecture on Columbus before Shaneka cut me off.

"Why do we have to do Columbus? We do him every year, and he ain't never fun."

I saw why the students might think Columbus boring. *If they do Columbus every year,* I thought, *why not move on?* "Okay," I replied. "Tell me what you know about Columbus. If you know enough, we'll skip him and go on."

"I think he discovered America."

"Is that all you know?"

"I ain't want to know nothin' more. Can we do somethin' else?"

"Yeah!" her classmate offered. "Like, let's learn 'bout Malcolm!"

We would stick with Columbus. But I subsequently learned just how right my intuition about making history interesting was: historical events were only as interesting to my students as the stories in which they were embedded. When an engrossing story could not be told, a lesson could still succeed only if I found a sexual reference or perhaps a curse or an especially pithy insult to include. Such references were like powerful magnets, attracting everything in their fields. If a lesson had such a reference in it, the students could remember as many names, places, and dates as I told them to. But without such a reference, they neglected to pay attention to even a few simple facts.

Unfortunately, most textbooks do not tell history as a story but as a collection of facts. The history books I consulted were usually better, but they would still have bored all but the best students in 10Y. Fortunately, I had a resource far greater than books: Mr. Gerard Sachsel, my seventh-grade history teacher. Ten years after sitting in his classroom as a student I can remember his lectures as vividly as I remember the best lessons I learned in college. To ensure that I retained all the details and nuances to his stories, I would call Mr. Sachsel and ask him to give me a particular lecture over the phone. An exceedingly generous man, he was always happy to do so. The Great Awakening, the events leading to the Civil War, the slave revolts—Mr. Sachsel knew just how to present the story of every subject in early American history so that it captured the imagination of the most recalcitrant students. For that reason, I looked forward to the spring, when the time even would be right to ask Mr. Sachsel to give me the Frank Sinatra of Lectures: the story of the duel between Alexander Hamilton and Aaron Burr. Like an athlete gearing up for the championship game, I spent a weekend in excited anticipation of delivering the Mother of All Lectures. So during first period on Monday morning, 10Y was the first class to hear Mr. Sachsel's great story.

Alexander Hamilton was a great political thinker, the main author of the monumental Federalist Papers, a brilliant economist who served as the first secretary of the treasury, a protégé of the childless George Washington, and a man of relentless ambition who probably would have been president if he had not been foreign born. A partisan Federalist, he was a man of intense loves and deep hatreds. He despised Thomas Jefferson, with whom he disagreed on practically everything except the wisdom of the Federalist Papers. Nonetheless, Hamilton worked out a back-room deal to ensure that Thomas Jefferson would become the president of the United States in 1800. Why would he do this for an enemy? Because there was one man Hamilton hated more than Jefferson, the man who would have been elected had Jefferson lost. That man was Aaron Burr.

The hatred between the two men simmered for years. In 1803, Hamilton attended a small dinner party for close friends and associates. He remarked, "Aaron Burr is the most despicable man I know." As usually happens with "secrets" told in public, this one got back to Burr. Burr responded the only way a gentleman could in those days. He sent his "seconds"—right-hand men—to Hamilton's house. Hamilton was home but was not expecting visitors. He opened the door and was greeted by Burr's seconds, one of whom slapped him across the face with a white glove. Hamilton knew what that meant. Aaron Burr was challenging him to a duel. Hamilton immediately accepted, but that hardly meant that a fight was imminent. A lot of decisions had to be made. Most of them were Hamilton's, for he was the one who had been challenged. The first choice was of weapons. Swords, rifles, or pistols? Which would Hamilton select? He had to consider his opponent, of course. And Aaron Burr was widely known as the second-best pistol shooter in the nation. Everyone shot pistols in those days, but only one man in the entire country was known to be a better shot than the sitting vice president of the United States. And it wasn't Alexander Hamilton.

Hamilton thought over his options and considered how his

response would affect his future. His dream of being president could never be realized, but there was something almost as good; Hamilton wanted to be the top general in the United States Army. What would happen if Hamilton rejected pistols out of an obvious fear of his adversary? Everyone would consider him a wimp, and wimps do not lead great armies. He chose pistols.

It is not clear who decided where the duel would be held. New York would have been the logical place, considering that both Hamilton and Burr were residents. But New York had outlawed dueling; the winner of a duel in that state could expect to be rewarded with the death penalty. Therefore, it was decided that the duel would be held on the plains of Weehawken, only a few miles from Jersey City.

Duels in those days were often not publicized until their completion. Thus, Hamilton was able to embark in a rowboat to Weehawken without telling his family where he was going. No doubt his family would have done everything in its power to prevent him from participating in the duel. This would not be the first duel for the Hamilton family. A few years before, Hamilton's son, Philip, had been drinking with a few friends in a New York tavern when he heard another patron make an insulting remark about his father. Philip immediately challenged the man to a duel, and the man accepted. The site was the plains of Weehawken. Philip lost.

Hamilton and Burr arrived in Weehawken, ready to begin. Their seconds tried to persuade their bosses to call off the duel, but neither Hamilton nor Burr would agree to do that. The duel would go on.

"Who," I asked 10Y, "will volunteer to participate in a reenactment of this famous duel?" We are going to do some role-playing and we need a Hamilton and a Burr. Walt raised his hand.

"No, Walt, I am not going to tell you who won first," I said, anticipating his question. "But you can be either Hamilton or Burr."

"I'll be Hamilton."

"Fine, who wants to be Burr?" Maura stepped to the front of the room.

"Now, don't do anything until I tell you exactly what to do," I said to Walt and Maura. I gave them each a loaded water gun and told them to face each other, holding their guns at their sides. "Now turn around and walk ten paces away from each other—and you better make them short paces because the classroom is small. Walt, you will shoot first, but not until I tell you to." I went over to Walt and gripped his shooting hand. "Fire!" I shouted. Walt turned and fired, but I jerked his hand upright so that he would not hit Maura but, rather, the top of the blackboard well over her head.

"Hey, man, what are you doing?" he asked incredulously.

"Hamilton missed on purpose. He fired over Burr's head and into the trees. Now it is Burr's shot, but not until I say, 'Go!'" I went to Maura and whispered in her ear. She nodded. After a count of three I said, "Go!" Maura fired, hitting Walt right in the stomach.

Walt hit the ground; he stayed there for a few moments.

"Walt, get up now."

"I'm dead, Mr. Gerson."

"No, you're not." I explained that Burr not only killed Hamilton but tortured him in the process: a shot to the stomach was deadly—but only after three days of intense suffering. Hamilton was put in a rowboat back to New York—as Burr had intended—where he died after a half-week of extreme pain. Burr fled to the West. And that was the end of legal dueling in America.

"Good," Maura commented. "Walt's got to stay there for three days."

"No, Maura, he can get up now. Hamilton was brought to a rowboat and taken back to New York, where he spent his dying days with his family."

After the role-playing it was time for questions and discussion. Almost every student in every class had the same first question: Why didn't Hamilton just shoot Burr as soon as he got the gun?

"It was as unthinkable to him that he would do such a thing as it is to you that he did not. He wanted to win, of course, but only with honor."

Charles raised his hand. "Maybe he didn't want to be called a fag or a punk."

"What?"

"Around here, anyone who refuses a fight is a fag or a punk. And I'd rather get beat up than to have people in my neighborhood think I'm a fag." Acquiescent murmurs filled the room.

"Good, Charles. So maybe now you can understand why Hamilton didn't kill Burr with a cheap shot."

"Why?"

"It's simple," Shanquilla explained. "He didn't want people then to think of him as a punk. If they thought he was a punk, he ain't get no props and would never be able to become the top general in the army."

"Exactly, Shanquilla. He wouldn't get any props. Shanquilla, maybe you want to try my next question: How do gunfights in 1995 differ from duels in 1803?"

"There aren't rules today. If some guy wants to kill someone else who did something to his girl, he'll just kill him. Without warning."

"And what would the friends and family of the guy who got killed then do?"

"They would go after the guy who killed him."

"And then what?"

"It goes on forever."

"Precisely. But you can be sure that no one in Hamilton's family tried to get at Burr. It was a fair fight: Burr challenged Hamilton, and Hamilton was able to choose the weapon. They both knew exactly what they were getting into and could have quit at any point. Because it was so fair and there were so many opportunities to cancel the event, Hamilton's family would never have sought revenge. The grudge was buried with Hamilton."

"Hamilton's stupid," Carmen volunteered.

"In what way?"

"Why did he go to the place where Philip was killed? That's just stupid."

"Carmen's right," Walt said. "We been there. How many of you have tipped the forty?" Most of the class raised their hands.

"Walt, forgive my ignorance, but what is tipping the forty?"

"Mr. Gerson, it happens when someone you know real well is killed. You go to the spot they was killed with a forty-ounce beer. You spill some of it on the spot and you drink some. You spill some and you drink some. You ain't ever did that?"

"No, Walt, I haven't."

There was a moment's silence before Maura broke it.

"Why don't Walt shoot me? If he did, I would never have been able to shoot at him."

"Good question. Simply, if both parties missed their shot, the duel would be over. Both people could return home with their honor intact. Hamilton probably figured that if he obviously missed on purpose, Burr would do the same. But Burr apparently had no such ideas. Or, some believe, Hamilton selected a defective weapon. No one knows."

I gave the same lecture to every class, and it generated the same interest every time. Later that week I received a call from Jamal's grandmother. "Mr. Gerson," she exhorted, "where you be gettin' those stories from?"

"You mean the Hamilton-Burr story, Mrs. Jones?"

"Yes. Jamal told me that the vice president got into a duel and killed a man. I told him he is talking like a damn fool."

"He is right. Vice President Burr dueled Alexander Hamilton, the secretary of the treasury, and won. A fascinating story, really."

"So Jamal says. You tell me that story, Mr. Gerson." So I gave her a recap over the phone, and she loved it every bit as much as her grandson did.

Discussions relating to this theme continued for several days, far longer than I intended. The students were fascinated by a rule-oriented gun culture. Just how did Burr know that Hamilton wouldn't turn around and shoot him as they were walking from each other? Luis in 10O asked. He just did, I told them. How did Hamilton know that one of Burr's seconds wouldn't kill him either at the duel or beforehand? Simon in 10E wanted to know. Same answer. The students concluded that some sort of self-interest must have been involved, perhaps Hamilton's seconds didn't kill Burr, they reasoned, because the seconds didn't want to be killed in revenge.

"Maybe," I said, "but that is not the main reason. There were set rules, rules that were not to be broken simply because they were not to be broken."

Because the students' interest in this subject was palpable, I had them write about it. I gave them an assignment asking what they thought of such a rule-governed culture of violence. If they liked it, would they prefer that such a set of rules govern fighting in Jersey City? And if so, what rules should govern modern street fights?

Almost all of the students reported great admiration for the rule-governed culture of violence in the 1800s. It fit into their exquisite sense of fairness. Carmen explained this in her paper:

> The difference between the Burr and Hamilton duel and fights today is that there is much more violence. When there is a fight now, it is never FAIR. Someone else always interferes. I understand that because if someone close to me is going to fight, so am I. I guess that is the way it has to be now. When Burr and Hamilton fought they only took one shot. But now when they fight even if they hit the person they have to use all the bullets just to make sure. It is very difficult living in a society knowing that the violence will never end. At least Burr and Hamilton knew when the violence would end.

Other students, realizing that the restraint and sense of honor that characterized fighting in the 1800s could not be applied to contemporary life, used their imagination to articulate a set of dueling rules. Jamal offered the most complete set:

1. The duel (fight) would be between the two persons.
2. The duel would be at one unknown area.
3. The people dueling are to come alone.

4. They will select to use weapons or no weapons.
5. When weapons are chosen, they are to leave and go to the unknown area.
6. When they arrive they are to fight immediately.
7. When the fight is over, the winner is to vacate the premises without looking back.
8. The winner is to never bring back the issue for any reason.

Just as the Hamilton-Burr lecture provided the students with an opportunity to consider the idea of honor and the relationship between rules and fairness, and between fairness and justice, so the story of the slave revolts, again provided by Mr. Sachsel, became the focal point for discussing a host of moral issues. The students' favorite was the story of Nat Turner.

Nat Turner was born a slave in Virginia at the turn of the nineteenth century. Almost from the beginning, everyone who knew him realized that he was not a normal boy but an extraordinary young man destined to transcend his station and its duties. Before he was ten, Turner developed a reputation as a seer. Slaves from all over his plantation would come to him to see what the future held for them. He acquired the nickname "the Prophet" because of the amazing accuracy of his predictions. Some people loved him, others feared him—but everybody respected him.

One day in his early teens Turner announced at a slave meeting that he had had a strange, portentous dream. With such an announcement coming from the Prophet, the room immediately hushed, as Turner prepared to expound on the insights that had blazed in his remarkable head as he slept. "I dreamed," he announced, "that I would lead a great slave revolt that would sweep the entire South." As exhilaration at this prophecy mixed with a realization of the seriousness of its implications, seventy to eighty slaves on the plantation immediately volunteered to do whatever was needed to make Turner's dream a reality.

Once a month all the overseers and slave owners in the region went to a meeting in town. It was a boys' night out: they would meet briefly and then play cards, drink whisky, and talk about women, guns, and cotton prices. On such nights the slave houses were completely unguarded; the whites were out and took their guns with them. After a bit of planning, Nat Turner decided that the slave revolt should begin on one such night in 1831.

Turner had a strategy, and his method was integral to his strategy. You do not, Turner instructed, merely take over the slave houses. You kill the whites inside. But not just kill the whites inside. You chop them up. Death was not adequate—torture was a necessary precursor.

First, Turner killed the family of his owners, the Robinsons, who were actually good to him. He butchered Mrs. Robinson and her nine children. Other slaves performed similar acts. When word of the massacre reached the slave owners and overseers in town, they immediately gathered a posse and covered the town looking for blacks. When they spotted a black person they did not ask whether he was slave or free—let alone whether he was with Turner or not; they simply killed him. The revolt was put down in a matter of hours, but several dozen blacks were killed in a few days. Many were brutally tortured first, as the whites tried to force them to answer the burning question, Where is Nat Turner?

Nat Turner had escaped. Many suspected that he fled up North or to Europe. He had not. Instead, he was staying on his plantation in South Carolina. He knew the place as well as a man could, and had dug a hole under a deserted woodpile. He was nocturnal, staying in the hole all day and emerging at night to drink water from a stream and to eat raw a chicken he would catch from a nearby coop and kill with his bare hands. But one evening, sick of eating raw chicken, Turner cooked his meat. Then he went back into his hole for the day. Two slaves went looking for Turner with dogs. The dogs directed the slaves to the ashes from the cooking fire, and Turner was soon found. He begged the slaves not to turn him in, but they knew that others were still being tortured in an attempt to ascertain his where-abouts. They turned him in.

Although it was extremely rare in matters concerning a slave, Turner was given a trial. He was convicted and sentenced to death. Because both slaves and slave owners were Christian, slaves were almost always given proper Christian burials. But not Turner. He was hanged and then left to disintegrate. Subsequently, various observers cut circles in his skin and peeled the skin off; then they put the body in a pot, melted it down, and put it into the soil for fertilizer. That was the end of Nat Turner.

A host of questions emerged from my lecture on Nat Turner, but the first one I asked my classes was one that easily initiated a class discussion: "If you were one of the slaves who happened upon Nat Turner, would you have turned him in?"

A short black girl named Celeste opened the discussion in 100. Celeste spoke in a voice that was exuberantly passionate when the material interested her. "There ain't no way I would ever turn in Nat Turner. The brother led our revolt against the slave masters so we could be free. I don't see how no one could say nothing else."

"That," I said, "seems eminently reasonable. Does anyone have anything else to offer?"

Kenny's hand shot up, and I called on him. "Kenny?"

"Celeste, you is all wrong. What was Nat Turner doin' when those slaves found him?"

"Mr. Gerson just said that he was in hiding, under the wood-pile."

"That's right, so what was he doing for us hiding under the woodpile? Was he leading another slave revolt?" That question was addressed to me.

"No, he was in hiding," I answered.

"So, why should others suffer when Turner wasn't doin' nothing? I'd turn him in."

"You," Celeste intoned, "dumb nigger. Dumb fucking nigger."

"Celeste," I said sharply, "cut out the language, *now!*"

"Kenny," I continued, "how could you aid the slave owners?

Turner, after all, was risking his life and leading a revolt so that you could be freed."

"Him, too."

"Yes, him, too. But so what?"

"If he ain't doin' nothin' for me now, why not turn him in?"

Quantina, an intelligent and soft-spoken student from Haiti, spoke up. "None of this matters."

"Why, Quantina?" I asked.

"Because they are all going to a better place afterwards. It is better to be dead than to be a slave. So if Turner dies or if other slaves die, who cares?"

Celeste, in the back of the room, was boiling. "You just a bunch of dumb fucking niggers. You're the problem—"

Kenny jumped in, "Mr. Gerson, throw her out! That's the second time. Give her Frank! You heard that!"

"Kenny, quiet. Celeste, I want to see you after class."

"For Frank!" Kenny pressed.

"Kenny, if you say another word, you're in for Frank."

"He played you out!" someone in the back of the room shouted at Kenny.

"Enough!" This was all a distraction from Celeste's comment and the issue of how I should handle it. Celeste had clearly breached classroom rules, and the class waited to see how I would handle the situation. I did not want to discourage her interest in history by removing her from the classroom; instead, I meant to speak to her after class about how her interesting ideas would be more convincing if they were presented in a modulated tone.

Kenny normally would have pressed even harder for Celeste's punishment, but the class was distracted by Luis and Jamal, who were laughing hysterically in the back of the class. I was furious.

"Jamal and Luis, I can't imagine what you are laughing at. I will see you both after school for detention."

"But," Jamal pleaded, "Mr. Gerson, you don't know what Luis said. It was about Nat Turner, I swear." I paused, an unspoken signal that I would hear the remark, grudgingly. "Luis said that he understood why Nat Turner cooked the chicken that alerted the slaves. He wanted free fried chicken!"

The class, except for Celeste, erupted in laughter. Luis was especially pleased with himself and got more of a response by adding, "Maybe he used the chicken's blood as hot sauce!"[1]

I told Celeste that I wanted to see her after class.

"Celeste," I told her after class, "you must understand something. No matter how upset you get at something, you must not handle it with such language."

"C'mon! You be hearin' them, Mr. Gerson.[1] That was Nat Turner, the great slave, you was talkin' about, and look at Kenny."

"Celeste, you can believe what you want, and I happen to agree with you here. But you can't call somebody a nigger if you don't agree with what they are saying, no matter how mad you get."

"But Mr. Gerson, I am black. I called Kenny a nigger, and he's black. He ain't hurt by it."

"I know you're black and Kenny is black, but there are nonblacks around. Lots of them, in fact. And it is very inappropriate for you to use that term in public. In fact, you should never use that term around nonblacks. You do not have to harm somebody directly in order to do something bad."

"Yeah, but you heard what that Kenny be saying. I learn on my black history retreats that we got to stick together, we got to be brothers and sisters or else we ain't goin' to survive. And to hear that shit in your class—I'm sorry about the word, Mr. Gerson— but to hear Kenny and Jamal talk like that just gets me mad."

"Celeste, I understand your anger at Kenny's remark. But you are not going to convince anybody of your point by cursing. If you are very angry about something, odds are that that is all the more reason to express it calmly."

"I'll try, Mr. Gerson. It's just that I get so mad."

---

[1]Jamal's detention did not affect his appreciation of Luis's joke. On the next test, he explained the Nat Turner revolt—flawlessly—also providing a pictorial accompaniment of Turner pouring liquid from a bottle labeled "hot sauce" onto the chicken.

"Celeste, you will have to try, and you will have to succeed. I am sure that the leaders of the black history retreat would not have been proud of you today. You didn't convince anybody."

She was silent for a moment. "Mr. Gerson, can I ask you a question about something I learned on the retreat?"

"Yes."

"You know when we did the Constitution?" (We had done a three-month unit on it.)

"Sure."

"Well, I learned that the amendment outlawing slavery, the Thirteenth Amendment, can be repealed and we can go back to being slaves."

"What?"

"Yeah, yeah, that's what they said. Is it true?"

"Celeste, that's the most ridiculous thing I have ever heard. The Thirteenth Amendment would never be repealed."

"But it could be, right?"

"Celeste, I guess any amendment *could* be repealed, but, believe me, it's not going to happen."

"But it could."

As February approached, many of the sophomores campaigned actively to do a massive unit on black history, covering the whole month. February is nationally recognized as Black History Month, and the students wanted to take advantage of that. In 10Y, Walt asked me a couple of times what special activities were planned for that month.

"Look, Walt, there is no such thing as 'black history.' Because blacks are an integral part of American history, we will study what some might consider 'black history' in the natural course of the curriculum. As you hopefully have seen, we do not need a special month to make room to study black people."

I don't know if he agreed completely, but the fact that we had just finished a long unit on slavery buttressed my point. In any event, Walt did not bring up Black History Month again, and his class dropped their concern as well. The same was true to a lesser extent for 10E, but not for the rest of the classes. 10W had the most prolonged discussion of black history—actually a series of discussions in which Shaneka took the lead most times.

"Mr. Gerson," she proclaimed on Monday, January 30, "February is in two days and we haven't heard *nothin'* about what we be doin' for black history month."

"You haven't heard anything, Shaneka, because, as I have explained, there is no more need for a special unit on black history than there is on 'military history' or 'political history.' 'Black history' is naturally incorporated into the curriculum."

"Yeah? Like what black history?"

"Shaneka, we just finished a week of lecture and discussion on the slave revolts of Nat Turner and Denmark Vesey."

"That ain't black history. They be revoltin' against the whites. We want to learn about just blacks."

"Shaneka, what exactly would you consider 'black history' then?"

"We should watch *Roots*, and the movie about Malcolm. And then we can talk about racism."

I was not about to spend seven hours of classroom time watching movies, and they knew that, but I offered a compromise. "Let's make a deal. If you can show me that you are serious about Black History Month, we'll devote two days to it. No movies, but we can talk about Martin Luther King, Malcolm X, racism, or whatever you want. No lectures, no notes, just your version of black history." The class murmured their approval, but there was a catch. "However, by February 15, six of you have to turn in an assignment—'What Black History Means to Me.' I don't care how long it is. And you get extra credit for doing it. That's not it, though. If fewer than six of you do it, then you cannot mention the phrase 'black history' until March."

On February 15 one student, Eunicia, handed in the paper—and she did an excellent job. Her C+ on a test was upgraded to an A+ as a result. But she was the only student to do the paper. On February 15 I told the class that they ought to do their papers over Presidents' Day weekend, considering the fact that Black History Month was ending. They murmured that they would.

But Presidents' Day weekend passed without any additional papers. I gave the class one last chance on February 23. I said that we could have a fifteen-minute discussion on race now to whet their appetite to do the assignment. They seemed satisfied. The discussion started well. I asked, "What does Black History Month mean to you?"

Eunicia replied, "It means we should learn more about our people. Black people need education more than anything else. If we had education, maybe we wouldn't blame the whites for everything. Maybe then we would blame ourselves."

"Very interesting, Eunicia. Now what exactly would you want to study in Black History Month?"

"What black people have done. You know, a black man did the first open-heart surgery, and another black man invented peanut butter."

Shaneka then chimed in. "And a black man invented the traffic light. I bet you didn't know that, Mr. Gerson."

"No," I admitted, "I didn't."

"See," Shaneka offered, "how can we learn about our people and succeed in America when our history teacher does not even know that a black man invented the traffic light?"

"Shaneka, I don't know how fair it is to blame the problems you see on my not knowing the race of the inventor of the traffic light."

"Of course you don't. Because you're prejudice. You know, this ain't right. If there were Jewish History Month, we'd do the whole month on that. We could talk about all the Jewish presidents."

"All the Jewish presidents?"

"Yeah, all the Jewish presidents. We talk about the Jewish presidents but never about why there be no black presidents. Well, I ain't doin' no mo' work for this class, yo." She put her notebook away and stared at the wall.

"Shaneka, you are not helping yourself at all. If this behavior persists, I will call your mother."

"Go right ahead. I was talking to my mother last night, and

she asked, 'What are you doing for Black History Month?' I said, 'We ain't doing nothin' because the teacher is a racist.'"

"Yeah," Shenia suggested, "Why do we have to write a paper to do Black History Month? This is *our* month! Just one month for our history! And you won't give it to us."

"You have to write a paper to show that you consider black history seriously and not just as a way to avoid hard work and have discussions on racism, instead."

"We ain't got to write no paper on George Washington, and we have discussions on him." I thought about this for a moment, before Shaneka commented on our first president. "George Washington was a fag, anyway."

"No, he wasn't," I assured her.

"Oh, yeah? Then why did he wear a wig?"

I did not initially plan to cover current events with my classes, but I decided during my first week of teaching that it would be a necessary complement to the history curriculum. From the start, I was struck by how sheltered many of the students were. I say *sheltered* because many of them had never been to New York City, which is a five-minute train ride away. Some had never been to the Statue of Liberty, which is a five-minute ferry ride from Liberty State Park, which is in the middle of Jersey City. Many had never read a newspaper before I required it for class, and their ignorance of the most basic current events was shocking. No one in the second-most-advanced class could identify a New Jersey senator; the best guess was Gorbachev. Another student identified Lautenberg as the deposed leader of Haiti, and yet another asked if Aristotle and Aristide were the same person.

Alarmed at my students' lack of knowledge of the news, I made current events a part of the curriculum. All students were required to read a paper every day. I strongly recommended the *New York Times,* but no one took me up on it regularly. Several of the students read (and brought in articles from) their ethnic (Puerto Rican, Filipino, and Brazilian) newspapers. I did not anticipate that, but I encouraged it in the hope of stimulating discussion of current events at home.

In the middle of the year two black students indicated that they wanted to learn about Africa. I said that that was perfectly reasonable and that I would be glad to discuss Africa in current events. "There is plenty going on in Africa, and plenty we can discuss," I said. "For instance, Rwanda. It is perhaps the greatest tragedy of the post-Communist world. Rwanda is the scene of decimation by machete. Every tenth person has been killed and with less sophisticated weapons than those used by the average Jersey City street cop. The war between the Tutsi and the Hutu is not even a civil war over ideas like ours was; it is over ethnic and race hatred, fueled by violent revenge." I committed myself to rehashing *New York Times* stories on Rwanda aloud to the classes whenever possible. One day in the middle of the school year, I was talking about the starvation and terror inside Tutsi concentration camps when several students in the back burst out laughing, including one of the students who had wanted to learn about Africa. "What is funny about this? What, exactly, back there? Didn't you hear me reading about the Hutu babies dying of starvation in camps because they will be massacred by the Tutsi if they come out?"

"Yeah, we heard," Jamal replied.

"Then what exactly is funny about that, Jamal?"

"Mr. Gerson, I am sorry. It is just that *Tutsi* reminded me of *Tootsie Roll*."

Celeste silently fumed; but her classmates were *amused*.

After several discussions about Rwanda, which in my slower sections never climbed above the level of the aforementioned exchange, I decided to stop talking about it in all but my top two classes. In those sections, though, discussions about Rwanda, as well as other African countries, continued regularly. The students were more interested in learning about the butchery in Liberia than in Rwanda because they had learned about the establishment of Liberia in conjunction with their study of American history of the 1820s.

Liberia was formed in 1821 to provide a home for American blacks who wanted to go back to Africa. Very few took advantage of the opportunity to emigrate; in fact, the number of blacks who went from America to Liberia from 1821 through the Civil War equaled the number of children born to slaves in any one month in the South. But Liberia was in the news in early May, and I relished the opportunity to tie current events directly to something we had just studied in history.

Until 1989, I explained, the President of Liberia was a descendant of Harriet Tubman, whose heroics we had studied earlier. President Tubman was an autocratic leader, and Samuel K. Doe, a Liberian expatriate living in the Ivory Coast, came home to restore a legitimate government. He had the power to overthrow the government but not to take control.

Carmen interrupted me. "That is like Jersey City. It is easy for one gang to win a battle with another, but that doesn't mean that it is going to rule the neighborhood."

"Exactly," I responded. "And in Liberia, as in Jersey City, several groups have been fighting each other ever since, for revenge and for control. None had a legitimate claim to govern, and none even had the power to do so illegitimately. The result? Anarchy. In the article I cited from the *New York Times*, a man in a Liberian hospital described the assault he survived. He was among seventy other members of his tribe when the enemy descended upon them. The enemy demanded that all the men in the field gather together in one place. A boy tried to flee, and he was immediately killed. The others did as they were told and were summarily, and without explanation, slaughtered. The one survivor, the subject of the *Times* profile, played dead after being clubbed in the head with a machete. To ensure his death, a soldier took a knife and cut off his ear. In spite of his injuries the man survived."

Maura said that this was just like *Lord of the Flies*. "There was no head of the group in *Lord of the Flies*, and they ended up killing each other. Like in what you just told us, there were no rules and no one to enforce them."

"Yes, Maura. Perhaps this can help us appreciate Jersey City more. You know that if you have a problem, you can call the police. They are agents of the government and have the power to enforce the law—the missing ingredient of life in places from the island in *Lord of the Flies* to Liberia."

"That's not always the case, Mr. Gerson."

"I know. But it's the idea. The great sociologist Max Weber wrote that an important sign that societies are progressing is when the government can acquire a monopoly on the legitimate use of force." I then realized that Walt had been laughing and said to him, "Walt, I am glad you appreciate my sense of humor. Unfortunately, I did not exercise it here."

"I ain't laughing at that. I don't know if Weber has ever been to Jersey City, but you can't call no cops here, man. They won't come, and if they do, they ain't goin to do nothin'."

Charles assented. "Walt is right. You got to take matters into your own hands."

"Walt," I said, "Cut out the double negatives. Now, while the police may not be as effective as we would want, you know that you can call them and that they are there. That is not so in *Lord of the Flies* or in Liberia. At least we have a government."

Carmen asked, "Mr. Gerson, are there drive-by shootings in your neighborhood?"

Walt answered, "Yes, there are."

"No," I told him, "There are no drive-by shootings in my neighborhood."

"Sure there are. When the temperature turns seventy, ten-year-olds hop on their bicycles, get mommy's money, go to the store, buy water guns, and shoot everybody along the way." The class laughed, and I quieted them down. But Walt felt the urge to speak once again. "Maybe in Short Hills you got a government. You get all the protection you need. Glee club sings too loud, and the Short Hills police are all over them. But if I got a problem here, I gonna cap the bastard. Or else he gonna cap me. Simply a matter of survival, Mr. Gerson. If I don't shoot the nigger, he goin' to kill me. And I don't think he'll wait for an hour after I call the cops."

The bell sounded, and Carmen approached me. "Mr. Gerson, you mentioned Weber the sociologist. What is a sociologist?"

"A sociologist is someone who studies society. Basically, he studies how people and groups relate to each other."

"That sounds interesting. Are there any American sociologists?"

"You're right, Carmen, sociology is very interesting. And yes, there are many American sociologists."

"Can I read what one of them wrote?"

"Of course, Carmen. I'll bring in something for you to read. You want to read the best? He's not an American, but he wrote a great book about America."

"Weber?"

"No, Tocqueville. He was a Frenchman who came to America in the 1840s to observe and write down his thoughts. The result was a great book—*Democracy in America*. And I'd think you'd like it."

"Okay, I'll read it."

I copied Chapter 13 of Part 2 of Book 2 of *Democracy in America*, "Why the Americans Are Often So Restless in the Midst of Thier Prosperity," and gave it to Carmen. As I was getting ready to leave at the end of the day, Carmen came to my room. "Mr. Gerson, can I see you for a few minutes?"

"Of course, Carmen."

"Tocqueville is right, at least as I see it. No one is satisfied with what they got and always want more. It is good because people are always working harder, but bad because they are never really happy."

"You have summarized Tocqueville's point exactly."

"I think I want to be a sociologist," Carmen said after a moment. "What do they do?"

Sociologists observe people, read a lot of books, and write about society. They write about how people and groups interact together. With that understanding of Tocqueville, I think you would be an excellent sociologist."

"Do they talk about it, too?"

"Sure."

"I want to be a sociologist who does more talking than writing."

"Carmen, great sociologists like Weber and Tocqueville did a lot of writing and a lot of talking. Their talking helps their writing, and vice versa. But you can't just talk. I'll tell you what. Why don't you start being a sociologist right now? You have done such a good job talking about Tocqueville. Write about either of the two chapters I assigned you, and I'll give you extra credit."

Carmen came back the next day, even more excited about Tocqueville than she had been the day before. She handed in her paper, and we discussed it at length. She wrote the following:

> Well, this chapter of *Democracy in America* was kind of interesting because it had some comparisons that could relate to today's society. For example, it talks about how a man can build a house for his old age and is quick to sell it even without a roof. These kinds of people are always eager to do something else, to go someplace else, to do something new, and are never happy with what they have. This relates to today perfectly. For instance, a person works hard to buy a car, buys the car and then sells it in a year. No matter how hard he worked for it or wanted it in the first place. Never is a person, back then or today, satisfied with what he has. Some people move from place to place because they don't like the neighborhood. Some people start businesses to sell something and as soon as they find a new and better way to make money, they forget about what they started off with. And some are like this because, as Tocqueville says, when they remember how short life is (supposedly), they feel they have to take advantage of every chance they get to make money. This is not always good; drug dealers think this way.

"Carmen," I told her, "I studied Tocqueville last year under a great Tocqueville scholar, Jeff Weintraub, with some excellent students. And your understanding of Tocqueville is better than that of most of the students in my class. Simply wonderful."

"Well, Mr. Gerson, Tocqueville is phat!"

Every year, the New Jersey Bar Association sponsors a mock trial competition for high school students. Students are presented with a hypothetical case and are assigned parts as witnesses, attorneys, and jurors. Winners of the county tournament go to the regional level and then to the state and national levels. When I participated in high school, we did a case about battered women's syndrome; the case for the 1994–95 school year was cocaine smuggling.

When I first told my classes about the contest in October, almost everyone seemed excited; dozens wanted to join. Having so many interested students would have been a problem, because there are only a small number of parts. But when the students saw that there would be practice every day as well as considerable homework, the number of participants decreased. Carmen, Maura, Shanquilla and many others had to work after school at the Newport Mall or local restaurants, and could not carve the necessary five or ten hours a week out of their schedule. Charles and several others had to care for younger brothers, sisters, and cousins.

But Walt and Henry signed up, as did several sophomores from my other classes and a number of juniors who heard about what I was sponsoring. St. Luke seniors were let out of school at 12:30 so that they could work; they would not be around for the 2:30 practices. The one exception was Randy, a senior to whom I had grown close. He arranged his work schedule so that he could come back to St. Luke between 2:30 and 4:00 every day.

After a few meetings, in which the students were to see which parts they wanted to take, one junior, Anita, stood out as a young woman of extraordinary talent. I knew that she was the top student in the junior class, and I was happy to have her. I did not know how happy until we met. In our first conversation Anita proved to be the most articulate student I had met at St. Luke, although she pronounced Beethoven "Beet-hoven" and vehemently "veh-e-ment-ly." I sensed that a girl as bright as she would want to be corrected, and I was right.

"You know why I get them wrong, Mr. Gerson?"

"No, why?"

"Because I have only read them, but I have not heard them spoken. It happens a lot, I think."

"That happens to everyone who reads a lot. What kind of books do you read?"

"Last summer, I read the entire encyclopedia, all twenty-six volumes."

"No kidding."

"You can learn a lot that way."

"Yes, I'm sure you can."

"And now I'm reading books about serial killers."

"Why serial killers?"

"Because I want to be a lawyer for the CIA, and I figured that reading about serial killers was the best way to go about that."

So I took Anita under my wing and made her the lead counsel on the mock trial team. Each night I would prepare general strategies for the case, which we would discuss the next afternoon. Anita invariably took what we discussed and came back the next day with refinements and elaborations of my arguments. We would stay after practice, sometimes for hours at a time. Anita did not have much of an idea of where she wanted to go to college. I told her all about my alma mater, Williams College, and showed her a book of photographs and text about the school. She was entranced by the beauty of the Berkshires (as is everyone), but said that she did not have money for college. I promised to help her negotiate with Williams for a program of grants and loans that would not be too burdensome. I said getting in was difficult but I had confidence that she would be admitted.

"Really?"

"Yes, and you know what? Richard Helms, the former director of the CIA, is a Williams alumnus."

Another bright junior, Liva, was the other attorney. Randy chose to be the defendant; he relished the opportunity to play an alleged cocaine smuggler. Walt assumed the part of the owner of

the yacht where the cocaine was discovered. Henry was the captain of Walt's ship, who had been at the helm when the yacht
was busted. The other parts were assumed by juniors and seniors.
Several sophomores and juniors signed up to be jurors; the only
responsibility they had was to be present on the day of the trial.

Starting in late October, the student lawyers came to practice
every day, and the witnesses showed up when the lawyers were
going over their parts. Anita's brilliance became more and more
striking each session. I planned on doing the rough drafts of the
questions the lawyers would ask the witnesses, but Anita soon
assumed that responsibility. In many cases her questions were
better than mine, and her strategies on how to elicit specific testimony from various witnesses matched or surpassed anything I
had prepared. When I decided to supervise this activity, I did not
have any plans to win the state tournament. I just wanted to
have a good time and help the students learn about law. But with
Anita, as calm and collected in front of groups as she was inci-
sive in private, I thought we might have a winner. As we
watched the videotapes of past championship matches, it became clear that no student attorney in the state had anything on
Anita. And as with a basketball team, one spectacular star sur-
rounded by decent teammates can carry a team to a high school
championship.

Anita was doing a wonderful job of leading the team. Inspired
by her example, the other students came prepared and eager to
evade one of the intellectual traps she would invariably lay for
them during her cross-examination. They rarely did. When they
came close, Anita would spend the evening improving her case,
often going over it with her uncle, a retired detective.

"I can't make it today," she told me a few weeks before our
first trial.

"Fine, Anita. I'll see you tomorrow. You might like this book,"
I said, handing her Alan Dershowitz's new novel, *The Advocate's
Devil*. Her absence was fine; students had to miss all the time, for
work and family responsibilities. But Anita missed the following
day as well, and although she came in the day after that, she ran

out in the middle, while Liva was cross-examining Henry. I had half a mind to follow Anita out the door to find out what was wrong, but I did not want to strand the other students. Since I did not have her phone number, I had to wait until the next morning to ask her if everything was all right.

She came to me first. "Mr. Gerson, we have to talk."

"Okay."

"I have to quit the team."

"What?"

"I am sorry to let down you and the team. But the government is cutting off my mother's welfare. She has no money, and she is going to send my eight-year-old brother to the Dominican Republic to live with an aunt. I know my relatives there. They are nice people, but they have a lot to worry about and won't be there for my brother. But he is going, anyway. So now I have to go to work at the movie theater in Newport so that I can get enough money to send to my brother every month so that he can at least take care of the basics."

I was stunned. Anita continued: "You are probably thinking, what about my father? Well, my father is not my brother's father. And who *is* my brother's father? I don't know; the man my mother claims is his father looks nothing like him and denies paternity. It's not a nice situation, but it's my situation. And I want to deal with it."

"Anita, look. Just look. Your situation is not ideal, and I am not at all surprised that you are taking control with a maturity most people twice your age do not have. But you have a future, too. You cannot quit this activity; you are the captain of the team that wins the county, or maybe the state championship, and a Williams scholarship is that much easier to come by. You have worked hard for sixteen years to put yourself in this position to get a scholarship to a great school. Now you just have five more months. Five months! Do you have any idea how short a time that is?"

"It's not that short."

"Anita, Anita. I'll tell you what. You come to practices when you want. You could go into the courtroom tomorrow if you had to. I'll take your part in practices when you can't make it. Just come whenever you want, and come to the match."

"I can't, Mr. Gerson. My grades have been starting to slip, too, while I have been worrying about all this, and I've got to get them up while I start to work so many hours. I am sorry, but something has got to go. I quit cheerleading last night, and I have got to stop mock trial, too. I appreciate your generosity and willingness to allow me to come whenever, but I just can't do it. I am very sorry."

I immediately went to Nathan Siderville, the guidance counselor, and told him the story. He was very sympathetic and told me that he would speak with Anita. "Mark, don't get your hopes up. Sad as it is, these things happen." He tried his best to convince her to remain on the team, to no avail.

I spoke with Anita again: "Anita, you can set your own schedule. If you want, we can meet at the school at 7 A.M. with one witness to go over your part. Let's make this as easy as possible. We can accommodate your new obligations and keep you on the team."

She reiterated how overwhelmed she was by having to work so much. "I just can't do anything else, Mr. Gerson. I can have nothing else on my mind except my brother and my grades. I am very, very sorry." I tried to stay close with Anita, but that did not work. She became more and more withdrawn. Although she was always polite, she seemed too embarrassed to remain close with me.

The rest of the team did not know what to think of Anita's absence. She did not tell anyone else why she had quit, and her reasons certainly were not mine to reveal. Another junior took Anita's part, but no one took her place. Despite a spirited effort on the part of all the students, we lost both our trials.

....
POLITICS

the president of Russia."

"No, Walt, he is not."

"He ain't?"

"No. Does anyone know who Bill Bradley is?" No hands were raised. "Anyone care to guess? We have eliminated the presidency of Russia, but there are plenty of other jobs you can guess from." There were no takers until Shanquilla volunteered one.

"I ain't know who Bradley is, but the president of Russia is Aristide."

"Nope," Maura corrected her. "That's Aristotle." Cynthia, a bright Haitian American student in 10Y, rolled her eyes.

Knowing my students would have to be engaged deeply in current events, I gave the following writing assignment to all my classes the next week: What are the differences between the Democratic and Republican parties? "If you don't know, don't worry. We'll learn plenty about the two parties. Just write down your impressions," I told each class.

No one in IOL, O, or W knew anything about the two parties. About half of the students in IOY and E knew just as little, but a few had strong opinions. Rosalita was the best-informed student in the sophomore class, and I read her paper first:

> There aren't really many differences in these parties. They will both make hypocritical promises come election time. Yet, personally I believe the Democrats are more hard-working than the Republicans. Take Clinton and Bush, for example.
>
> Clinton grew up in an abusive home. He said he did not let his stepfather hit his mother. He worked hard to keep his family and personal life comfortable. Bush, on the other hand, grew up in a rich home, went to all of the best schools, and was privileged in every way. He never had to work hard.
>
> Democrats like my father want to represent poor, hard-working people. Republicans are there to represent snotty, lazy, nose-picking rich people.
>
> There is also a difference between these parties when it comes to

the betterment of minorities. I believe if Michael Dukakis would have won the 1988 elections, many minorities would have been better off. Because of the 12 years of Republican torture the minorities had to endure, we have suffered more than the majority. During the recession we were laid off more, and lost our jobs more. We have tried more than anyone and I firmly believe that if a Democrat would have followed Carter, we minorities would find life a little easier.

While Rosalita's was the most well developed, several other papers reflected this same feeling toward the two parties. Maura opined, "Republicans are for the right people, in other words for whites. Republicans only worry about them as a race. They worry about keeping the white race on top, as always." Others continued in the same vein.

Walt:

I think that Republicans are greedy, conceited people. The majority of them don't care about anyone but themselves. They are only concerned with other high class people, they are not concerned about lower or middle class people. Democrats on the other hand are not greedy. They want to help all classes of people, and are well mannered. I am a Democrat.

And Carmen wrote:

Well, politically speaking, a Democrat works more for the middle class and poor people. They try to meet their needs through government help and other aids. A Republican, on the other hand, works more for the rich and upper middle class population. They tend to want to get lower middle class and poor citizens off public help not just to so-called "better the community," but to prevent the rich from giving away more taxpayer money.

Now, personally speaking, I feel that neither party is doing anything for anyone because they do not want to come to the inner city community to see what the problem is. Both parties want to spend government money on UFO sightings projects and stuff like that. This whole Democrat-Republican showcase is one big JOKE.

In class the next day I began to discuss the homework assignment when Shanquilla called out, "Mr. Gerson, you ain't be tellin' us somethin'."

"And what might that be?"

"You didn't say what party you are."

"Okay," I said. "I am a Republican." The class snickered. "Look, I know that very few of you are Republicans, but it doesn't matter to me. Many of your papers were superb even though you were supporting the wrong party. You don't have to worry about pretending to agree with me."

Walt shot back, "Don't you be worryin' about that. We ain't never goin' be Republicans. If you and you white friends want to be Republican, that has nothin' to do with us."

"Fine, then. But in order to understand why I am a Republican and why most of you are Democrats, we'll do current events. I have broken current events into five categories: international, national, local, sports, and wildcard. International refers to another country. National refers to anything to do with the United States. Local is the New York–New Jersey area. Sports are sports, and wildcard is anything you want.

"You will present one current event a week. It must be an article from a newspaper. No 'I saw it on TV, Mr. Gerson, or my aunt said that we invaded French Guiana.' I want you to read the paper, and I will require that you bring in a copy of the article. If you have trouble getting a newspaper, let me know. I read the *Star Ledger*, the *New York Times* and the *Wall Street Journal* every morning before homeroom, and you are welcome to have the papers to keep after homeroom. If everyone just takes one section of each paper after homeroom, you will have more than enough news for the day, and in the correct categories. Are there any questions?"

Rosalita raised her hand. "Yes, Mr. Gerson, does crime count as a current event?"

"Good question, Rosalita. The answer is that of course you can use crime. Usually it will fit into local, but I could see it fitting into national or even international. For instance, if President Clinton passes a federal law cracking down on drug dealers, that could fit into national. If he makes a deal with the Colombian government to curb the cocaine trade, that could be international."

"But if someone caps someone in Jersey City, that's local," Walt stated.

"That's right."

We started current events the next day, and the top class was the best prepared. The student assigned to local reported on a stabbing in Jersey City, and the student assigned to national presented a story about the murder rate in American cities. The student assigned to the international category did not have anything, and the student responsible for sports reported on the baseball strike. Charles was assigned to wildcard.

"My current event," he began, "is not from the newspaper. My cousin—"

"Charles," I interrupted, "I am sure that whatever your cousin did is newsworthy, but your current event must be from the newspaper. That is the assignment. I think I made that perfectly clear."

"But it should have been in the newspaper," he stressed. "C'mon, Mr. Gerson. I ain't understand you, and this is all I got. I'll read the paper next time, I promise."

"Go ahead, Charles, this time."

"I was at my aunt's house, right? And my cousin—actually not my real cousin but my aunt's boyfriend's son—comes in with his girlfriend. He heard that she was talking with this guy. And he smacked her. She screamed, and he smacked her again. Harder. Then I stopped him, and she stopped crying. That was a crime and he should have gotten reported."

"Charles," I said, thinking that this should be discussed in private, "why don't we discuss this after school?"

Students in every class did what 10Y had done: they fit a crime story into every conceivable category. This lasted for weeks. I tried to steer them to other subjects, mainly by insisting that the stories they presented had to derive directly from the newspaper. This did not work; the students proved adept at tying in a newspaper article with something they had witnessed or experienced. Many students spoke of visiting relatives in prison, who were there for anything from murder to dealing drugs.

While the students disapproved of the acts that landed their relative behind bars, this sentiment did not extend to the convicts themselves. Many had warm feelings for their imprisoned relatives and spoke about them freely and with affection. One day in the middle of the year Maura came to school with a Bible carved out of soap, which she was showing to everybody.

"Maura, what is that?" I asked.

"Oh," she replied, "my cousin made it in jail. He makes things for me all the time."

"Yes," Rosalita added, "my uncle is in jail in Pennsylvania, and he just sent me a handkerchief with Mickey Mouse sewed into it. I'll bring it in tomorrow."

When Rosalita brought this (rather well done) product to class, Shanquilla broadened the issue. "Look," she announced to the class, "I know more people in jail than probably all of you put together." Several students nodded, granting her that distinction. "But this ain't right. Jail is so easy. Everyone I know there just lifts weights, plays ball, and makes phat stuff all day."

"Yeah," Walt added, "that ain't right. No punishment there. Maybe I'll go sometime."

"Just don't bend over for the soap if Maura's cousin drops it while making his Bibles," Carmen warned.

"I'll cap anyone who tried to do me up the butt!" Walt fired back. "I'd die before I let some faggot near me. No bullshit here. Not with faggots."

"Yeah, Walt," Maura offered, "I am sure some big motha' is going to be scared away when you scream, 'Don't touch my butt, don't touch my rear end please, sir.'"

"Enough!" I exclaimed.

Homosexual rape in jail was the great fear of my students. Toward the end of the year I noticed that Charles—who had been bright and alert all year—had ceased paying attention. I told him to come after school, and he did.

"Charles, you have not been the same in the past couple of weeks. Your homework has not been in, you have been—"

He cut me off. "Mr. Gerson, we gotta talk."

"What's up?"

"You know my cousin is in prison. My brother's joinin' him now."

"Oh, Charles, I'm sorry."

"Yeah."

"Charles, if you don't mind me asking, what did he do?"

"It don't matter."

I thought for a moment. "No, I guess it doesn't."

"I am worried that someone is going to, you know, Mr. Gerson, up his ass. That might happen, right?"

I didn't know how to respond to this. From what little I knew of prison, I thought his fears were well-founded. "I understand your fear, Charles," was all I could say. I felt terrible about not being able to offer more to assuage the pain of my student, but what else was there to say?

"Isn't rape against the law?" he asked.

"Yes."

"So, they can't really rape in jail. There are guards all around."

"Well," I conceded, "as you know, the law isn't always enforced."

"But my brother can kick anybody's ass."

"That might help."

"But a lot of guys in jail probably think the same thing."

Most students had at least some respect for the criminal justice system because they knew the horrible things their imprisoned relatives had done. But they were far from being satisfied with it. "The criminal justice system," Walt declared in the beginning of the year, "is racist." His class murmured in assent.

"What do you mean, Walt?"

"How much crime do you see in Short Hills?"

"Not much, Walt."

"Right. But you got lots of cops, I bet. To do what? We got murders, drug dealers, rapes, stabbings, and combinations of those. We ain't able to walk home without running from someone who either wants to rob or kill us or we think wants to rob or kill us. There be crack all over, and people on the crack be committin' mad crimes. And who stops 'em? Nobody. And who controls the government? The white man controls the government. If he was not a racist, why he let our streets get like they are and your streets like they are?"

Maura joined in. "He's right, yo. You ever go into a white neighborhood, Walt? I drove into one once when my cousin came over with his new car. You know how many liquor stores we saw? One. Go to Jersey City, and how many liquor stores are there? Every block, there are a few—and sellin' that cheap shit that gets people drunk really quick on forties of MD. Walt's right. It's racism. If they opened up cheap liquor stores or peep shows or crack places in a white neighborhood, the army would be in there to stop it and protect the scared whites. But when that happens here, in our neighborhoods? Nothin'. If the Declaration of Independence is right that "all men are created equal," why ain't we protected the same?"

Rosalita followed up by asking why rapists do not receive the death penalty. If rapists can't be executed, can't they at least be castrated? Why don't murderers get the death penalty automatically? Why are drug dealers allowed to live?

In 10E I introduced Bill Bennett's idea to behead drug dealers in public parks, and it was very popular with the students. When I explained the Singapore system of justice to the students in another section, they greatly admired it; many wanted to try caning in Jersey City. A Filipino student spoke of how his beloved Marcos government used to carry prisoners naked in carts through the public square. The other students thought that was an excellent idea and could not understand why I did not think we should try it here.

We moved from crime to religion. "Let's consider school prayer," I said. "Do you think prayer in school or at graduation would make nonbelievers feel uncomfortable?" The students thought this was preposterous, pointing out that they were in Catholic school, that few of them were Catholic, and that no one felt uncomfortable during prayers or mass. So what is the problem, they wanted to know, with public school children praying?

After going through a few more such issues and eliciting similar responses, I let my students in on a secret: "You are more Republican than most Republicans."

"C'mon, Mr. Gerson," Maura answered. "The Republicans just be for the rich. You are just tryin' to convert us to your party."

On the morning of November 9, 1994, the day after the landslide Republican congressional victory, I was looking forward to current events. I had my top class first, and Maura was set to report on national current events. I was sure she would provide a blistering analysis of the Republican victory, but no such luck. She reported on a murder in New York that seemed to resemble one she saw in Atlanta as a child. No one else mentioned the Republican victory, either.

"All right," I said. "You know the elections were yesterday. Who won?"

No hand went up. "C'mon, you don't know? Anyone have any ideas?"

Finally, Rosalita had something to volunteer. "At breakfast, my father was muttering about the 'goddamn Republicans,' so I guess they won or else he would have been happy."

"Very good, Rosalita. The Republicans won a huge victory, and I am not just saying this because I am one. Some consider the Republican victory a transformation—even a revolution—signifying that the country has made a major swing to the right, that is, to the Republicans. Talk of political transformations is usually exaggerated, but that does not mean that this election won't prove to be very important."

"Shit," Walt offered.

"Anything else?" No one had anything to say for a moment

until Charles raised his hand. "Charles, you have a comment or opinion on the Republican victory?"

"Actually, I wanted to do my current event, if that is okay with you, Mr. Gerson."

"Sure, Charles, go ahead." The NBA season had just started, and Charles evaluated an article that reported that the top pick in the 1995 draft, Glenn Robinson of the Milwaukee Bucks, would not be Rookie of the Year because of his contract holdout.

In one respect, I thought it healthy that the students were apolitical: they did not see politics as their salvation or as a substitute for what must be accomplished by their own efforts. Nonetheless, I thought it my duty to encourage them to be informed about the political life of their nation. While party politics, and even discussion of political issues, did not interest them much, the moral ideas and philosophy infusing politics proved to be of considerable interest. Our best discussions of current events rarely focused on specific incidents or issues—and never on who was up and who was down on the national political scene; they focused instead on the ideas infusing the news. What was right and what was wrong? Who was getting away with murder (literally or figuratively)? Which politicians acted in concert with their principles and which ones didn't? Who had the best interests of the citizens of Jersey City at heart, and who used them as a tool to advance self-interest? These were the political questions that captivated my students, and I tried to bring them to the fore whenever possible.

I discovered another way to interest my students in politics, one that I never would have guessed at the beginning of the year. One day I was driving to school and listening to what consistently made the morning drive immensely enjoyable, to *Imus in the Morning.* Senator Al D'Amato of New York, a regular, was a guest on the show. Imus asked him a question about the O. J. Simpson trial, and D'Amato launched into a mock imitation of Judge Lance Ito, replete with a mock Japanese accent. I could not believe what D'Amato had just done. *He will surely be vilified,* I thought. *What an educational opportunity this will be for my students!*

I did not mention it that day, but the newspapers had the incident plastered all over the front pages the next day. Senator D'Amato, in response to the outcry, had to be hospitalized with a heart ailment. Everyone in the metropolitan New York area knew of what happened, and that included my students. In three of my classes the current events discussion was dominated by that event, with students loudly stressing that the offender—Senator Al D'Amato, a *Republican*—was acting like REPUBLICANS do, like a racist. I gladly accepted the teasing that accompanied the *faux pas* of a senator from my party—I had been trying to teach my students who Senator D'Amato was all year, and nothing had worked until his *faux pas* on Imus. On the identification section of the final exam, most of the students identified D'Amato correctly, adding a brief and accurate description of the Ito incident.

On the heels of the D'Amato incident was an even bigger political event. In May the major news organizations picked up the revelation in the *New Republic* that Senator Phil Gramm had financed a pornographic movie. Though none of the students knew who Gramm was before the incident, or much cared when I told them, their interest in the race for the Republican presidential nomination was suddenly ignited. They despised hypocrisy, and they despised Republicans; Republican hypocrisy provided for a great teaching opportunity. I only wish that Watergate had happened in 1995.

If my students' efforts to find Republican hypocrites sounds like something of a game, it is because it was. The "ha-ha, I got you" manner in which their comments were made and their ideas articulated also revealed something greater: my students did not take politics seriously. They hated the Republicans in the same way I hate the Knicks; just as I delight in John Starks's downfall (for inflicting on former Nets point guard Kenny Anderson a career-altering injury), so my students delighted in Phil Gramm's failure.

Moral ideas proved to be a more lasting source of political interest for the students. And there was never a case in American history where moral ideas intersected politics more directly than in the formation of the Republican Party—on July 6, 1854, in Ripon, Wisconsin. The Republican Party, I explained to all my classes, was formed to oppose the Democrats, who were split on the issue of popular sovereignty, that is, the idea that states should be able to determine for themselves whether they wanted to be slave or free. Some Democrats wanted slavery, and the rest said that states should be able to decide whether to be slave or free. The original charter of the Republican party declared as its foundation three principles: (1) Slavery is a great moral, social, and political evil. (2) The Kansas–Nebraska Act (which allowed for slavery in northern territories) and the Fugitive Slave Law (which required every state to capture and return escaped slaves) should be immediately repealed. (3) All Republicans should forget about political differences and unite in the battle against the extension of slavery until the fight is won.

I reported this historical fact somewhat triumphantly, with the hope that it would at least open the students' minds to perhaps not hating Republicans so much. Alas, it didn't work. Carmen was the only student who chose to respond. "Mr. Gerson, that platform sounds fine. But it was a long time ago, and the Republicans are against minorities now. Except for you."

"Thanks, Carmen."

Most of the students' political views were formed from personal experience or firsthand observation, and they took a kind of pride in this parochialism. I thought that the United States–Haiti crisis in the fall of 1994 would stimulate interest among the students, if for no other reason than the fact that several students were Haitian. The Haitian students stayed quiet about our involvement in their country of origin, but their classmates did not hold back. Shanquilla exclaimed, "I don't see why we is going to Haiti. They ain't never do nothin' for us. If we got a bad leader, do you think that Haiti would send its army over here to help us?"

"Shanquilla," I pressed, "your opinion is certainly a valid one. But the issue is more complicated than that. After all, we are the

United States and—according to my lights, anyway—ought to intervene to help people around the globe who could never help us. That is what makes us a superpower."

"We got mad problems here. So we shouldn't help Aristotle overthrow Cédras."

"Aristide, Shanquilla."

"Whoever he is, we shouldn't be there."

Nearly all of the students in Shanquilla's class, other classes, and in my homeroom (where live reporting from Haiti blared regularly over Channel One) agreed with her. I did not think much of the parochial opposition of my students to intervention in Haiti until the spring, when more blatant moral disasters came to the fore, namely, the atrocities in Bosnia, Rwanda, and Liberia. No matter how graphically I described the tragedies in those places, no matter how devastating the photographs I showed, no matter how much exhorting I did, I could not stir the slightest interest in any of those human graveyards among any of my students. This was a great disappointment.

We had a long unit on the Constitution, which the students loved because this document is packed with fascinating moral ideas with political ramifications. We spent a good deal of time on Article I, Section VIII, which enumerates the powers of the federal government. In this era of renewed interest in federalism, this is an especially important section; it defines, or should define, the terms of the debate between the federal and state governments. As I was introducing the unit to her class, Shanquilla raised her hand.

"Mr. Gerson, I know all about Section Eight already."

"Really? That's great. What do you know?"

"I know it is unfair."

"How is Section Eight unfair, Shanquilla?"

"Because it doesn't apply to everybody."

"You must be thinking of something else," I told her, "because everything in the Constitution applies to everybody. Especially Section Eight, which covers the federal government—which by definition covers everyone."

"Sorry, you're wrong. My mother applied to get Section Eight housing, right by the Lafayette Projects on Communipaw Avenue, and she got turned down. So you *is* wrong, Mr. Gerson. Section Eight does not apply to everyone."

After school later that week I witnessed a rather heated exchange between two juniors. As I went to break up what I feared might develop into a fight, one of the students called the other a "POW."

The other was obviously incensed; it was a good thing I was so close by. I defused the situation and then turned to one of the onlookers, a student of mine. "What is a POW?" I asked.

"A really bad insult."

"Okay, but what does it mean?"

"Puerto Rican on welfare."

Welfare was an omnipresent issue for the students and did not always come up so directly. During the unit on the gold rush in California in 1849, I spoke of the hordes of people who risked everything to trek to the West in search of quick wealth. In 100 Quantina asked if there was anything like that going on today. "No, Quantina, there's not. As least as far as we know, there are no hidden sources of gold or diamonds or any other valuables. You can't get something for nothing anymore."

"That ain't right, Mr. Gerson," Luis said.

"Luis, do you know of hidden sources of gold? Please let me in on it—after class because I think we should go there alone."

"Okay, Mr. Gerson. I'll let you in on it now. It's called welfare."

"Yes," Celeste exclaimed, "Welfare is the gold rush of today. Everyone wants money, but no one wants to do any real work to get it."

"You is on welfare, Celeste," Luis proclaimed.

"My momma works, so fuck you. *Fuck you!*"

"Celeste, calm down. It's okay," I assured her.

"Yeah, Mr. Gerson, my family is on welfare," she said. "But we is getting off. My momma said that just last night. And I promised her that I is never, never goin' to be on welfare. That is why I work hard in school. I ain't never goin' marry no one like

Luis. But everyone on welfare ain't like me. I was watchin' MTV on Monday or Tuesday, right? And Ol' Dirty Bastard said—"

"Forgive my ignorance, Celeste," I pleaded, "but who is Ol' Dirty Bastard?"

"He's a rapper. He ain't sound like Frank at all. He went on MTV and said that he gets both welfare and food stamps, and is happy about it 'cause it's free and he doesn't have to pay anything to get it. He then showed the food stamps in front of the camera, and said that everyone should try to get them. That ain't right. That just ain't right."

"You know the real bad thing about Ol' Dirty Bastard?" Luis asked.

"His music?" I asked.

"Ain't nothin' wrong with his music," Luis interjected. "He may be mad wrong on welfare, but he sings dope." The class loudly indicated their assent.

"Okay, fine. Continue, Luis."

"The worst thing is that my mother works so hard. She should earn a thousand dollars every two weeks, but she only gets eight hundred dollars because the government gives the rest to people like Ol' Dirty Bastard and Celeste."

"*Fuck you!*" Celeste shot back, exasperated.

"Luis, that was uncalled for. I'll see you for detention," I told him.

"You know," Jamal cautioned, "I know what you is saying, Luis, but some people really need welfare."

"Fine, and they should get it," Luis added. "But most don't. It's free money, and it's not just money. When you is on welfare, you go to the doctor free, you get cheap housing, and you even get free abortions. Is this fair to people workin' to support themselves and their families?"

For homework that night, I told the class to write on any political issue that interested them. Judging by the day's discussions, I suspected that most would write about welfare. However, I didn't want to require it because I knew how terrible some of the students on welfare felt about it and I wanted to give them an exit from this potentially painful assignment. But most of the students chose welfare, anyway. Their papers expressed views similar to those heard in class:

Celeste: I feel that people want welfare because it's free money. This is not fair to people getting up every morning to work to support themselves and their families. Some of these people need help, too, but most welfare money is mostly going to people who send their kids to school and sit home and do absolutely nothing. And that's not fair.

Luis: I think that welfare should be given only to those who need it and it should only be given to that person for a year. During that time, they would have to get a job. That means getting over their attitude that they can sit at home and watch television all day because the government owes them something. Meanwhile, my parents are out working to pay the government to pay these people.

Quantina: Personally, I think that people on welfare are generally lazy. My reason for saying this is because I work. Should I support someone who won't work? I don't think so. I work hard for my money to have my own things, not to borrow or take someone else's stuff. These people should get their behinds up and a job because I'm sick and tired of supporting them. If we could get a job at 16, don't tell me someone older can't get one.

Jamal: I think that welfare should only be used by those who really need it. People think that welfare is bad and they don't like it. The reason they think that way is because some people abuse it. Some people are on welfare and don't really need it. That's one of the reasons why the President of the United States wants to end welfare. The people who are cheating on welfare are hurting the people who really need it. Like I said, welfare should only be used by those who need it. I don't think welfare is automatically bad but there should be a law to contain cheats.

Rafael: The view on welfare I have is negative. I think it was a very stupid idea. People now are just taking advantage of the situation. People on welfare have kids after kids, when they can't support them and don't have the responsibility to get a job. So, my parents end up paying for it. It gets me very upset, because they have more babies just to get more money. And they are degrading themselves and their children. I hope I never have to go on welfare. But if I do, I will never take advantage. Don't get me wrong; there are people that need it badly but they do work to support themselves. So I guess I'm not against welfare, but just those who take advantage of it. Having kids for more money. It's really a disgrace.

We had similar conversations in other classes, and the reactions were the same. Toward the end of the discussion in my top class, Carmen said, "It all boils down to work. If you are willing to work, you can always get a job and make mad money."

"Yeah," Maura added, "but too many people don't want to work. And it hits all ages—from teenagers to adults."

"Why, Maura," I asked, "do some people not want to work?"

"I can answer that," Carmen interjected, "from what I see. I work every day after school at the Gap. People I know come through the mall and stop in to ask me to get them a job. They ain't really lookin', they just talkin'. So I say, 'Get your own ass a job.'"

"That's true," Maura concurred. "The same thing is on the streets. People sit around, doin' nothin' and blame the Man."

"And when they get jobs," Carmen added, "it ain't easy getting them to come to work. Or to do it right. That huge store B.J.'s opened, and said that there would be plenty of jobs. Last week there were long lines to get the jobs."

"Yeah," Walt said, "and did you see what they be doin' on the lines?"

Carmen did. "Yes. They be smoking pot. While they were waiting to be interviewed for a job."

The students' attitude toward work was substantiated by the fact that most of the students did work—and worked hard. During my job interview in July, Sister Theresa told me that some students reported working until 1 A.M. stocking at a supermarket or washing dishes at a restaurant, and she was not exaggerating. Charles told me that he had made five thousand dollars the year before, and I don't doubt him. He had all the telltale signs of a student who was putting in long hours at a demanding after-school job, but he was also studious and polite and exhibited a determined seriousness of purpose. Students who worked hard rarely received detention; they were mature, polite, and disciplined. Perhaps more to the point, they did not have time to stay after school. Trained to respect their bosses and their customers, this attitude figured into the way they treated teachers and other authority figures as well. Their bosses would not tolerate any lapses in behavior, and the hardworking students understood why—the customers would go elsewhere. In the nearby Newport Mall, where many students worked, there were competitors not ten feet away, and the margin of difference in price and quality of the goods was minimal. Work habits and attitudes relentlessly conditioned by fifteen or twenty hours a week on such jobs did not shut off when these young people came to school.

Because they worked hard and wanted and expected to work hard as adults, my students took an almost instinctive interest in money and economics. One of the parts of the Constitution that captivated them was the interstate commerce clause, because it allowed the government to limit the number of hours they could work. I did not expect to spend much time on this, but the students were fascinated by the idea that the federal government could regulate working conditions in a Jersey City restaurant on the basis of the fact that the tablecloth was made in New York. I was surprised that this point generated significant ire among my students. Carmen reacted first: "No one should tell me how much I should work except my mother. How does Bill Clinton know how much money we need or how many hours I can work and do well in school?"

Walt added, "She be right, yo. And if I ain't workin', you think I'm studyin'? No. I am out with my boys."

Every student who commented on the interstate commerce clause agreed with these assessments. The unanimity was striking, but so was the fact that most students did not allow themselves to become too upset in light of what they considered a grievous violation of their liberty. Why? Because, as Charles told me, no one paid any attention to these laws. He had worked sixty hours a week in a restaurant for several years, and no one had ever threatened to stop him. Moreover, Charles added, it was not just small businesses that do not keep official records; his younger brother had worked similar hours in a branch of a large supermarket chain, and no one had bothered him, either. I would never have thought of it before, but now I would not be surprised if statutes restricting the number of hours teenagers work are the most violated laws in the city, and there is nothing the government can do about it.

The interest generated by the interstate commerce clause spoke to one of my students' great interests—economics. Next to religious history, the kind of history my students liked best was economic history. Not, to be sure, the monetary policy of the Second Bank of the United States, but supply and demand, the invisible hand, and other concepts they could recognize in their daily lives. This interest was apparent from the beginning of the school year, when I planned a lesson on the joint stock companies that financed Columbus. Actually, it was not so much a lesson as a brief explanation, but the top two classes were so fascinated by the concept of stocks that we ended up spending the rest of the week on the stock market and other methods of investment. Several students came to see me every day that week during lunch to learn how to read a stock page, and another group came after school. My brother Rick, an expert on the stock market who was managing one of the nation's largest student-run funds, read, faxed and overnighted to me the material I used. The material was new and fascinating to the students. I decided to take advantage of our proximity to New York and told Rick to organize a trip for my class to the financial district during his Christmas break.

Our first stop was the Stock Exchange. The students took advantage of all of the attractions of the visitors' gallery, which included a variety of computers offering different information, a movie, and a gift shop. Others stood transfixed in the alcove overlooking the trading floor, listening to the market being explained in the language of their choice. The New York Stock Exchange provided a presentation and tour free of charge to the students.

"How much do you think it costs to buy a seat on the New York Stock Exchange?" the woman leading the tour asked.

I saw Rick whispering something to Shanquilla, and her hand shot up.

"Yes, young lady?"

"Six hundred and thirty thousand dollars."

"Why," the tour guide said, taken completely aback, "you are right. How did you know that?"

"'Cause I bought one," she answered, sporting a huge smile.

From there we visited my cousin Rob Goralnick, who ran a commodities clearinghouse, and then went to see his brother-in-law, Jon Yeager, who traded oil in the World Trade Center. The students liked watching the commodities floor not only because it is anarchic and exciting but because it was in the Eddie Murphy movie *Trading Places*. Jon came up from the floor, and made excellent sense of the chaotic trading going on below us. And he pleased Maura and Shanquilla greatly by naming some of the traders on the floor they had identified as especially good-looking; he pleased them even more by inviting one of these traders to meet us. (That trader was flattered and shocked; apparently, he was not used to being a sex symbol to adoring teenagers in the visitors gallery of the commodities exchange.)

Finally, we visited two of my friends, Dave Ruder and Adam Scheer, investment bankers at top New York firms. I warned them in advance that my students would ask two kinds of questions: The first would concern things about a teacher that a college buddy would know but a student would not (I told Adam and Dave to use their own discretion on those). The second type of question would be, How much money do you make? Although this is not a question asked much in bourgeois society—it is con-

sidered impolite—I knew my students would have no compunction about asking it. I told Adam and Dave to answer honestly. It
would, I stressed, be good for my students to know that people
fresh out of college can, so long as they work hard in school and
are willing to continue doing so after graduating, make upward
of fifty thousand dollars. The fact would have been a bit removed coming from me.

We met Adam and Dave at the fountain in the World Financial Center, which the students proudly identified as the site of
the big party in the Eddie Murphy movie *Boomerang*. Dave came
down first, and my brother went to greet him. "Mr. Gerson,"
Shanquilla said, pulling me aside, "he's cute!"

"He's also as good as engaged."

Adam met us a couple of minutes later at the dock near the
World Trade Center, and they both gave a short talk and then
took questions. "Dave, what kind of girls does Mr. Gerson like?"
Shanquilla asked.

"Good-looking ones."

"More specifically?"

"You'll have to ask him about that."

"Shanquilla," I asked, "do you have any other questions for
Adam and Dave?"

"I do," Maura said. "How much money do you guys make?"

"More than Mr. Gerson," Shanquilla offered.

"That's true," Dave said with a laugh.

"No, really, how much?" Maura persisted.

"Enough to live comfortably," Adam answered. "And in a condition where we can hope to continue living comfortably."

"Well, okay how much money do you make?"

"After taxes," Adam did a quick calculation in his hand,
"when you consider how many hours we have to put in here, it
comes to about six dollars an hour."

"What?" Maura looked at me. "Six dollars an hour?"

"Six dollars an hour?" Shanquilla shot back. "That means you
got to work over a hundred thousand hours to buy a seat on the
stock exchange!"

"Huh?" Adam and Dave did not know where that came from.

"Never mind," I assured them.

Maura was not giving up. "I can't believe you only make six dollars an hour. That's nothin'."

"Well, I have never figured it out precisely, but I think that is basically it," Adam conceded.

"What's the point of this?" Maura asked. "I make six-fifty an hour at Pathmark!"

"There is more to life than money," Adam replied. "It is more important to enjoy your job, to get up each morning and look forward to going to the office. It is, after all, where you spend most of your waking hours."

No answer.

"I am just curious; why do you care so much about money?" Adam asked.

"Because you buy things with money," Maura responded.

Issues of economics were more complicated when they were re-moved from my students' lives. When we watched the movie *Glory*, the part that received much applause from all the classes was when the ex-slave, played by Denzel Washington, refused to assume a position of command and told his patrician comman-der from Massachusetts, played by Matthew Broderick, that after the war he would return to the comfort of his big house in Boston while the ex-slaves would have no future. Similarly, the jokes my students made about Short Hills sometimes had harsh edges to them. It was not that they were automatically jealous or resentful of people who live in the comfort of the suburbs. They were confused—confused primarily because they had no idea how people accumulate sizable sums of money. And without knowing how wealth is acquired, they didn't know whether to admire or revile wealthy people.

In the middle of the year Rosalita volunteered this observa-tion in class: "The rich just sit around all day, reading the stocks on CNN and counting their money at the country club."

After determining that she indeed was being serious and that most of her classmates agreed with her, I said, "How do the rich accumulate their money? It doesn't grow on the trees lining the golf course at the country club."

"Mr. Gerson," she said, "you should know. A lot of rich people inherit it. Anyway, they could not work as hard as my father. Because they get their wealth naturally, they can go on fancy vacations, drive fancy cars, belong to fancy clubs where they count their money after playing golf, and never talk to those who ain't rich except their servants. They don't earn their money any more than people on welfare earn theirs."

The teachers at St. Luke were very much like the students in one way: they were apolitical and did not get excited about the tribulations of national politics. We talked politics around election time and when something major happened, but that was it. I did not hear the term *Contract with America* mentioned once; for that matter, I did not hear one conversation about Newt Gingrich. School choice was the only topic that generated any excitement or stimulated any partisan comments, as when the nuns, referring to school choice, said to me, "I guess we are all Republicans now."

The issue of school choice in Jersey City died during the year, to the dismay of the students, parents, and the faculty of St. Luke. The original school choice plan proposed for Jersey City would have given every student in the city a $1000 voucher to be applied for tuition at any participating school in the city. So tuition at St. Luke would have dropped from $2200 to $1200 immediately, lifting an immense burden from the shoulders of the parents of our students—and from the St. Luke administrators as well, who had to collect the money from even the poorest parents so that the school could remain financially solvent. Everyone at St. Luke supported the school choice program, from the students to the principal, though some teachers and administrators worried that the program would become an invitation to the state to regulate Catholic schools.

On Sunday, October 16, 1994, Mayor Bret Schundler hosted a nationwide rally for school choice in Liberty State Park, and I brought eight students on a field trip to the event. We met at St. Luke early in the morning and walked to a nearby Catholic school, which had agreed the day before to give us a ride to the rally. It was a perfect day for the park—sunny, with a mild breeze. As soon as we arrived there, the students began eating (an activity that lasted throughout the day). The easy availability of inexpensive pretzels, hot dogs, ice cream, sodas, and French fries was apparently overwhelming. There were all kinds of booths set up by various groups; the students snatched up the free offerings of pens, pads, and balloons and engaged in intense conversation with advocates of causes like the Elimination of All Government.

Soon after we arrived, I spotted an old friend and soon discovered that he was working for Mayor Schundler. Walt greeted my friend with a street handshake, replete with closed fists, a thumb wrestling grip, and a few other moves. My friend participated gladly, but when he left, I sternly informed Walt that that was no way to greet adult strangers. Walt said he understood, but I did not know whether to believe him or not. This would be tested a few moments later, when I spotted Mayor Schundler and told the students that we would introduce ourselves to him. Walt shook his hand the conventional way, offering no cracks about Republicans.

Rosalita was a bit self-conscious when she met the mayor—she had a mouthful of French fries—but she recovered herself soon enough. "Mayor Schundler," she asked, holding out her plate of fries, "would you like some?"

"No thanks. I'm too nervous to eat," he replied.

The most exciting part of the day for the students was the speech by Republican National Committee Chairman Haley Barbour—they weren't paying any attention to Barbour but, rather, to the commotion developing ten feet behind where we were sitting. About a hundred off-duty Jersey City policemen from the Police Officers Benevolent Association (ununiformed but wearing POBA hats) formed several lines behind a barricade behind us and chanted, "Bret must go!" They were not protesting school choice, they were upset about a union contract. But as one of the people attending the rally (a father with a small daughter) attempted to leave, one of the POBA members would not let him. The man tried to push his way out, and a POBA member decked him. Walt bolted toward the fighting officer, and I moved quickly to restrain him. Walt indicated that I shouldn't worry, that he was trying to take a close-up photograph with the camera that was draped around his neck. I let Walt go as the state police quickly arrested the POBA cop. Schundler's people then produced the POBA permit, which only allowed the police to protest 250 feet back from the assemblage, not in the middle of the grass, 100 feet from the stage. Walt got several pictures of the melee. I had the film developed, hoping that one would be good enough for a newspaper (none was).

This incident was quite disillusioning. Here were the police, the protectors of law and order, blatantly promulgating lawlessness. Intricate arguments about the First Amendment can be made, but there can be little doubt that the police violated the spirit of free speech by drowning out the speaker. It is inevitable that the mayor and police union should disagree on contract issues, but they should present a united front to the public, especially in a place like Jersey City, where the bad guys need to fear the good guys. My fifteen-year-old students, who had a tenuous and ambivalent relationship with authority and were taught on the street that the police are their enemy, were confused. Only slightly less confused myself, I could be of little help. And what was there to say? I admitted to my students that the police were wrong, very wrong—something I never planned to say to these children who desperately needed to revere and trust the police. When the police decided to protest, did they consider that the audience would be filled by impressionable schoolchildren? They must have, considering that much of the audience were Catholic school students. But they did not care.

Though school choice was the only explicitly political issue to captivate the St. Luke faculty and students, politics has a way of finding its way to educators, whether they are prepared or not. In

April our principal announced that we would have a half day on May 5. This was odd; half days were rare. Sister Theresa explained that the occasion was very special: we were going to attend a seminar in multicultural education at St. Peter College.

The seminar consisted of a lecture by Marina Herrera, Ph.D., who worked for the Catholic Church and is a respected figure in multicultural education. She provided several handouts, which included lessons for teachers involved with "multicultural communities," lessons replete with "practical steps for overcoming prejudice." The first step was to "acknowledge your ethnocentrism—the belief that any one culture is the paragon after which all cultures should strive." I did not see myself as an ethnocentrist and considered my colleagues the least ethnocentric people I had ever known. After all, they devoted their lives to serving children from all over the globe—as had, presumably, the other educators in the audience. But when Dr. Herrera exhorted us to acknowledge our ethnocentrism, everyone sat there nodding politely, murmuring assent. She admonished us "to be watchful in ourselves and others for any sexist or racist overtones in our teachings or the organizations to which we belong[ed]." No one seemed especially put out by that, although it seemed to imply that we were either prone to or actively promulgating sexism and racism—descriptions that, to put it mildly, did not fit the St. Luke faculty. Dr. Herrera also stressed that we had to make every effort to include in our teaching both sexes and every conceivable ethnic group and religion, including "promoters of popular religious devotion." I didn't quite know what popular religious devotion was, but I wondered why, if it was so popular, we had to make a special effort to protect its practitioners. Moreover, Dr. Herrera warned of "the tokenism that passes for the just due of different racial, ethnic, and cultural groups in textbooks, film, and other media." I made a note of that: Beware of politically incorrect political correctness.

Dr. Herrera expanded on the role of multiculturalism in the schools, suggesting that lack of a bilingual program sent a racist message that one language is better than another. Employers, she suggested, should adjust to a more diverse workforce and should be more accepting of those who do not speak English. She stressed that this was not a strictly American phenomenon, that these same principles could be applied worldwide. She said that during the cold war she wanted Americans to stop making weapons and learn to love the Soviets. Now that the cold war was over, her solution, she said, could be adapted to conflicts all over the world, from Bosnia to Rwanda.

Acknowledging that this was a lot to digest at once, Dr. Herrera explained that everything was developed fully in the packets she had handed out. She suggested that we look especially for the definitions in the handouts of key terms in American citizenship that would help us identify how the words we used and the ideas we had internalized contributed to an ethos of racism and ethnocentrism. Three key terms were defined as follows:

Acculturation. The process by which an individual born in one culture and moving to another becomes, as far as humanly possible, similar in thought patterns, language, idealism, etc. with people of adopted culture or adoptive culture. Assumes the host culture needs no change.

Pluralism. A dynamic of competition: each group tags the other groups with disparaging labels; this dynamic is often accompanied by recrimination and isolation; true communication in this setting is impossible; the contribution of each to the whole is decided by the controlling group; they remind each other how different they are and how difficult it is to communicate and to work together. The outcome of this dynamic is confrontation, the "race" to control, dominate, and even eradicate the group perceived as intruder, resulting in periodic conflagrations. It is a race for the survival of the fittest.

Unity in Diversity. A dynamic of collaboration; each group names itself, chooses how it wishes to participate in the culture and what it wants to contribute. Each group sees itself as having gifts that are indispensable to the building of human community; each contributes from a position of strength because each contribution is seen as valid and essential for the well-being of the whole; differences are accepted as the most marvelous manifestations of the grandeur and creativity of God. The outcome of this dynamic is celebration of all that is good in our humanity. There are only winners whose humanity is enhanced by the exchange with others.

Dr. Herrera did not mention how the multicultural constituency she proposed to serve would have reacted to all this. From my experience, not very well. The parents of my students wanted their children to become acculturated into a positive American culture reflecting and affirming Judeo-Christian values, and they expected St. Luke to help them do just that. I had many parents call to enlist my help in disciplining their child and had several discussions with parents about how to best prepare their child for the American work world that lay ahead. But I never had parents call to demand that my curriculum incorporate their native culture. And for good reason. Miguel, who left his family behind in Cuba to swim through shark-infested waters and throw himself on church steps in Jersey City, probably did not believe that Cuban communism was a manifestation of the grandeur and creativity of God. The same can be said for Mary's parents, who remained in China but found a way to send their daughter to America. These people probably believed that America is some kind of paragon of something; why else would Luis risk and Mary sacrifice so much?

It is not surprising that Dr. Herrera should have these views. They can be found in some form in numerous pronouncements from organizations of Reform Judaism, the Catholic Bishops, or the National Council of Churches. The striking fact about this seminar on multicultural education was that people who clearly believe that acculturation and pluralism are the best methods of American social integration, people who devote their lives to making these ideas a reality for poor and marginalized children, did not take offense at Dr. Herrera's talk. My colleagues in Catholic education devoted their lives to ideas that were diametrically opposed to those presented by Dr. Herrera, but they did not seem to realize it. Their code of ethics was being impugned, but they were not offended. If the word *multicultural* (to me an ideologically charged buzzword connoting the opposite of the pluralistic ideal) did not tip them off, Dr. Herrera's clear and direct explication of her philosophy did not, either.

As a reference point, I thought back to my college graduation, when the Phi Beta Kappa oration was delivered by a professor who castigated whites, capitalism, heterosexuals, the traditional family, men, and so on. Given the state of our academic culture, there was nothing surprising about that, but the same cannot be said about the reaction of the audience of lawyers, doctors, professors, CEOs, bankers, brokers, and students—loud and persistent applause. These intelligent and successful people sat through a speech blasting the very ideas that ordered their lives and brought them to Williamstown on this beautiful weekend, and they cheered! Politeness is certainly a virtue, but . . . Then I remembered Irving Kristol's 1970 discussion of the popularity of *The Graduate:* "There is something positively absurd in the spectacle of prosperous suburban fathers flocking to see—and evidently enjoying—*The Graduate,* or of prosperous, chic, suburban mothers unconcernedly humming 'Mrs. Robinson' to themselves as they cheerfully drive off to do their duties as den mothers." The bourgeois are sometimes so comfortable and so unaware of the importance of ideas that proud parents at Williams happily cheered a champion of the adversary culture who was rebuking everything they presumably believed in, lived for, and asked of their children.

The reaction from the Williams audience was perhaps not surprising. But Catholic clergy and lay teachers? There is no one in the world who understands the power of ideas more than Pope John Paul II, and the Catholic Church is as sensitive to the power of ideas as any institution in the world. When men and women who have dedicated their lives to the Catholic Church do not automatically respond with a potent emotional, if not in-

tellectual, rebuttal to the likes of Dr. Herrera, it shows the intellectual dominance and strategic successes of multiculturalism.

Of course, one cannot escape politics altogether, even if one is
not as strident as Dr. Herrera. When politics did come up among
the teachers at St. Luke, it was usually in association with moral
ideas and public philosophy—and related to teaching a specific
class. For example, at the beginning of the year the new teachers
went out to lunch, and a religion teacher admitted that she felt
she might have trouble instructing the students in some of the
stricter tenets of Catholic social thought. She was pro-choice (as
were most of the new teachers) and felt that she could not bring
herself to teach her students that abortion is murder. She
planned on avoiding the topic altogether. But if she couldn't, she
would state her position alongside that of the Church. "How are
you going to deal with homosexuality?" another teacher asked.

She replied, "That will not be a problem. The Bible is mixed
on that."

"Not really," another teacher interjected. "Romans, Chapter
one, and Leviticus, Chapter twenty-two, verse twenty-one,
make things pretty clear."

"What do they say?"

"Romans, Chapter one, says that evil people will be punished
by an affliction of homosexuality, and Leviticus says that any
man who lies with another man shall be put to death."

"Well, then I guess I'll have to avoid that, too."

She might have tried to avoid it, but I doubt that her students
let her. My sophomores struggled with issues of race, gender, and
ethnicity, but never homosexuality. I learned this early on, when
I decided to sponsor debates on important public issues as a way
of stimulating interest in current events. Two of the classes—the
10Y and 10O—chose to debate gays in the military, one of the
many topics I suggested. After picking the four people who
would participate in the first debate in each class, I talked to
them individually. The first question was obvious enough: "Who
wants to do which side?" Everyone wanted to oppose gays in the
military. "You can have your opinions," I assured the students,

"but realize that debates sometimes require that participants defend things with which they strongly disagree." Two students from each class agreed to argue for gays in the military, and I laid out a few ground rules: "This debate is to be mature, and that means that I don't want to hear what you personally think of homosexuality, one way or the other. The issues should focus on combat readiness, unit coherence, and other similar topics that you will come across in your research." The students came to see me a few times before the debate. Finally, having prepared with articles they had taken from the Jersey City Public Library, they were ready to debate.

The debate in one of the middle classes occurred first. In 10O the resolution was "Homosexuals should be allowed into the military," and Jamal, who was on the pro side, began. He laid out a succinct and coherent case for allowing gays into the military, saying "I ain't gay or nothin'" a few times more than was necessary (in fact, it was entirely unnecessary), but that was okay.

Then it was Kenny's turn: "I ain't want to shower with no faggot. My opponent don't care, though."

"Kenny!" I exclaimed. "This is not what we discussed."

"I wouldn't shower with no faggot, either! Fuck you . . . you . . . you faggot!" Jamal yelled back.

"Jamal!"

A member of the audience chirped in: "Jamal, you would have to shower with fags if there are fags in the military. What are you going to have, yo, a shower for fags only?"

"Well, then, I'm switching sides. I ain't want to shower with no faggots. Mr. Gerson, I ain't takin' this side no longer."

"This debate is over!" I commanded. With the debate canceled, I went straight into a lecture and hoped that things would go better in the top class.

10Y had done more research, and two speakers presented their views before we heard the "showering with gays" argument. But that debate had to be called off as well; at least I was ready this time. After aborting this second debate, I realized that it had been stupid of me to let my students choose such a topic for a debate. 10E did a marvelous job with the death penalty, and we should have stuck with topics like that.

As I later discovered, the very worst accusation one Jersey City youth could hurl at another was "Fag!" One day Walt decided that his classmate Johnny was effeminate and told the class that Johnny was gay. Johnny whimpered a reply, and the class laughed along with Walt. I had never seen a student so crushed by an insult—not even when their mothers were insulted—as Johnny was that day. This was compounded when I tried to get Tommy's attention and mistakenly called him Johnny. "Hey, Mr. Gerson," Tommy pleaded, "I ain't gay." Johnny muttered something, and the others demanded that he be given a Frank for muttering. That was definitely not going to happen, and I let the incident slide. I was tempted to punish Tommy or Walt, but dreaded the question that would be asked in the hallways—"Why did you get a Frank?" I hoped that if I just let it pass, the insults to Johnny would abate.

Nor was this feeling toward gays limited to the boys. One day in 10O Celeste began stroking Rafael Emiriez's hair (Rafael sat in front of her). "Celeste," he asked, "would you please stop that?"

The class laughed lightly, and Celeste was clearly flushed with embarrassment. "What are you, a fag or something?" she asked.

"Nope," Rafael replied, turning violently toward her. "I think you're really a dyke."

"That ain't true! I get more butt than you! I get more butt than you, you faggot! I get more butt than you!"

"Celeste," I pleaded, "cut it out. To say the least, you are not being ladylike."

"Maybe I ain't, but Rafael is!"

Prejudice against homosexuals extended to all of my classes, and it was much stronger among boys than among girls. Some girls believed that some people are gay and that we should not dislike them for it, but they were few in number. Most shared the boys' attitude but held it less intensely.

In a discussion of prejudice in 10W, I asked if prejudice against homosexuals existed.

"No," Shenia answered, "definitely not."

"Why not?"

"Nobody ain't born like that."

"Shenia, many people—myself included—believe that most gays are born that way."

"Aw, c'mon, Mr. Gerson."

"No, really. It is hard for me to believe that so many people would choose a sexual orientation where AIDS is rampant, where you will often be ridiculed or at least unwelcome, and where you will never experience the joy of having a family and raising children. Who would choose that?"

"Oh, c'mon, Mr. Gerson. How can you be born like this?" Shenia asked, displaying limp wrists and saying, "Oooo, ooo."

Shaneka agreed. "Mr. Gerson, Eunicia be right."

"Why do you say that, Shaneka?

"Because Jenny Jones said it," Shenia noted, referring to the daytime talk show host.

"She did?"

"She had on this guest yesterday who said that she became a lesbian because men always broke her heart."

"Yeah, Mr. Gerson," Shenia said, "you think she be born with a broken heart?"

The only person to back me up even slightly was Eunicia, who said that she saw a psychiatrist on Ricki Lake testify that homosexuality may indeed be inherited.

Although the students were curious about the homosexuals they saw on television, the issue was still quite removed from reality for them. Lecturing them on tolerance toward homosexuals would have been futile. I knew that prejudice against gays could not be reversed through talking any more than anti-Semitism or racism could. But there were other opportunities to discuss homosexuality. In a discussion about the O. J. Simpson case in my top class, Maura said that O.J. looked as though the trial was wearing on him.

"No, Maura, I disagree," I informed her. "I think he still looks great."

"You think what?" Walt asked in a clipped tone.

"Walt, I said that I think that O.J. still looks great. He has always been a good-looking guy, and I don't see anything different now."

"You think a man is good-looking?" he stammered.

"Walt, need I repeat myself? O.J. is a damn good-looking murderer!"

Walt recovered himself. "You a fag?"

"Walt, just because I think he is good-looking doesn't mean that I am attracted to him. There is no chance, Walt, that you'll admit it here, but you know as well as I do that O.J. is good-looking. But if I asked you, you would respond—as I would have at your age—'I can't tell if a man is good-looking or not.' But that is just silly."

"*Bullshit.*"

"Mr. Gerson," Maura asked, "you know any gays?"

"Yes, quite a few."

"You like them?"

"Some I do, some I don't."

"You mean you have gay friends?"

"Sure."

That set the class off. "Mr. Gerson has faggot friends!" Walt exclaimed. "Do you guys swim together?"

"I haven't yet, but I would have no problem doing so. Maybe I will this summer."

"Mr. Gerson," Maura inquired, "what are *they* like?"

"Gays?"

"Yes."

"The gay friends I have are normal people that any of you would like if you got to know them."

The class moved on, but Cynthia came to see me at lunch. "Mr. Gerson, can I speak with you for a moment?"

"Of course, Cynthia, what's on your mind?"

"I'm just worried about you."

"Oh?"

"I mean, do your gay friends ever hit on you?"

"No, Cynthia, most of them have boyfriends. They know that I am not gay and would want nothing to do with them romantically."

"But, still, I saw on Ricki Lake that gays sometimes seduce other men. Like this man was sharing an apartment with his fiancée went away for a while. The man's male cousin stayed with him, on a sofa in the living room. The man and his cousin had gay sex and talked about it on a radio show the next day. The fiancée was driving home and was listening to that radio station. She went inside and beat the guy up."

"Good for her. He deserved it. He should not have cheated on her."

"But that kind of thing must happen all the time, and I don't want it to happen to you, Mr. Gerson."

The influence of shows like those hosted by Ricki Lake and Jenny Jones on the thinking of my female students cannot be overestimated. My students could quote these programs as accurately as an Evangelical can quote the New Testament. For many of the students, these shows constituted their only contact with the world outside of Jersey City. Rhoda was a student with no motivation whose comments sometimes revealed an intelligence that far surpassed her poor marks. The morning after I gave her a D in the third marking period, she submitted the following note:

> I never been so lazy in my life until I saw that children on t.v. show don't show no respect for their parents on tv. So then I felt like it was a good thing that you can get what you want and come in when you want. So my momma just give me anything I want. Mr. Gerson, you really have some good reports and ideas to talk about, but I just get so lazy. History has always been my best subject, but all this violence around me is just bringing me down. I'm just hooked to all the violent t.v. shows and the talk shows and the tv movies and rappers. I love rap.

Most students were far less blunt, and most would not have so easily blamed their failures on television. Moreover, though my exhortations to the students to read instead of watch television did not always resonate with their inclinations, a few students were able to come to this belief on their own. Grace was the most mature student I had; her self-confidence, sense of justice, religious piety, and commitment to hard work were inspiring to other students and to her teachers. In a paper on the Benevolent Empire—the amalgam of religious groups that spearheaded the temperance, Prohibition, Sunday School, and other such movements in the mid- to late-1800s—Grace offered a contrast to Rhoda's experience with the entertainment world:

> Television portrays morality as being a trait for the strange. That's the junk you see on talk shows and sitcoms, and on other shows as well. If that is the case then I'm just strange because moral values and the methods of morality that were instilled in my heart is the reason why I am who I am today. I am fortunate enough to have an intelligent, spirit-filled mother and a pastor who pours in his cultural-revelational knowledge into my heart every Sunday.

O.J.

"HE AIN'T DO IT. HE WAS FRAMED." JAMAL HAD COME TO SEE ME DURING homeroom.

"Yeah, Jamal," I said, "right."

My freshman homeroom was watching Channel One, the controversial news program brought to high schools by Christopher Whittle (controversial because it has commercials). I was not too worried about advertisements defiling my students' minds but was rather disturbed by the Generation X reporters who came on television in T-shirts and jeans. That is not how mature people dress for work.

When news on O.J. came on, the homeroom quieted down immediately. The silence was disturbed only by the students who felt the need to proclaim Simpson's innocence to the reporters on television—and to proclaim it proudly, with evidence and facts. These ninth-graders were as knowledgeable about the case as they were convinced of Simpson's innocence. They knew every major player associated with the trial—from Johnnie Cochran to Paula Barbieri to Denise Brown to Christopher Darden—and they were eager to learn more about the trial and about anything that could possibly be related to the case.

Among the sophomores in all of my classes the Simpson trial was something of an obsession. This fascination was not simply prurient or voyeuristic (though there is no doubt some of that). The trial was a terrific teaching tool that helped to illuminate important aspects of American history curriculum. The best way to interest students in a subject they suspected was irrelevant was to tie it directly to a pressing contemporary concern. This worked in isolated cases; for instance, interest in the duel between Alexander Hamilton and Aaron Burr appealed to my students' experiences with violence.

The O.J. case provided a consistent frame of reference that was useful in a variety of lessons throughout the year. Because of the case, the students were able to understand the multifaceted workings of the jury system; the roles of the judge, lawyers, and witnesses; how and why evidence is admitted and impeached; and the significance of terms such as *direct examination, cross-ex-*

amination, contempt of court, grand jury, sequester, recess, objection, discovery, sustained, and *overruled.* But there is more. Students love history when they can see justice and injustice, fairness and unfairness in it—and when they can take sides. O.J. allowed them to do just that—and about far more than just the trial itself.

The best example of how the subject of O.J. helped me teach American history is seen in our study of the Constitution, on which we spent more than two months. The fourth through the eighth amendments are about crime, and the O.J. case was the vehicle for studying them. When explaining the search and seizure requirements of the Fourth Amendment, Shanquilla pointed out that the defense was trying to nail Detective Mark Fuhrman on this because he had no search warrant when he climbed over the fence at Rockingham. "Exactly," I replied. "Given that, do you think that he should have scaled the fence anyway?" Shanquilla and her classmates vigorously agreed: what if someone was being killed while Furhman was calling a judge asking for permission to go to O.J.'s property? "Good point," I then explained the exclusionary rule and asked, "Should evidence that is acquired illegally be used in court anyway?" This provoked a heated discussion, and all but three said that illegally obtained evidence should be included. If someone is guilty, the consensus was to get him off the street no matter what. Why force us to live with murderers and rapists just because the police made a mistake? my students asked.

That brought us to the discussion of the jury, as delineated in the Sixth Amendment. We covered this amendment in early January, which was perfect because that was when Robert Shapiro was demanding that O.J. be tried right away. The students reasoned immediately: Shapiro wants a speedy trial, just like the amendment says. Right. But the public aspect of the "speedy and public trial" part of the amendment caused some disagreement. "This amendment," Carmen declared, "makes no sense."

"Why?" I asked.

"It says you get a public trial in front of an impartial jury, right?"

"Yes."

"How is O.J. going to get an impartial jury if the trial is in public? Everyone in Los Angeles knows about the case, and the media is making it worse. Ain't no way O.J. is going to get a fair trial under these conditions."

"If it wasn't public, Carmen, we wouldn't be able to talk about it all the time," Walt added.

"It's not for your amusement, Carmen," Shanquilla shot back, "it's for O.J.'s innocence."

And that, for my students, was no laughing matter. No more than 4 of my 120 students thought O.J. Simpson was definitely guilty, and few were willing to admit the possibility that he might be. This faith in Simpson was strongest among black girls. They enforced something resembling social control to govern opinions on the case. One girl suggested in February that the case against O.J. wasn't that crazy. Bad move. She was viciously attacked until she admitted that she was just kidding and that of course O.J. was innocent.

Why was O.J. so important to these students? If he was guilty, they seemed to think, his race was guilty. Of what? That was not clear. When I mentioned that I thought O.J. was guilty, they dismissed my opinion with a smile, convinced that I wouldn't understand. Remembering Sidney Hook's question to a die-hard supporter of Alger Hiss—"If Hiss were to come out tomorrow and announce, 'I'm guilty!' would you believe him?"—I asked my students, "If O.J. were to come out tomorrow and say, 'I did it!' would you believe him?" Like Sidney Hook's interlocutor, they replied, "Absolutely not." They reasoned that Simpson would just be covering up for somebody else. We agreed to disagree, and that only made our discussions even more interesting. Though my students identified with Simpson on racial grounds and for racial reasons, they must not have internalized the case too deeply because they were not offended at my belief in Simpson's guilt. They thought I was merely naive, nothing worse. And at least I admitted that O.J. would never be convicted.

Why, my students asked, do you think that O.J. will get off even though he is guilty? "Simple," I replied. "There is bound to be at least one holdout on the jury. If one juror is confused, the defense wins." While nearly all the students disagreed with me over the question of O.J.'s innocence, my contention that he would nevertheless be acquitted produced some spirited discussion. Wanting to explore this issue, I handed out an article by Kenneth Noble from the *New York Times* that showed that the overwhelming majority of blacks believed O.J. to be innocent while the inverse was true among whites. Many students reacted viscerally to this, charging Noble with everything from "racism" to "ignorance" to being a "poor writer."

While my students were well aware of the role of race pervading the case—especially as concerned the relationship between Nicole and O.J.—they refused to concede that jurors might vote for O.J. because he was black. The notion that some blacks might vote to acquit O.J. because of his race was, to these students, profoundly offensive. They insisted that their belief in O.J.'s innocence had nothing to do with his race and that O.J. should get off because he did not kill Nicole and Ron.

But they were not willing to leave it at that. Like most observers of murder trials, my students had a need to identify the real killer. Such crimes cannot go unaccounted for. And my students were more than willing to supply the real culprit. Maura suggested that Ron Goldman killed Nicole before killing himself and somehow disposing of the knife. Shanquilla believed the Akita did it. Shenia suggested that Al Cowlings did it. Eunicia believed the killer to be O.J.'s son. Kenny, who argued vociferously that O.J. could not possibly have killed two people, blamed "that fag dude who wants to marry O.J." That would be Kato. How, I asked him, could Kato kill two people if O.J. couldn't, especially considering that Kato is weak and dumb while O.J. is strong and smart? "He just did, Mr. Gerson, he just did." LaToya didn't know if Kato was gay, but she thought that O.J.'s son Jason was, that Jason's affair with Ron Goldman had gone awry, and that Nicole was an unfortunate innocent bystander. Her friend

Shaneka said that might be correct, but she had a slightly different take on it. "Mr. Gerson, I know who did it," she volunteered.

"Who?"

"Marguerite."

"Putting aside the question of how Marguerite had the strength to commit a crime that the Juice was physically unable to pull off, how did O.J.'s blood get all over the place? How was his blood at ten o'clock and two o'clock on the steering wheel of the Bronco, at the murder scene, and in his room? Moreover, Shaneka, how did Ron Goldman's blood get in the Bronco and O.J.'s room, and how did Nicole's blood get into O.J.'s room?"

"Marguerite did it."

"You have already said that. But how?"

"She and O.J. were still friends even after the divorce, right?"

"I think so, yes."

"Marguerite went up to O.J. and cut him—"

"With what?"

"I was getting to that, Mr. Gerson. With a knife. She cut him lightly on the finger. See? Then, she took his blood and put it on the murder scene and in his house."

"And Goldman's blood?"

"She put Goldman in the car and splattered O.J.'s blood around. Then she went to his house when he was sleeping and did the same thing."

"Why, then, wasn't Marguerite's blood all over the place if she killed them?"

"Maybe she didn't bleed."

"Doubtful."

"Maybe she had similar DNA to O.J."

"Nope. Everyone has their own DNA. Not even parents and children have the same DNA. And, anyway, Marguerite and O.J. have nothing in common genetically."

"DNA ain't nothin' anyway."

After hearing this exchange, LaToya came back with a revelation. "Mr. Gerson, I have it! Did Nicole have an open or closed casket funeral?"

"I have no idea."

"Well, maybe you should get an idea if you want to talk about the case," she shot back.

"Why?"

"Because if Nicole had a closed casket funeral, as she probably did, then I don't believe she is really dead because then the police could get O.J. without having a white woman killed."

"You mean you think Nicole's alive?"

"That's what I just said. As of now, you can't prove that she ain't."

"So, maybe she's with Elvis?"

"No. Elvis is dead and Nicole's alive."

Walt had his own theory of what happened: O.J. was shaving and cut himself. Kato took the blood from the shaving cut, brought it to the crime scene, and dumped it. "Why," I asked, "did O.J. collect his blood after he cut himself shaving?" Walt called me a racist, and that was that. As usual, this insult was not to be taken seriously; it was just a shorthand way of saying, "Shut up. I don't want to continue this discussion any longer."

Kenny called me a racist in one discussion after I reiterated my confidence that O.J. was guilty. "How, Kenny," I replied, "can you call me a racist for thinking O.J. is guilty? Celeste, sitting not two feet from you, just said that she thinks O.J. is innocent, and that the real killer is Al Cowlings. A.C. is, of course, black."

"That's okay for Celeste. She black. You ain't." True enough.

Though the students believed Mark Fuhrman to be a vile racist—well before the existence of the damning tapes was made public—most were very impressed by his composure on the stand. Carmen, one of O.J.'s most fervent supporters in 10Y, came to class with a definitive judgment after Fuhrman faced down F. Lee Bailey's cross-examination: "That racist detective is slick." No argument there. The students knew a smooth character when they saw one, and they accorded him at least grudging admiration.

Though my students were very sensitive to issues of race, they were neither moved nor shocked by Bailey's constant invoking of the "N word" (maybe because they used it so much themselves) in his cross-examination of Fuhrman. The fact that they neither liked nor trusted Bailey did not prevent them from accepting his craziest theories. Bailey's theory that Fuhrman put O.J.'s glove in his sock and subsequently dumped it at O.J.'s house, getting blood in the Bronco at some point, was neither accepted nor rejected. As Walt said, "Well, it *could* have happened, right?" Can't argue with that.

But the Fuhrman testimony brought to light a deeper issue that tapped a nerve center in each student—the police. My students had an ambivalent, complicated relationship with the police, which is one reason why the police demonstration at the school choice rally in October was so disturbing to them. Several students had police officers in their families and had great respect for the work those men and women do. Moreover, the students knew that a lot of criminals had been jailed, and they were grateful to the police for that. However, they saw violent crime in their neighborhoods every day and could not understand why such blatantly illegal conduct existed in plain view. One explanation they considered was the racial one; my students believed that if their neighborhoods were white, the police would crush every crime. I was not in Jersey City during the Rodney King trial, but the behavior of the police officers in the King incident occupied a major place in the psyches of my fifteen-year-old students, behavior that told them that the police are capable of vicious racism. The Rodney King incident touched the rawest emotions, which in turn triggered a host of antipolice and antiauthority sentiments bathed in racial hostility.

While my students did not regard police as foot soldiers for a racist enterprise (they did not even regard them as racists themselves), they were suspicious enough to blame the police for aspects of the case that incriminated O.J. In their minds, the police did not have to be in a *conspiracy* against blacks or O.J. to plant evidence against him. I asked them over and over again how O.J.'s glove could have landed in his back yard. Easy, they said, the police planted it. And how did O.J.'s blood get on the glove alongside that of Nicole and Ron? Simple—the police did it. And how did the police get O.J.'s blood to plant it? Walt reiterated his shaving cut theory, surmising that Kato and the police were in cahoots on this. "Then how," I asked, "did Kato apply the chemical solution needed to preserve the blood?" "Mr. Gerson," Walt responded, "this is the police. They can do anything."

While my students harbored suspicions about the police, the police were for them, in a sense, just a stand-in for the rest of society. They are symbols of authority, and my students' complicated and, at times, bitter feelings toward them indicated a deep, pervasive insecurity. Nowhere was this insecurity more evident than in their evaluation of the most highly publicized criminal cases in America. It seemed to them that many prominent blacks were being hauled before courts. When Shanquilla made this observation, I asked her to explain.

"C'mon, Mr. Gerson. There's Darryl Strawberry, Mike Tyson, Tupac, that mayor in Washington, Michael Jackson, and now O.J. Whenever a black man gets too big, he gets brought to trial. At least O.J. can still get off, even if his brothers couldn't."

"Shanquilla, in the American criminal justice system, justice adheres in the individual. We shouldn't make blanket statements based on a few examples, at least not without considering these cases individually. Anyway, which one of those men do you think innocent?"

"Maybe all. Definitely Mike Tyson."

"Mike Tyson?"

"What was that girl doing with him in his hotel room at two A.M.? Shit, he gave her a booty call and she came," Shanquilla opined.

"Ain't that the truth. Plenty of other hours in the day to drink and talk," Maura answered.

"Wait," Walt counseled, "just because a girl goes to a guy's room doesn't mean she is going to have sex. Maybe he did rape her, maybe he didn't. But goin' to his room don't prove nothin'."

"Yeah, okay, Walt," Shanquilla answered. "If you invited a girl to your room at two A.M., would you want to talk to her?"

"After sex, sure."

"See?" Shanquilla was on a roll. "Only Mike Tyson probably didn't want to talk with her and kicked her out for being the trick that she was. So she sued him."

"Are you saying that this is a man's world?" Rosalita asked.

"Absolutely, girl, absolutely," Shanquilla replied. "And if you ain't know that, honey, you are going to find yourself in big trouble."

As Shanquilla's comment suggests, there was a profound sentiment among my students—especially among the black girls—that this is a man's world in which a girl has to follow the rules. The rules were distilled into a fairly simple one: A woman better not get on the wrong side of her man, or else she is going to pay. This is how my students understood Nicole. Many disapproved of interracial relationships, a sentiment that accounted for some, though not all, of their animosity toward Nicole. Because O.J. was the accused in a trial that had assumed such racial significance, my students could not take their anger out on him. So they dumped it all on Nicole. This became clear to me when I discussed the case with Shaneka outside of class one day in the middle of the school year. She had come in with her most recent theory, something about Ron Goldman and O.J.'s son having had a homosexual relationship, and I was painstakingly reconstructing the case against O.J. Shaneka seemed at a loss for words and finally said, "Look, Mr. Gerson, I just don't care about your theory about O.J. bein' guilty."

"Why not?"

"Because the bitch deserved it."

That same week I assigned an in-class writing assignment to 10W, something I did periodically. The goal was to give the students an opportunity to write their ideas on any of the topics we had discussed in class that week. Eunicia, always soft-spoken and polite, asked if she could write a dialogue in addition to the essay for extra credit. "Sure," I replied. Here is what she wrote:

NICOLE AND ME

by Eunicia Jefferson

Eunicia: Hi Nicole, what's up? So you still messing with those drugs?

Nicole: Yes I am, I have to come up with some money so I can pay for it, I mean, I paid for some of it by selling my body. I feel I'm going to get killed by the mob. They don't care, girl, they will kill me.

Eunicia: You really shouldn't do that to O.J. You had a good thing going.

Nicole: I sure did, he was supporting my drug habit and he would always try to stop me, and we would get into big fights, that when I put pictures of me in my bank vault.

Eunicia: You better watch your back, and start thinking about your kids because they are the ones that is going to suffer.

When I discussed this paper with Eunicia the next day, she said that Nicole got what she deserved for messing with a black man. "Wait," I said, "if you think that it is wrong for O.J. to marry a white woman, doesn't he deserve some of the fault?"

"No," answered Shaneka, who had been listening in. "Women control these types of situations, and Nicole roped in O.J. to get his money. If it wasn't for Nicole, O.J. would have stayed with his first wife [who was black]." Eunicia nodded in agreement.

"But wait," I pressed. "When O.J. left Marguerite for Nicole, O.J. was a national hero and Nicole was just a kid—just a few years older than you, in fact. Can't you imagine a situation where Nicole was so awed by O.J.'s fame and fortune that she simply fell for him?" No, again, I clearly did not understand. To them it was simple: Nicole was the woman, and O.J. was the man; if the relationship were ill-fated from the start, there is no question whose fault it was.

What, I asked all my classes, about the beatings? Even if you do not believe that the prosecution has proved its case, you can surely deplore the wife beating that no one denies."

"Wrong, the beating did not bother Nicole too much, so why should it bother me?" Shaneka responded.

"Why do you think the beatings did not bother Nicole? She sounded quite frantic and desperate to me on that 911 call," I said.

"It was just for show. Otherwise, she would have left him."

Another student pointed out that Nicole did, in fact, leave. But no matter. According to Shenia, she did not leave soon enough. Since Nicole did not leave O.J. immediately after the beatings began (presumably because she wanted his money or fame), she was playing with fire—and we all know what happens to people who do that.

"Look at what has happened since the marriage," said Shenia. "Nicole was a slut. She gave some other guy oral sex in O.J.'s house, and then there was all those guys before she got married. It is only right that he became very jealous and took out his jealousy in some way."

Eunicia added, "Nicole stayed, didn't she? If she didn't like it, why didn't she leave?"

"If Nicole were a black woman, she would have fought back," said LaToya. "No black woman would take that."

Shaneka echoed an especially common belief: "Nicole hit O.J. first. Of course he was going to hit her back. If she did not want to be hit, she should not have hit him first."

I was somewhat shocked the first time I heard this. "Shaneka! Don't you think it is one thing for a woman to hit a man and another for a man to hit a woman?"

She looked confused. "No."

Usually, I let opinions fly freely, but I decided to draw the line here. "Listen. Under no circumstances ever is it okay for a man to hit a woman. If a woman hits a man, he should at most gently restrain her but never, never hit her."

Shaneka and the others were unconvinced. "Mr. Gerson, why do you say that?"

"It is very simple. Men are stronger than women. Much, much stronger."

"Then you obviously ain't seen the women in Jersey City."

The anti-Nicole bias was most prevalent among students from broken homes—which was most of them. Walt, always vocal, honest, and forthright, came from a strong two-parent family, and he never complicated his defense of O.J. with criticism of Nicole. He thought that Kato did it, and that was that. According to Walt, Nicole was the unfortunate victim, in no way an accomplice to her own murder. Walt's refusal to blame Nicole for her misfortune and his capacity to see her as a person was reflected in his regard for the members of the opposite sex in his personal life; when he wanted to date a girl, he wrote her impassioned, eloquent love letters. He knew how to treat women, and he knew that O.J. did not.

How about Ron Goldman? He was clearly a bit player in this drama, mentioned only in relation to Nicole. Was he sleeping with Nicole? How did O.J. kill Nicole if Ron was there with her? In ignoring Ron Goldman, my students were doing just what the nation was doing. Maybe we ignored Goldman because he was rarely mentioned separately in the media; maybe we ignored him for the same reasons the media did (whatever they might be). I don't know; it is probably a combination of both. But it certainly is strange that Goldman, as much a victim as Nicole, was rarely mentioned and that the tragedy of his death was rarely felt. If it were not for his father, Goldman might have been ignored by the media altogether. I wanted to discuss this with my students, but I did not know the answers myself—or even where to begin to look for answers.

Though my students had an enormous intellectual and emotional investment in Simpson's innocence, the brighter classes were not completely immune to the sheer weight of facts against him. In late May, after I pointed out that tests of DNA by several labs indicated that there was something like a 1 in 21 billion chance that O.J. wasn't involved, Maura appealed to the good sense of her classmates: "Look, I used to think he didn't do it, but he just did it, all right, yo?"

"Mr. Gerson, if O.J. did it and didn't plan it, that ain't first degree murder, right?" Charles responded.

"No, Charles, it wouldn't be. But if O.J. didn't plan it, how did he do it?"

"Maybe it happened this way. O.J. goes to Nicole's house to slap her around a little. Okay? She made him mad by goin' out with other men, so he goes to straighten her out. He is at her house, and guess who stops by? Ron Goldman, with the glasses she left at the Mezzaluna. Goldman sees O.J. start to beat up Nicole and tries to stop him. O.J. says, 'Hey, mothafuckuh, she is my bitch. Who the hell are you?' Goldman doesn't like that. He still wants to fight to protect Nicole, and now himself. So they fight, and we all know who wins. Nicole saw it, so she has to be killed, too. That's maybe how it happened."

"Charles," Maura countered, "how does that explain O.J. wearing gloves and carrying a knife? If he just wanted to beat her, he wouldn't need that stuff."

"As we learned in the Constitution unit," Walt informed her, "even if O.J. did it, it doesn't mean that he gonna get in trouble. You know what I hope, Mr. Gerson?" Walt asked.

"No, what's that?"

"I hope O.J. gets off, and then calls a press conference on the courthouse steps, where he tells everyone that he did it."

"What would be the point of that?"

"Then he couldn't be convicted because of double jeopardy. Fifth Amendment, baby. Can't try a man for the same crime twice. And if he doesn't say that he didn't do it—if he doesn't testify—he can't get perjury either. So, O.J. will go free."

But it was also Walt who came up with what I considered as damning a piece of evidence against O.J. as I have heard. "Look at what happened when the cops called O.J.'s hotel room in Chicago to tell him, 'Your ex-wife has been killed.' O.J. responded, 'My God, Nicole's been killed.'

"How," Walt asked, "did O.J. know the cops were talking about Nicole and not Marguerite?"

"Walt," I responded, "that's a terrific point." One of the other students turned to Walt and asked, "Does that mean you think O.J. might be guilty?"

"No way."

IMMIGRANTS

ELLA FITZGERALD MIGHT HAVE SEEN THE CHARM OF JERSEY CITY FROM THE solarium of the Empire State Building, but millions of soon-to-be Americans have seen it as they passed the base of the Statue of Liberty, en route to Ellis Island. St. Luke had students from forty-two different countries. I taught sophomores from Cuba, the Dominican Republic, India, Guyana, Poland, Thailand, Russia, Cambodia, mainland China, Korea, Indonesia, and Haiti. The proper home of the Statue of Liberty and Ellis Island, it is only fitting that Jersey City is the most ethnically diverse city in the world.

I decided to do everything I could to honor this distinction, and museums at those two monuments to American immigration provided the perfect opportunity. I took different groups of students on field trips on weekends throughout the fall and spring, when the weather permitted. These trips were among our most pleasurable experiences all year and were educational as well—and not just because of the exhibits we saw in the museums of the immigrants whose heritage we researched at Ellis Island. The exhibits also included photographs of scenes from America's past—for example, the one of a New York storefront with a sign that read "Japs Keep Walking"—and posters, such as the one advertising a meeting for the "anti-Chinese" in Tacoma, Washington. These items taught the students more about racial progress in this country than I could communicate in a year of lectures and discussions. And it was not just those reminders of a sad era in our history that taught the students about how America has made such astounding gains in race relations. It is a powerful experience to visit monuments to America's ability to assimilate in unplanned and unplannable ways people of every conceivable race, ethnicity, and history, an experience made even more potent by the realization that so many different peoples have found happiness here.

But as the gift shop in Liberty State Park (the embarkment point for the trip to the Statue of Liberty and Ellis Island) attested, progress can be confusing and ambiguous. Lots of things were for sale at the dock—from T-shirts and mugs to books.

Next to miniature replicas of the Statue of Liberty were driveway signs that targeted several ethnic groups; there were, for example, signs that said "Parking for Italians Only—All Violators Will be Towed" and "Parking for Irish Only." I was thinking of this irony when Maura nudged me.

"Mr. Gerson, are there signs for those of mixed ethnicity?"

"Yes, there was one over there that said, 'Parking for Irish-Bolivian-Dominican-Jewish-PuertoRican-Chinese-Icelanders Only.' There were a lot left."

"You be playing too much."

"Yes, I *am* playing—conjugate the verb *to be*, Maura—but, not, I think, too much. I suppose you can't get a sign for mixed ethnicity. You can get an American flag, though."

"There are no signs for you, either. I don't see a 'Parking for Jews Only' one. Maybe it's that they don't like Jews."

"Doubtful."

When we started taking these trips in the fall, I decreed an ironclad rule: No field trips during school time. I stuck to it— and I was wrong. Exposing every sophomore to Liberty Island would have been valuable because of the education about immigrants that the trips provided; I regret not taking all the students. Still, a lot of students did come on the weekend trips, and they learned a tremendous amount not only about history but about contemporary America and immigrants today.

During our study of the politics of the 1850s, I explained to my classes that while the Democrats were busy advocating the "on this hand, on the other hand" theory of popular sovereignty regarding slavery and the Republicans took an unequivocal moral stance against it, a new party was formed, the Know-Nothing party, originally called the American party. The nickname came about because members would reply cryptically, "I know nothing," whenever they were asked by outsiders what they did at a party meeting.

After one such lecture Kenny asked, "Why didn't they say nothin'?"

"They wouldn't say anything because of the nature of their

platform. Let me tell you their ideas, and see if you can guess why they didn't want anyone to know what they were up to. They believed in three things: they were pro-slavery, anti-Catholic, and anti-immigrant."

"All right!" Kenny exclaimed, "I want to join that party!" Several other students cheered.

Thinking he might just be seeking attention, I asked, "Kenny, why would you want to join that party? It is pro-slavery, and you are black. It is anti-Catholic, and you are Catholic. And—"

"Because they are against immigrants. I hate immigrants, too."

"Kenny, that's terrible."

Before I could explain, he cut me off. "Why do you like them?"

"Kenny, immigrants are the backbone of this country. Their unwavering patriotism, hard work, and strict adherence to family values continues to renew our national spirit and invigorates the country."

"That ain't right. You just sayin' that because you is white."

"Kenny, first, an idea should be evaluated without regard to the skin color of the person holding it. Second, your objection is especially off-base in this circumstance, considering that immigrants come in all colors. Literally, Kenny. People of every race and ethnicity in the world have immigrated to America."

"And they take the black man's jobs."

"Kenny, that is simply not true. Immigrants create far more jobs than they take. Look around any neighborhood in Jersey City, and you can see all the grocery stores and gas stations that would not exist were it not for immigrants, many of whom still barely speak English. And look at how many people they employ in the stores, and all those who make the goods, all those who drive and load the trucks to bring the things you buy to the market."

"And how do they be getting the money to build businesses in our neighborhoods? What about us blacks? We want businesses, too."

"No one is stopped from opening a business here, Kenny. There are a lot of successful businesses run by people of all ethnicities, including many owned by blacks."

"Name some."

"How about some of the big ones? There are of course, scores and scores of small businesses run by blacks that I don't know the names of. But you can look at the late Reginald Lewis's TLC Beatrice International Holdings, Johnson Publishing Company—you may read *Jet*, one of many magazines that John Johnson publishes—Essence Communications, Dave Bing's steel company in Detroit. And there are many more."

Jamal, who had been sporting a skeptical glance throughout the conversation, remained unconvinced. "Mr. Gerson, what about the exchange program for cab drivers?"

"What?"

"Yes, the United States sends cab drivers to Araubia, and Araubia sends its cab drivers here. That is why there are barely any black cab drivers."

"First, Jamal, there are plenty of black cab drivers. Second, Araubia does not exist. If you are referring to Aruba—well, one does not go there to drive cabs. If you are thinking of Saudi Arabia, one does not go there at all. I can assure you that there is no exchange program for cab drivers, let alone one designed to keep blacks out of the industry."

"Yes, there is such a program, yo. And it is run by the government for immigrants to take jobs away from blacks."

Anti-immigrant attitudes were common among my students, and not just among those whose families had been here for generations. Second-generation immigrants, sons and daughters of immigrants, often displayed hostility to immigrants as well. They did not buy into conspiracy theories about cab drivers from "Araubia," but they were convinced that immigrants were taking jobs from native-born Americans, and they believed that closing the gates would solve that problem. With only a couple of exceptions, they did not see my point; there was no sense of "there but for the grace of God go I." As strong as the anti-immigrant sentiment remained among many of my students, it informed their abstract beliefs only. None of the students, regardless of their beliefs, were prejudiced against immigrants, classmates, and neighbors. Insecure high school students often identify peers who are different and affirm their own sense of acceptance by tormenting the outcasts. In September, when I first noted the strong anti-immigrant sentiment, I anticipated that the immigrant students would be mercilessly teased by the native-born students. But that was not the case. Immigrants were never at the receiving end of the taunting. And they did not dish it out, either. They protected themselves from adolescent nastiness by keeping to themselves. The students who bore the brunt of the teasing were native-born students who tried unsuccessfully to force themselves into the social mainstream. A student suspected by his peers of being gay would suffer more brutal teasing in a day than any immigrant student would in four years of high school.

The immigrants kept to themselves not because they had any hostility toward the native-born but because they were simply different—very different and in significant ways. Compared to their American-born peers, the immigrants behaved differently and thought differently—and even interpreted American history in different ways. For instance, I explained that the Mexican War was a classic case of a war that could have been avoided. President Polk sent General Zachary Taylor to the border of Mexico with his army, but he simultaneously sent a negotiator named Slidell to talk with the Mexicans. The Mexican president refused to meet with Slidell, instead starting a war that the Americans won easily.

"Why did the Mexican president refuse to meet with Slidell?" Jamal asked.

"The guy was a hardheaded leader who overthrew his predecessor in a coup."

"What's a coup?" asked Cynthia, an immigrant student from Haiti.

"Good question. Now, get this down for the SATs, if nothing

else. A coup is when someone or some government overthrows the sitting government."

"I ain't care about no SATs, Mr. Gerson," Jamal informed me. "They are culturally biased." A couple of his classmates contributed their "amens."

"Yes, Jamal, they are biased," I admitted, "biased against people who don't study."

The class jeered, and Jamal brought the class back to the discussion at hand. "Is a coup like what Aristide did to Cédras?"

"Good point, Jamal. In a sense, yes. But more like what Cédras did to Aristide. The U.S. put Aristide back in power because he was the rightful leader overthrown in a coup."

"Did we ever have a coup here?" Cynthia asked.

"Never. And that fact is extraordinarily remarkable, a testament to America's great strength."

"Why is it so remarkable?" Jamal questioned.

"Well, look at it this way. Some time ago, around 1976, a great sociologist named Daniel Bell was asked by someone considering awarding him a fellowship to predict something in the future. Bell gave the following prediction: in four years there will be another presidential election. The winner will serve as the president."

Cynthia asked, "Who did he say would win?"

"He didn't."

"Why not?"

"I guess he didn't know. And he was not going to predict what he didn't know for sure."

"Mr. Gerson, what is the big deal about Bell's prediction?" Jamal asked. "Luis," he said, looking at his friend, "could get that one right."

But Cynthia got the point. "Jamal, it is a big deal. In the Dominican, people overthrow each other all the time. Elections don't mean much, especially because you could get shot on your way to the polls. You know, Mr. Gerson, that Bell guy should have said that, too. Not only will there be an election where the winner takes office, but no one will get shot voting for him."

"Terrific point, Cynthia. That would have been an excellent addition."

"Tell Bell."

"I don't know him."

"Oh."

The understanding the immigrant students brought to American political culture was reflective of their appreciation for this nation and their desire to immerse themselves in all its abundant offerings. The school and the archdiocese recognized the great will and tremendous potential of these youngsters and made a monumental effort to help them. Of course, no one checked into whether or not they were here legally. That was a running joke at St. Luke ("I wonder if there are any illegals in my classes. Hmm.") because teachers often found out which of their students were illegal—but never disclosed the information. On the field trip we took to the financial district of New York City, a few students and I sat down together to lunch at a McDonald's across the street from the World Trade Center. Leeza, an excellent student in 10E who quietly burned with intellectual curiosity, sat down next to me. In the course of conversation she casually mentioned that she was a Pakistani immigrant. There were several other students sitting at our table in the restaurant, so I pulled her aside right after the meal.

"Leeza, it is fine with me that you are here illegally. But never tell anyone again unless you absolutely trust him."

"I trust you."

"Yes, but there is no way you could trust the five or six other students at the table, and absolutely no way that you could trust the strangers who could have overheard the conversation. You have got to be more careful."

"Don't worry, Mr. Gerson. No one is going to deport me. My grandmother said that she would never let anything like that happen to me." I tried to convince her that she should be careful, not worried—a distinction I knew her grandmother would surely appreciate. But it was simply incomprehensible to Leeza—who pored over the stock pages, asked me about computers and the Knicks, did her homework vigilantly, and was always engrossed in an American novel—why anyone would want to kick her out of this country. A week after our lunch I told her about Proposition 187, which would require teachers in California to report illegal immigrant students to the authorities. I could see my point getting through; Leeza turned progressively more pale.

"Is that here?"

"No, only in California."

"But it could come here."

"Not anytime soon. But the governor of that state, Pete Wilson, is probably going to run for president. He'll lose. But if anyone pays any attention to him, Wilson will make Proposition 187, which is very popular in California, a campaign issue that will generate national attention. Even if he doesn't run, immigration, and especially illegal immigration, will be a major issue for at least the next two years and maybe more. Another candidate will make a big issue out of that because a lot of people agree with Wilson's position. Most people, actually. I am not telling you this to scare you. I just wanted you to be more careful about who you tell you are illegal because there are—contrary to all reason and right thinking—people who want to, for lack of a better word, deport you."

"Teachers would have to report me?"

"Yes, I believe so."

"So you would have to tell on me, Mr. Gerson? To send me back to Pakistan?"

"Technically, yes, I would have to, but I would never do it. I would go to jail before I turned you in. And no other teacher at St. Luke would turn you in, either, I am sure. People at St. Luke love you; you have nothing to worry about here. But the law does not only apply to teachers; it is a general proposition designed to deport illegal immigrants and to prevent them from arriving in the first place. All you need is one person to turn you in. If you know a thousand people and nine hundred ninety-nine would go to jail before they turned you in, that doesn't matter if the one does it. In short, you should never mention your status as an illegal immigrant to anyone." She got the point.

The Newark archdiocese had a strong commitment to bringing immigrants into the United States and to helping those already here acclimate and feel comfortable. Many priests and sisters helped to rescue kids from totalitarian countries like Vietnam and China and bring them to the United States, where they could live in a parish. One priest took in a half dozen kids a year and cared for them until their parents arrived—if they ever did. Often, parents living in misery in other countries sent their children to Jersey City, realizing that they might never see them again. Once in America under the auspices of the Church, the children were well clothed, fed, housed, and loved. The priests kept track of their academic performance and made sure that the students became actively involved in athletic and church activities. These immigrants were given part-time jobs so that they could make money and learn about the American work world; at the same time, their tuition was guaranteed and college scholarships were arranged.

Most of the political refugees to St. Luke in the 1994–95 school year came from Cuba. One junior, Miguel, swam to Guantánamo Bay during the October exodus, telling no one but his family that he was going. After making his way to the United States he hooked up with a network of Cuban Americans who directed him to a friendly church in Jersey City. Appearing on the church steps one night, he asked the priest to take him in. The priest did and immediately arranged for Miguel to go to St. Luke. Never having had a conventional education and without any parental or familial support, Miguel initially had a difficult time learning how to act in an American school. When his typing teacher told him to begin the in-class assignment, he flatly refused. Mr. Murphy set Miguel straight and told the priest with whom he was living about the incident. Miguel's behavior improved dramatically; as he told me, he didn't come to America to get kicked out of school and deported. There can be no disciplinary mechanism better than a feeling of gratitude; once that is tapped, behavioral problems evaporate almost immediately. And if there was one sentiment shared by all the immigrants, it was gratitude—gratitude to parents for making tremendous sacrifices, gratitude to their school for educating them properly, and gratitude to a country that was providing them with freedom. This feeling of appreciation made the immigrant students a pleasure to teach.

Because there were so many Cubans and other Spanish-speaking students, Miguel, ironically, did not learn English as quickly as the immigrants who spoke other languages. The Spanish-speaking immigrants always had someone to interpret for them. Vietnamese and Chinese kids did not have that luxury; in order to conduct the most basic communication they had no choice but to learn English. Instead of participating in a bilingual program, St. Luke students who did not speak English or who spoke marginal English spent an hour or two a day in a trailer across the street learning the language and receiving help with homework. Doing homework was an especially time-consuming process for immigrant students; their papers often reflected the fact that nearly every word had been translated from a foreign-language dictionary.

The toughest aspect of forming a bilingual program at St. Luke and, I suspect, elsewhere would have been deciding what the *bi* part of *bilingual* would be. Everyone assumes Spanish, but why? There are plenty of immigrant kids defined as Asian—those from India, China, Vietnam, Cambodia, and Korea—but they speak different languages and even different dialects within those languages. And then there are all the students from former Iron Curtain nations. They speak their native languages and come to the United States speaking only a bit more English than their Asian peers. Much of what they know needs to be re-learned, anyway. An immigrant from Poland came to St. Luke around Christmastime speaking very little English. In her ESL (English as a second language) class she created quite a scene in the lesson on parts of the human body. In one minute she identified "tits," "dick," and "asshole." She was not trying to be irreverent; quite the contrary—she was merely quoting correctly from a workbook she had been given before leaving for the United States.

Besides the daunting number of languages spoken by the immigrant students at St. Luke, there were the numerous dialects of those languages, which would have made a comprehensive bilingual program impossible to create. Most foreign languages have several dialects, which often have loose ties to the mother tongue. One of the ESL teachers was explaining to a Vietnamese student what coleslaw was. *Kimchi,* she explained. The student was very confused and then broke into laughter. The teacher looked to another of her pupils, also an immigrant from Vietnam, for an explanation for this reaction. The second student was laughing, too, but was able to explain that in some Vietnamese dialects *kimchi* means "your father frequents prostitutes."

Since the beginning of the year I was friendly with a very bright senior—an editor of the yearbook and a class officer, Carlos. We would talk basketball or politics most mornings; he was a die-hard Miami Heat fan, and we would have impassioned arguments about who was better, the Nets or the Heat (yes, we would both have admitted that the real question was who was worse, but no matter). Only at the end of the year did I find out that Carlos had come to the United States from Cuba as a freshman, speaking not a word of English. By his senior year he was one of the most articulate and acculturated students in the school.

But the word *acculturated* can be tricky when applied to the inner city. So much of the culture there is not one to be admired. It is a culture that requires fourteen-year-olds to change from street clothes to school uniforms after getting to school in the morning to avoid getting pummeled on the bus, a culture that makes a two-parent family a rarity, a culture where a kid can cut a month of public school without being caught, a culture that has fifteen-year-olds report their skin color on college search material, a culture where race relations are so bitter that everyone knows that one disagreeable jury verdict or errant comment from an authority figure anywhere can set off a riot.

In different ways and for different reasons, the immigrant students avoided becoming acculturated to that kind of culture.

Those with relatives in the United States had strong family structures that inculcated traditional religious values. Some of those without families here were reminded constantly of how difficult and unpleasant school was in their home country; others were painfully reminded by their loneliness how fortunate they were to be in America. And almost all were very poor; they were responsible for taking care of younger siblings or for earning money after school. They did not have the free time some of their native-born peers enjoyed. But none of this was ever taken with any bitterness or resentment; the very fact of being in America was seen as something to be cherished and celebrated, a dream from which responsibility is born.

One day when I was on lunch duty at the beginning of the year, Maura came running up to me to say that Jack, the Filipino student in 10Y, was sobbing as a result of something that had happened in my class. *What could it be?* I wondered. I found Jack in the bathroom crying and asked him what was wrong. His head remained buried in his arms, so I tapped him gently. "Jack," I insisted, "what is the matter?" He slowly reached into his backpack and pulled out a piece of paper. It was the test I had just handed back. "Jack, what is the problem? You did well," I said, pointing to his B+.

"B+ is not well! I need A."

"Jack, hold it for a moment. No one in the class got an A on this test; yours was, I think, the second- or third-best mark. You should be proud of yourself."

"Mr. Gerson," he said, emerging from his sobs, "Can I do some extra credit? Anything. I'll listen to a lot of Frank. I'll read some chapters in the textbook and outline them for you. You said we should outline. I'll write an essay. Anything, but I need the A."

"Jack, for God's sake, you don't need the extra credit. It's not even the semester grade."

"I need the A. My father won't understand. He wants me to get A. And I always did, until now."

What the hell, I thought, *I am not going to set this father straight. And he is, it seems, pretty straight already. Only a good man could raise a son as industrious and polite as Jack, even if his demands are a bit stringent.* So I gave Jack the A, and he came through with an extra-credit essay even though I did not ask him for one. Maybe, though, that wasn't the best idea. While respecting the demands of his father, I should have tried to teach Jack to keep things in perspective. I thought he would take things a bit easier when he saw my A on his report card, but that was not the case. For the rest of the year, whenever he did not set the curve on a test or come very close to doing so, he became very upset with himself. Nothing I said—no assurances that an occasional A- was perfectly fine, no guarantees that I respected his intellect a great deal even if he got something wrong on a test—would deter him from his relentless pursuit of perfection. A pursuit, surely, to be admired, but also one that was clearly demanding and potentially tormenting.

Unlike Jack, for whom directives were clear and obligations certain, many of the native-born students at St. Luke lived in a conflicted, torn world. The message they received in the home and in the classroom was directly contravened by what they were taught by their friends in the streets. The immigrant students knew as well as anyone the world of the street, but they were not tempted by it; their lives inside of school and out reinforced each other. However, the worlds the native-born students inhabited were locked in a fierce battle; one misstep on those mine fields by a naive and insecure teenager could be devastating.

10E started the year with two immigrants—Leeza from Pakistan and Sallie from Indonesia. They were best friends. I didn't think anything of their relationship; after all, any two people can be best friends. Then Mary came from mainland China, speaking not a word of English. Leeza and Sallie immediately took her in—I mean on the very first day—and remained close friends with her throughout the year. The three girls socialized together, and Leeza and Sallie (both of whom spoke good English) spent many patient hours helping Mary with her homework.

One day in early December I noticed Mary weeping as she left my class. "Mary," I asked, "are you okay?" Mary stopped walking but she did not reply. She kept on crying, shielding her face from me as though she was ashamed of something. She slowly pulled out of her notebook a test I had just handed back in class and showed it to me. She had gotten a C.

I had no intention of grading Mary conventionally at the end of the marking period. A student who came into class knowing no English and with no exposure to American history could not be evaluated in the same way as those who had spent their entire life in Jersey City. But I did not want to deal with the matter on an individual test. I knew that if a native-born student saw that he received a lower grade for the same raw score as an immigrant student, there was a good chance that he would become very bitter—and might take it out on the student receiving the preference.

As I attempted to find out what was wrong with Mary, her friends Leeza and Sallie approached her and attempted to comfort her. I did not have to worry about Sallie and Leeza's worrying that they needed to do better than Mary to earn the same mark. So I had no compunction about reassuring Mary right there. "Mary, you didn't really fail. Don't worry. I think you deserve an A." I crossed out the C and wrote an A on the top of the paper. "There you go, you got an A. Congratulations." Mary was a bit confused and not at all happy, but the effusive congratulations of Sallie and Leeza told her that she should be proud of herself for receiving the A. The fact that neither of them had gotten an A although their raw scores were far higher than Mary's did not deter them from praising their friend for what was indisputably a top-notch effort.

A couple of months after Mary came to St. Luke from China, Peggy came into her class from Taiwan. Mary, Leeza, and Sallie adopted her right away. Unlike her new friends, Peggy was a spunky girl who saw no problem with talking back to her teachers. She might have thought this was acceptable on the basis of her observation of the behavior of the native-born students, but Mary, Leeza, and Sallie told her otherwise. Peggy stopped her rude behavior and directed her active spirit toward productive class participation.

The immigrants were fully aware that they were different—

and not just because they came from another country. They knew that they had created an alternative community, one whose values differed from those that characterized the youth culture of their native-born classmates. The immigrant students were outside the social mainstream, but they did not care. In an assignment on individualism, in which I asked the students to assess individualism today and in the days of the frontier, Sallie wrote the following:

> What makes me a better or a good person is that I don't have to put up a facade for my friends or my family being something I'm not or someone I'm not. That takes a lot of pressure off so I can concentrate on other things like my education and what I want to do in my life or what I want to become.

There was probably much pressure on the immigrant students to become acculturated to the destructive culture of their native-born classmates. The immigrant students were often the victims of vicious prejudice. One might think a natural reaction to this would be to try to become an indistinguishable part of the mainstream culture, at least outwardly. But no. In a paper I assigned on the question Where do ideas come from? Leeza responded as follows:

> Most of my ideas come from books, T.V., people and, of course school, but as one gets older one starts forming one's own ideas and opinions. A large percent of my ideas come from my parents. I would say my morals; my religion, my rules of everyday life; knowing what is right and wrong, come from my parents. Parents give you your ideas about values, morals, and what is good and bad, but they also protect and shelter you from wrong worldly influences. Parents shelter you from things like racism, sexism, etc.
>
> I remember the first time I experienced racism. It was my first year here in this country and I had just started school. I was very homesick and I didn't know too much English and I felt totally lost in school. I didn't know what to do, what to say, half the time I didn't know what we were doing and I had to have everything explained to

me. I remember the first 2 weeks all I did was keep my head down and cry. After a while I got better, a lot better in fact.

My teacher at that time was an African-American teacher. At the end of the third marking period that teacher thought I said a cuss word to her and she said she heard me say it, at that time I did not know the meaning of any cuss words. Well she came right over to me and told me exactly what she felt about my nationality and about other Indians and then she went and failed me for the whole year. Of course she was fired immediately.

My second experience with racism was with a group of people called "Dot busters." I know they beat up on a lot of old ladies and men. I remember once my friend and I had bottles thrown at us. I don't know if the people were Dot busters or not because we didn't want to find out. There have been other things since then like remarks and etc. It's funny because I find that the races who get discriminated against the most discriminate against others. I feel very strongly about racism.

One thing that initially surprised me concerned the way in which the immigrant students spoke English. Of course, their English was halting, and they often misused words (generally in much less spectacular ways than the girl who revealed her knowledge of English during an anatomy lesson in the ESL class). But they never used slang. I never heard an immigrant student use a double negative, knowingly curse, or say *yo* or even *ain't*. The best English in the sophomore class was spoken by Cynthia, the Haitian student in 10Y. She came to see me once during lunch and misused a word.

"Cynthia," asked, "do you translate from the Creole as you speak?"

"Yes, Mr. Gerson, I do."

"Do you dream in Creole?"

"Usually. It depends upon what I am dreaming about, but usually."

"Then, how is your English so good? I can't even imagine you speaking English the way most of your classmates do."

"True. Mr. Gerson, when you need to learn English after speaking another language, you learn the right way. And that lesson doesn't go away, and you are not influenced by other kinds of English that you may hear spoken by your peers. It is hard enough to learn one kind of English."

In addition, there was a more substantive reason why the immigrant students did not speak slang or nonstandard English. The immigrant students never attempted to adopt the language of the native-born students, that is, the use of double negatives, the *yo* to end sentences, the failure to conjugate verbs, or any of a host of more subtle indicators. They wanted to become acculturated into mainstream American culture and had no use for language that did not correspond to that goal.

I made an effort to read as much as I could about the native cultures of my immigrant students, partly because their excellence sparked my curiosity and partly because I wanted to better understand where they were coming from. I made a point of discussing what I read in the *New York Times* about Haiti with Cynthia each day. My reading was basically just preparation for whatever she was going to teach me that day. I did not realize the extent of Cynthia's lessons until one night when my mentor from Williams College, Jeff Weintraub, called. We were discussing the political situation in Haiti when he remarked, "Mark, I didn't know you were such an expert on Haiti. Am I mistaken, or have you learned all of this recently?"

"Recently, Jeff. Actually from a Haitian student of mine."

"She must be extraordinary. Her understanding of the country for a fifteen-year-old is really astounding." I told Cynthia about this exchange, and she was extremely proud.

Cynthia and I talked mainly during lunch; she went home every day after school to take care of three younger siblings and a younger cousin while her mother and father each worked two jobs. Her parents needed money not only to raise a sizable family in America and to send the children to a Catholic school but also to send to needy relatives in Haiti, several of whom were in real danger. Cynthia came to my classroom one day during lunch, having mentioned to me after class an hour earlier that she really needed to talk.

"Mr. Gerson," she said after she sat down, "I'm scared."

"About what, Cynthia?"

"My parents are going to Haiti tomorrow."

"They go all the time."

"But this is different. My father's brother, my uncle, was assassinated two days ago. He was talking on the phone, and Aristide's men bombarded the house with bullets, killing two of his daughters as well. It was a setup, Mr. Gerson. Aristide's men called him so he would get the phone, which is near the window. Then they shot him and his family as he talked. And now my family is going to the funeral, and there might be violence at the funeral. They have security, but my uncle had security, too."

"Cynthia," I said, "I am very sorry to hear about your uncle and your cousins. But just keep in mind that your parents are very intelligent and know the country extremely well. They love you and your siblings and would never do anything to endanger themselves. I am sure they are sure of their safety, or else they wouldn't go."

"They have to go, Mr. Gerson, no matter what. But no one knows they are going into Haiti, and no one is going to meet them at the airport. Still, I am very scared. I don't want to be an orphan, Mr. Gerson."

Her parents went, and Cynthia stayed behind to care for her three younger siblings. I was worried about her staying alone in a bad section of Jersey City, but she assured me that she would be okay. She had my phone number and promised to call if she needed anything, and her next-door neighbor, who was her elementary school principal, promised to stop by periodically to check on her.

Cynthia was fine, and her parents came back safely. Though such incidents were rare, no one who knew Cynthia was surprised that she was given the responsibility of caring for her siblings, and no one doubted the ability of this fifteen-year-old to care for three children. It was unthinkable for her to turn to gangs, drugs, alcohol, promiscuity, or general irresponsibility. Cynthia did not have an adolescence, and she accepted that fate. Every Monday she heard her classmates discuss their activities of the past weekend, and every Friday she heard them make plans for the coming weekend. No matter how enjoyable those plans may have sounded to her, she accepted the fact that they would never involve her. She had too much to do at home. If she ever felt deprived of anything, she never mentioned it to me—and there was not much she held back in our lunchtime discussions. She loved her family and her adopted country, and she accepted the responsibilities that each handed to her.

In February the Hudson County Bar Association sent flyers to every history teacher in the county announcing their annual essay contest on the Bill of Rights. I announced this opportunity to win a prize and a savings bond to my classes. Some students expressed interest and I was hoping for plenty of submissions, but there was one in particular I intended to seek.

"Cynthia," I said to her at one of our lunches, "you have to enter that essay contest about which I told your class."

"C'mon, Mr. Gerson. I would never win."

"I think you just might. Your understanding of this country is, to say the least, unique and special."

"You really think I should try?"

"Absolutely."

Cynthia often stressed how much this country meant to her family, who had risked so much to come to this land where obstacles can be overcome by hard work and good values. A couple of weeks before the contest she handed me her essay, which eloquently articulated many of the themes of our discussions. We mailed it in, and I received a letter from the bar association three weeks later. Cynthia had placed second in a contest entered by hundreds of high school students. She was ecstatic, as was her family. Her father must have taken three rolls of pictures of Cynthia at the award ceremony, which I attended with him.

When Cynthia called me in July asking for a recommendation to attend Academic High School in Jersey City, I was delighted to oblige. I knew Academic High all too well: it was Jersey City's magnet school and its mock trial team obliterated the one I coached at St. Luke. So I was not surprised when *New Jersey Monthly* ranked Academic the Number One public high school in the state. It was perfect for Cynthia, and it was free.

Cynthia called me again in August to say that she had not heard from Academic and had a tuition bill for St. Luke. "Mr. Gerson, what should I do?" I told her that I would ascertain whether she had been admitted and would get back to her right away. I reached the vice-principal in charge of admissions, who took my call immediately. "Yes, Mr. Gerson, how can I help you?" he asked.

"I was a teacher at St. Luke last year and wrote a recommendation for Cynthia Raston in mid-July. She has not heard anything from you yet, and I am wondering if you could tell me if she has been admitted or not. I am sorry to bother you, but her tuition check for St. Luke is due, and she needs to know where she will be going to school in two weeks."

"Of course, of course. I'm surprised she didn't hear. Let me check the files. Hold on for a moment, please." He returned to the phone after a few minutes.

"She was a very strong candidate, Mr. Gerson," he informed me. "But unfortunately we could not find a place for her."

A sinking feeling went right down to my stomach. "Oh."

"It wasn't her, it was her ethnicity. We determine admissions by ethnicity, and we had hers filled."

I was stunned and did not know what to say. "You mean," I sputtered, "you have enough Haitians?"

"No, we don't get that specific. She would fall under black. We have enough blacks."

"That's it?"

"Yes, that's it. Again, she was a strong candidate. If a spot opens up for her in the next week or so before school starts, we'll surely keep her in mind. Please tell her so, and thank you for calling."

I sat down for a moment, still stunned, and then went outside to shoot baskets and try to make some sense of this. I couldn't. Then I remembered that I had to call Cynthia. What would I tell her? The truth? I pondered this for some time, and came to a simple realization: there was no way that Cynthia would understand why she had been rejected. Her skin color was a nonissue to her. Whereas most of her classmates at St. Luke considered their race and ethnicity an important part of their identity, Cynthia did not. She would have had an easier time believing that the tooth fairy had married Santa Claus than the fact that her race had an effect on her admission to Academic High School. So I told Cynthia that while the vice-principal said that she was a strong candidate, they did not have many slots open this year. She was crushed.

Without telling Cynthia, I called the vice-principal back the next day. "Sir," I said, "I am sorry to bother you again. But I spoke with Cynthia, and she very badly wants to attend Academic. I would greatly appreciate the opportunity to come down to Academic High School to plead her case in person and convince you that she is just the sort of student you are looking for. I can be there in a hour or at any other time that is convenient."

"That's no use, Mr. Gerson. There is simply no room for her, as we discussed yesterday."

"I would like to understand your policy a bit better. Is it because Cynthia is not of the proper ethnicity?"

"It is not a matter of 'proper ethnicity.' We only fill in. If two white kids leave, we put two white kids in. If four Hispanic kids leave, we put four Hispanic kids in, and so on." Their goal, he told me, was to attain equal representation of the four ethnic categories they had designated: white, black, Hispanic, and other. "If we just took them as students," he explained, "the school would be filled with sixty percent other."

"Other? What's other?"

"You know, Oriental, Indian, and so on. If we went just by the scores, it wouldn't be balanced at all. It'd be all other."

Remembering that most applications offer a box designated DECLINE TO RESPOND in addition to various ethnicities, I asked him whether it would be best for students applying in the future to take that option.

"No, we don't offer it. If they don't declare, we'll call home. We have to put the students in one of the four categories."

THE CITY AND THE SUBURBS

IN HIS NOVEL *SYBIL*, DISRAELI WROTE, "TWO NATIONS, BETWEEN WHOM there is no intercourse and no sympathy; who are as ignorant of each other's habits, thoughts and feelings as if they were dwellers in different zones, or inhabitants of different planets; who are formed by a different breeding, are fed by a different food, are ordered by different manners, and are not governed by the same laws . . . *the rich and the poor.*" Disraeli, of course, was describing Victorian England, but he might as well have been writing about modern America. It was Disraeli's idea that was at the crux of Michael Harrington's call for "the nation of the well-off . . . to see through the wall of affluence and recognize the alien citizens on the other side." Harrington's book *The Other America* served as the intellectual inspiration for the Great Society and the modern welfare state. The powerful resonance of *The Other America* can be traced to the importance and precision of Harrington's central question: How can two entirely different societies coexist within a nation devoted to universal ideals?

Harrington's answers to that question may not have been correct, but the prevalence of bad solutions does not mean that there is no problem. Harrington was absolutely right that there are two Americas, and it is not hard to find the other one. In my experience, it is 19.8 miles away—the distance between my home in Short Hills and St. Luke in Jersey City. While Short Hills is a suburban paradise, the embodiment of the American dream, Jersey City has all the problems and promise of contemporary urban life. As Disraeli and Harrington suggested, these two worlds are distinguished by an enormous difference in wealth, but ultimately they are separated by a comprehensive social system that encompasses much more than money.

Because they are blunt and quantifiable, money and the things money buys are easy tools with which to analyze the two Americas. But like judging a man by the car he drives or the clothes he wears, analyzing America by its wealth neglects the rich textures of life that compose most of the world we recognize and experience. To assess the differences and similarities between the two Americas, a good place to begin is with education.

Why? Irving Kristol said it best almost four decades ago: "[Education] involves above all the image of man into which we should like to see the child mature. It is a clash of visions, of philosophies of life, loyalty and death." Through schoolchildren, we can see relatively uninhibited embodiments of the two Americas. And it is through the education of children that we can see the visions, philosophies, and ideas that ultimately create the two Americas.

"Two nations . . . who are as ignorant of each other's habits, thoughts, and feelings." I graduated from Millburn High School in 1990 (Short Hills is part of Millburn Township) and adored my childhood in that wonderful community. Millburn High is one of the best public schools in New Jersey and one of the best in the country. Dedicated teachers, several with doctorates, teach a student body where more than half the students score better than the ninety-fifth percentile on the SATs. Almost everyone in the top 25 of my class of 180 went to Harvard, Yale, Princeton, Williams, MIT, or Stanford. Millburn has historically had excellent athletic teams (especially in soccer), and the spacious trophy case in the high school entryway has to be cleaned every couple of years to make room for the additions supplied by the quiz bowl, debate, and mock trial teams.

Raised in this milieu, we were aware that it was rare, but we didn't really know *how* rare. It was the only environment we knew, and stories from relatives who had been reared elsewhere seemed improbably distant. As I taught at St. Luke, I often thought back to my high school days and wondered, *What was Millburn High School really like?* Specifically, how did the quintessential citizen of one America differ from the quintessential citizen of the other America? I sifted through my memories of Millburn, only five years old and still vivid, but they did not lead me to the answers I sought. The half decade between seventeen and twenty-two is a very long one in which perceptions and perspectives are revolutionized by the process called "growing up." In order to better understand my students at St. Luke, I wanted to learn about Millburn. So I asked my seventh-grade history teacher, Mr. Sachsel (who was then teaching sophomore U.S. history), if I could spend my spring break with him, visiting Millburn High School under his auspices.

"Of course!" he replied.

So I began my time at Millburn on a Thursday in the spring. Given that Millburn students are reared with books, magazines, and serious discussions ingrained in the fabric of daily life, I knew where to start: the library. The library, which had been constructed in my time at Millburn, is a splendid modern building with a vast collection of books and periodicals. It had been computerized and had a microfilm room where students could check back issues of magazines, journals, and newspapers. There were cubbies for those who wanted to work individually, tables where materials could be spread out, and rooms where students could discuss a project without disturbing anybody else.

I exchanged warm greetings with the librarian, whom I had known as a student. I asked her for back issues of the *Miller,* the school paper, and she provided me with over a year's worth. I sat down at an empty table and began reading. There were editorials and op-eds on a variety of topics, most of them exceptionally well written and well informed. This was especially so when the articles branched out from straight news analysis and into issues of public philosophy. An exchange on the death penalty, for instance, featured one student opposing it by citing a 1987 article from the *Stanford Law Journal* on wrongful convictions. His adversary used government statistics to document a 13% decline in violent crime since 1980, which he attributed to the widespread adoption of the death penalty. Other articles, reflecting the same rigorous standards of informed debate, focused on issues such as feminism, Bosnia, abortion, and term limits.

Something was missing—there was a big dog who was not barking—and it made itself known to me soon enough. I read through the papers again and confirmed that there were no articles on the American city or the problems that engulfed the teenagers only ten miles away in Newark. I broached this issue in a discussion with one of the editors of the school paper, Jonathan Greenblatt. (I had asked Mr. Sachsel to introduce me to Jonathan, who had written an impressive analysis of a Republican budget proposal in a recent issue.) Jonathan and I went out on the large patio attached to the Millburn High School cafeteria. Like the library, the patio was built during my years at the high school; the district must have had a lot of money when it made all these improvements in the late 1980s. The patio was being used as it had been when I was a student at Millburn: students were playing ball, drinking sodas purchased from the cafeteria, flirting, or watching a match on the nearby tennis courts.

I complimented Jonathan on his article and told him how impressive I found the paper as a whole. We chatted for a few minutes before I asked him the main question I had in mind: "Jonathan, did you send a reporter to Liberty State Park in Jersey City on October 16, when a rally for school choice, cosponsored by President Bush, attracted thousands of people from across the country?"

"What was that?"

"You know, school choice. The most important rally for it nationwide was held in Jersey City in the fall."

Jonathan looked at me. "I'm not familiar with that. What is school choice?"

I explained that school choice was perhaps the most important educational reform in America today, that it would provide state vouchers for schoolchildren to be used for private, parochial, or public schools of their choice. I told Jonathan that the nation's foremost proponent of school choice was Mayor Bret Schundler of Jersey City and that all eyes were on Jersey City to see how a revolutionary pilot program would work.

"It didn't take off, did it?" Jonathan asked.

"No, it didn't. It looked like a sure thing, given that it is a cornerstone of the national Republican agenda and the mayor, governor and both houses of the state legislature are Republican. But it looks dead now, at least in New Jersey."

"Well, this is, as you know, a very Republican town and I often talk about politics with my parents and sometimes with my friends but school choice has never come up."

Theoretically, Millburn students could be aware of the "habits, thoughts and feelings" of Jersey City students without knowing about the political issues affecting New Jersey's cities. Millburn/Short Hills is a literate and politically astute community, where even the high school students are conversant in complicated issues. And it is much easier to know about urban issues than urban people. Very few of the Millburn students with whom I spoke had a friend who did not grow up in Millburn/Short Hills or a comparable suburb. It was not as though these students were unwilling to branch out; they just did not know how to do so. One Millburn student said that she met a bunch of girls from Newark at a track meet. They became friends and exchanged phone numbers. But no one ever called.

No one else had even had this level of contact, except for two bright students with whom I spoke, Christine and Frances. Mr. Sachsel chose them to join me in his office during a class period. Both Christine and Frances were immediately interested in Jersey City, demonstrating more than intellectual curiosity about a strange world. They spoke with such knowledge and authority about the other America that I could not help but ask how they knew so much.

Christine explained, "I have two cousins in Newark public schools. They tell me that the attitude of their classmates toward school is totally different from ours. If they don't do their homework; it's no big deal. There's no teacher to tell them to do it. And parents of students in Newark, if they are around, are indifferent and don't know if they have homework. It is not socially okay to do well in school, so no one does. They would rather get pregnant."

I asked Frances how she knew so much. "Oh," she replied, "I went to St. Rose [the local parish Catholic grammar school and junior high] through the eighth grade. I knew a lot of kids from Newark, Elizabeth, Irvington, and East Orange there."

"How did you meet kids from the cities when you were at St. Rose? I thought it was a local school."

"No. Kids from the cities hop on the train near their home and get off in Short Hills. The Short Hills stop is down the street from the school."

"And now that you are in different high schools, do you stay in touch?"

"Of course. We're friends."

What separated Christine and Frances from their peers? They had had intimate association with their urban age-mates as social equals. This was not the case with the vast majority of their classmates, whose relationships with the other America were of two kinds:

1) Strictly economic: Many Millburn/Short Hills families had maids, and those maids lived in the cities. But no matter how well Short Hills families got along with their maids, there could be no relationship of social equality here. Also, suburban kids go into the cities to buy things. One example that a student brought up, which reminded me of my friends' adventures in high school, concerned alcohol: a store in Irvington was known for selling beer to minors, so Millburn kids would flock there for the beer—then get out, recounting their dangerous mission the whole way home.

2) Service: There was some (though not as much as I expected) feeling of *noblesse oblige* among Millburn students. These students, primarily through religious youth groups, volunteered in various capacities in the cities and thus garnered some impressions of urban life based on that experience. Most volunteer work by high school kids is done for the homeless. Though helpful and admirable, this work does not lead to the establishment of social bonds between the inhabitants of the two Americas. If anything, it gave Millburn kids the idea that all inner-city residents are like the homeless people they served in soup kitchens.

"*Two nations, between whom there is no intercourse and no sympathy.*" In May I came to school one day with new glasses. Walt began our class by indicating his approval. "Mr. Gerson, those are some phat glasses!"

"Why, thank you, Walt."

"Did you get them from New Eyes for the Needy?" Carmen asked.

"Carmen, why would I get glasses from New Eyes for the Needy?" I was vaguely familiar with New Eyes for the Needy, a charity, headquartered in Short Hills, that provides glasses to those who cannot afford them.

"Because it's in Short Hills."

"Carmen," Walt said, "Short Hills is a rich town. Why would they get their glasses from a charity?"

"I don't know. Mr. Gerson, what does New Eyes for the Needy do?"

"People who no longer need their glasses donate them to New Eyes for the Needy, which sends them to people who do not have enough money to buy new glasses."

"In Short Hills?"

"No, the donors live in Short Hills. The recipients don't."

"Do the recipients live in Jersey City?"

"I am sure some of the glasses donated at New Eyes for the Needy find their way to Jersey City."

"Why would people in Short Hills want to give their glasses to poor people in Jersey City?" Carmen asked.

That discussion prompted one on what life is really like in the suburbs. Maura suggested in all seriousness that suburban kids relieved their interminable boredom by playing chicken with their cars or Russian roulette with their guns. I told her, "Look, Maura, I have lived in those 'boring' suburbs all my life, and, first, they aren't boring and, second, I have never known anyone who played either game."

She remained unconvinced. "Are you saying, Mr. Gerson, that no one does those things?"

"I am sure that people do those things somewhere, for some reason. People do stupid things all the time everywhere. But Russian roulette is surely uncommon."

"No, Mr. Gerson, it goes on all the time in the suburbs."

"Two nations . . . ordered by different manners." There was probably no greater surprise to me when I began teaching than the attitude of the inner-city students toward teachers, school, and authority figures in general. Millburn students respect their teachers until given substantial reasons not to; students at St. Luke respect their teachers only after having accumulated substantial reasons to do so. St. Luke kids, very sensitive to any slight against their honor, reacted viscerally when they felt their dignity had been violated. It did not matter whether the violator was a school administrator, a teacher, or a friend. School, education, and the future may have been important to them, but nothing could trump the thirsty demands of violated honor. Fights provided one example of a common reaction to violated honor, but more subtle examples abounded.

On the very first day I noted that no students were trying to ingratiate themselves with me. No one was trying to answer all the questions, make small talk after class, ask me about my background—all behaviors that came naturally to me when I was a student and to pretty much everyone I knew at Millburn and at Williams. And this was not first-day-of-school shyness.

Right before the midterm Simon approached me before the exam.

"Mr. Gerson, I'm worried about the exam."

"Why? You have done well all semester, we reviewed thoroughly in class, and it's not that tough, anyway."

"But I didn't study."

"Why not?

"I just didn't."

"Simon, why are you telling me this?"

He was confused. "Tellin' you what?"

"That you didn't study. I mean, why do you want me to know that you didn't study?"

He was thoroughly bamboozled at this point. "Because I didn't, Mr. Gerson. We are talking about the midterm. I didn't study, so I told you I didn't study."

"Yeah," his friend Jermeine interjected. "What do you mean, Mr. Gerson? He didn't study, so he told you. What up?"

"Put it this way," I asked, "Don't you think it would be better for you to let me think that you studied very hard?"

Simon looked at Jermeine and then back at me. "What?"

"Let's say that you get an eighty-six and an eighty-six is either a B or B+, depending on how I scale it. If I think you didn't study—or in your case, Simon, because I *know* you didn't study—I will give you the B. But if I think you gave it your all, I'd give you the B+. Get it?"

Simon's brutal honesty was no anomaly. When the students were bored with a lecture, they told me so; when they were not prepared, they volunteered that fact; and if they did not like my tie, that was promptly reported as well. This way of dealing with authority was completely different from anything I had ever experienced or practiced, and I thought long and hard about it. *So, I wondered, is it better for a student to disguise his boredom or to explicitly proclaim it? When it is explicitly proclaimed, maybe I can avoid wasting a class period. Shakespeare, after all, said that there is no profit where there is no pleasure, and that statement is certainly true in education.*

Alas, no. Honesty may be a virtue, but a bad habit was reinforced each time a student told me that a lecture was boring. The students suffered by not understanding how to interact with authority figures. I felt that if I could even begin to teach them how to deal with authority, that lesson would be far more valuable to them than a semester's worth of lectures on Columbus, the Boston Tea Party, and the Second Bank of the United States.

When Kenny told me in class shortly after the midterm exam that a lecture on the French and Indian War was "very, very boring," I stopped the class and said, "Let's analyze Kenny's last comment. He can phrase that statement—that truth, actually—the way he did and come right out and say how much he disliked the lecture. Or Kenny could say this: 'Gee, Mr. Gerson, your lecture on the French and Indian War was interesting, and I learned a lot, but the book handles that material pretty well. Do you think we can even have more lectures like the one you gave on the Boston Massacre? That way, while telling me the lecture is boring, you are saying that you have been doing your reading, have enjoyed lectures in the past, and would like to help me teach you better. Therefore, in place of me being the impersonal producer and you being the discriminating consumer, we all work together to improve your education."

No one in Kenny's class agreed; for that matter, no one in any class agreed when a similar situation arose there. Walt, though, got right to the point: "Mr. Gerson, are you telling us to kiss up?"

"Absolutely, Walt," I replied, giving him a taste of his own honesty.

As it happened, Walt was the only student I almost convinced of the merits of kissing up. He came to see me midway through the second marking period, when deficiency notices went out to parents warning them that their child might be failing. Walt's parents apparently received four such notices, and he was desperate. He was willing to try anything.

"Walt, teachers will always reward a student who they believe is working hard," I explained.

"Teachers always say that."

"Probably because it's true. Clichés generally are. But, Walt, it's not sufficient in your case."

"Because I'm a black man?"

"No, but because you are smart and capable enough not merely to work hard but to get A's for doing so. With you it is not a matter of you trying your best but still coming up short. You are easy for a teacher, at least in one respect. We know that you are trying if you ace our tests and papers."

"Okay, okay, I'll be working harder. But what can I do now?"

"That's easy, Walt. You write notes to each of your teachers saying that you are very disappointed with how you have done and would like to improve in the future. Then, you see each one of them individually to explain that you are now ready to work. And you ask them what extra work you can do."

"But that's kissing up, Mr. Gerson."

"Call it anything you want except late for dinner. Just do it. And we are not finished. You should also do what my friend Dorothy used to do in college. Whenever a teacher gives you an assignment, turn in a rough draft as early as possible. If you can, turn it in a week, or even ten days, early. That way, the teachers know that you are planning ahead, giving their assignment serious thought, and working hard. Moreover, the teachers will likely give you back your draft with corrections and suggestions. That way, they will have a vested interest in you doing well—because it is really them doing well, too."

"Okay, Mr. Gerson. Can we do one at a time? Let's say I do the notes and show them to you before I put them in the teacher's mailboxes?"

"I hope you do, Walt."

Walt came in the next day with identical notes for every teacher. He gave me the handwritten note he wrote for me:

Dear MR. GERSON,

I am ashamed of my work this marking period and for disrespecting you by doing bad work. I know I could do better, and will work harder from this day into the future until the end of the year. I enjoy HISTORY and will show my enjoyment by doing better in your class. I hope you don't mind if I come in and see you to discuss the material from time to time before or after school.

Yours Sincerely,

Walter Barnett

P.S. I hope you don't think that I am kissing up.

"So, Mr. Gerson," he said nervously as I looked up, "what do you think?"

"Generally, Walt, it is excellent. Almost perfect, in fact. But there are a couple of flaws that you will have to correct before you can put these in your teachers' mailboxes."

"Aw." He looked crushed. "Mr. Gerson, these took me mad effort."

"I know, Walt, and, as I said, it is a great start. But you will need to do a few things. First, it is not a good idea to write one note, make photocopies of it, and insert the person's name and subject."

"Oh."

"Yes, you want to make it personal. Also, don't mention kissing up."

"Ain't that what I am doing?"

"In a manner of speaking. In any case, it is better not to broach the issue at all. It calls attention to what you are doing. Trust me on that. Kissing up, though everyone successful does it in one way or another, carries with it a negative connotation."

"Also," I added just to be safe, "don't tell any of the other teachers that you consulted with me on this. Better for them to think it came from you alone."

He nodded in agreement and said that he would show me the revised notes the next day. Walt came back, having made the requisite corrections. "Mr. Gerson, can I deliver these now?"

"Yes, you may. You have done a masterful job." He thanked me and turned to go.

"Walt," I called to him, "one more thing."

"What?"

"Before you put these notes in the teachers' mailboxes, Walt, consider something. You will have to follow through. Kissing up is the easy part, especially for someone with your charm. But kissing up will only work if accompanied by genuinely working hard. It will backfire if not complemented by serious real effort. The teachers will think that you are being fake, and they are going to like you even less if you don't work hard from now on. So you better be sure you are willing to put in extra work if you are going to do this."

Walt came to me a couple of days later and said that his teachers loved the notes and were quite willing to give him a second chance. He wanted to know how he might start acting on the notes.

"You have two stories to read for English this weekend," I said, "but only have to answer questions on one. Why don't you answer questions on both? It won't take much time, and it will surely impress Sister Patricia—and convince her that you are serious about improving your attitude and work habits."

"To convince her that I was not just kissing up?"

"Something like that." Walt did as I suggested, and Sister Patricia was very impressed, not to mention more than a bit surprised. I felt a tinge of guilt for encouraging Walt to ingratiate himself with my unsuspecting colleagues. But, then again, he had asked me for help, and I would have been disingenuous if I had not advised him as I did.

Millburn kids, unlike Walt, Simon, and other St. Luke students, find ingratiating behavior perfectly natural. They have a very different sense of honor, embedded in a code that neatly coincides with their self-interest. They view school as their vocation. To them, doing well academically is a moral duty, what one owes oneself and one's parents. Educational achievement is also a practical responsibility, the key to college and the world beyond. Millburn students treat their teachers as they will one day treat their employers, demonstrating the utmost deference, ingratiating themselves whenever possible, and reserving expression of their negative feelings only for discussions that could not be overheard by a potentially aggrieved party. If a Millburn kid is disrespectful to a teacher, it is a big deal, because it is both exceptionally rare and exceedingly stupid. Honesty may be a virtue, but at Millburn so is prudence, and the students there, unlike their counterparts at St. Luke, always allow the latter to temper the former.

The idea of deliberately ingratiating oneself with a teacher, which is perfectly acceptable to Millburn kids, is so far removed from the mind-set of St. Luke students that the latter act as if they intend to establish the opposite relationship with their teachers. Consider, for instance, their favorite game to play with them: "shock the bourgeois." St. Luke kids act as if they think they have invented sex and feel it their duty to teach their teachers about it. Every young teacher confronts this behavior, and only a few accept it comfortably. The first-year health teacher, Jenny Smith, was not one of these people. "We will discuss sex in this class," she explained during the opening week of school, "as a part of sex education. But we will do it maturely. We will use proper terminology and not say anything to get a cheap laugh. You can speak as freely as you want and ask any questions you want, so long as they are serious. I won't set any specific rules because you are all young adults and I trust your maturity. Are there are questions?"

A student in the back of the class raised his hand. "Yes, Rasheed?"

"Ms. Smith, if I rub a woman's clitoris hard enough, will she come?"

As a freshman, Rasheed was precocious in playing shock the bourgeois, but the MVP of this game was Sandra, a 250-pound sophomore with three great passions in life: food, doing things she believed would shock the bourgeois, and telling the bourgeois all about them. Her great conquest, as she told everybody, was publicly humiliating her young English teacher, Will Donaldson. She asked him first if he had a girlfriend.

"Yes."

"How long you been going out with her for?"

"Two years."

"When did you first have sex with her?"

In March I took Sandra and several other students on a field trip to the Statue of Liberty and Ellis Island. Outside of school any residual inhibitions against shocking the bourgeois were gone, and Sandra was in top form. She started by talking incessantly about her twenty-six-year-old boyfriend, who was, she informed everybody, doing very well in a methadone clinic. But Sandra's first attempt to shock this bourgeois did not concern sex: In the space of ninety minutes, from when we met at the school to when we were ready to board the ferry to the Statue of Liberty and Ellis Island, Sandra consumed a shocking amount of food: First, she stopped at the bodega near school and ate a sandwich. Then, as we walked to the park, she went to the corner store and bought a very large bag of cookies. Not satiated yet, she bought a hot dog in the park. Then she bought peanuts and popcorn, both of which she consumed while waiting to board the ferry. Furthermore, she made prolonged stops at the snack bars at both Liberty Island and Ellis Island, eating a hamburger at the former and an ice cream sundae at the latter. I had never seen a female eat that much, and I told her so. But that is not the shock she wanted.

"Those waters, Mr. Gerson, are disgusting," she said, pointing to the Hudson River.

"Why, Sandra? They look fine to me."

"If you look at night, they are full of condoms. And I should know; my boyfriend will often throw three or four of them into the river at night. Used condoms, that is." I didn't respond the way she wanted, so she kept saying that she couldn't wait until Wednesday.

Finally, I gave in. "Okay, Sandra. What is the big deal about Wednesday?"

"Every Wednesday my boyfriend takes me out to dinner."

"That's nice."

"But we don't order dessert."

"I can't imagine you would have to, Sandra. You probably have four dinners."

"No, that's not it, Mr. Gerson, although sometimes I have two or three. My boyfriend knows the owner, so he don't charge me. After dinner, we have dessert. It's just not the kind you are thinking about."

"Okay, Sandra. I get the point."

"You know what I mean?"

"Yes, Sandra, and it does not interest me one bit."

"Sometimes I suck his lollipop for dessert," she said, giggling. "You know what that is?"

"Sandra, grow up."

Though the students were eager to shock the bourgeois teachers by letting them in on their revolutionary invention of sex, they thought it improper to share their discovery with the sisters.

I helped advise the literary magazine with Sister Peter and another teacher and was quickly reminded that teenage creative writing is often an outlet for sophomoric prurience. One junior, Clarissa, who was on my mock trial team, read a short story she wrote. Clarissa dreamed of being a sophisticated and sought-after woman; she was constantly telling the mock trial team about an older boyfriend (who may or may not have existed). In her short story a man came into the school and asked her for directions to the office. As she gave him directions, he stroked her hair and whispered into her ear. That was the whole story. When Clarissa finished, another student said, "You know, that is a good story but maybe you shouldn't read it with Sister Peter right here." Sister Peter, with a smile, brushed it aside. "No, no, that's okay. Clarissa, you have interesting ideas, but you probably should develop the relationship a bit more. I have been around for a long time and have seen things change quite a bit, but I have never seen such quick moves especially in a hallway in the middle of the day. Let's work on it together."

Though Millburn kids show far more reverence toward teachers, St. Luke students are much more effusive in expressing affection for parents. Millburn students generally speak of their parents in reference to something specific (my mother grounded me, my father is a pediatric oncologist, I am going with my parents to Puerto Rico over Christmas break, etc.). They rarely quote their parents as moral instructors or cite them as role models and almost never openly declare their love for and gratitude toward them in public. This is not to say they don't feel these emotions. Of course they do; they are just trained to believe that such feelings are private and should not be discussed in public. St. Luke kids on the other hand feel them and proclaim them. From the very beginning of the year I was struck by how often they cited their parents in papers, in conversations with each other, and in class discussions. Statements like "I think taxes are bad because my father loses so much of his money to the government" or blatant declarations of affection were heard frequently. It was socially accepted—even encouraged—to speak freely of love and admiration for parents. A telling example occurred when I asked 10W to write a short paper on the historical figure they most admired and another on someone in their lives who had been a great influence. Shaneka did the second assignment first and was showing it to LaToya, who was sitting next to her, when I commented. "Shaneka, this is your work, and you need not show it to anyone while they are trying to do theirs. Get started on the other one."

"But," LaToya stressed, "it's really good. You have to read it now, Mr. Gerson." LaToya handed it to me.

> Sholanda Washington my mother she is the greatest black women in the whole wide world. Because she teaches me from right and wrong. What to do and what not to do. When I'm in trouble or when I'm about to be in trouble she talks to me to help me stay out of trouble. She's the greatest she is always there for me through thick and thin. When I need her she is there for me. When I need someone to talk to she is there for me. And when I need a shoulder to cry on she is there to talk to me to see what the problem is. My dearest mother.

I thought that was beautiful, and saved it to show her mother on parents' night. Unfortunately, her mother could not make it. She had to work.

What accounts for this difference in attitude toward parents? For one, the same honesty that led Kenny to tell me just how boring he thought my lecture on the French and Indian War was led his classmate to openly declare her love for her mother. The complex array of unwritten rules and mores that restrain behavior in the suburbs does not exist in the other America. But it is more than a matter of inner-city kids not having WASP-like reserve. Suburban kids take a lot more for granted than do their age-mates in the inner city. The latter see the enormous sacrifices their parents and loved ones make for them; they know what happens when sacrifices are not made and when responsibilities are not honored. The idea "there but for the grace of God go I" becomes quite evident when one has neighbors and relatives from broken homes (or no home at all) turning to drugs, violence, and crime.

Millburn kids are vaguely aware that such a world exists, but it is emphatically not their own. Illegitimacy is all but unheard of at Millburn High School. Moreover, few Millburn parents divorce and those that do almost always stay in contact with their children. Suburban youths come to regard this social environment as normal and expectable, as something they are entitled to in the sense that this is how things are. Urban youths have a different sense of what they are owed by their parents and are correspondingly appreciative of the small and great sacrifices their families make for them. Having very different views of what is normal, urban and suburban youth have different ideas of what they are entitled to and what to expect from the worlds they inhabit.

"*Two nations . . . not governed by the same laws.*" This difference in the concept of normalcy among students in the suburbs and those in the cities is important in ways that extend well beyond the realm of the family. I graduated from Williams College in 1994. It was a beautiful school in so many ways, a rare place this side of heaven made even more by the fact that it was so safe. But this extraordinary safety was unacceptable to some of the students. They did not want real crime, of course, but they wanted to imagine that there might be danger, so they would have something to worry about. Thus, campus groups held marches, rallies, and protests to warn the college community of the dangers literally lurking behind the bushes on the snowy, sleepy Williamstown campus—often in the form of "Take Back the Night" rallies and marches. Knowing the nature of university administrators and our litigious society, these students were aware that the college would go along with them to avoid controversy and potential lawsuits. By the time I entered my senior year, Williams had spent over $2 million on rape prevention lights, trimming of shrubbery, and state-of-the-art police cars for campus security. I have little doubt that if a sociologist in the year 2000 goes to Williamstown to study the issue, he will find that Williams College spent more money on crime prevention per crime in the previous ten years than did any other institution on earth.

In contrast, Jersey City has real crime—and lots of it. What would have horrified anyone from Millburn or Williams was treated as perfectly normal by my students. This phenomenon, identified by Daniel Patrick Moynihan as "defining deviancy down," is a way of life in Jersey City. According to Senator Moynihan, our habit of considering normal what was once regarded as deviant is a source of great moral confusion. He cites the example of the St. Valentine's Day Massacre, in which a few gangsters in Chicago killed a few others. This event warranted two entries in the 1942 *World Book Encyclopedia;* now reports of similar killings are buried in the back pages of newspapers, if they appear at all.

Toward the end of the school year I was in the middle of teaching 10Y when gunshots rang out, followed by a bloodcurdling scream. I looked around to see if everyone was all right, and several of the students were laughing—I had panicked and apparently did not know how to hide it. Walt told me to calm down because the shots had come from a distance, were clearly not going to hurt anybody in the room, and were therefore no big deal. My students had been a lot closer to gunfire than that and found my naïveté rather humorous. After a minute, so did I. That afternoon I drove Randy, a senior on my mock trial team, home after practice, and I told him about the incident.

"That's nothing, Mr. Gerson. Ain't nothing at all," he said.

"What? It was gunshots in the middle of the day. Is your neighborhood worse?"

"My neighborhood is not bad, although there is some crime."

"What kind of crime?"

"You know, drug deals and everything that comes from that. If one guy owes another a lot of money—twenty bucks or more—the second guy will beat up the first and steal whatever he can. And then I saw a guy shot last week because he knocked this girl up and wouldn't admit it—so her brothers took care of him. One of the brothers will get killed now, because the family of the guy who screwed his sister is going to get even, and you know how it works. But as long as you stay out of the cross fire, you are okay. And people get shit stolen all the time, and most of the time no one is killed because the robbers just want to bug out with the shit, and no one can get him back because he doesn't usually get caught." The next day Randy told me that he discussed our conversation with a policeman that night, who confirmed that his neighborhood was one of the quietest in Jersey City.

Differences in urban and suburban perceptions of deviancy and normalcy may be less striking, but they are everywhere and are still important. For example, parents of students at Millburn and St. Luke had very different ideas about what constitutes normal parent–teacher interaction. St. Luke parents had a much more trusting attitude toward their child's school than did their suburban counterparts. St. Luke parents had great faith that the teachers and administrators were doing the right thing, and they rarely, if ever, questioned them. Even the most supportive, caring parents had little education themselves, especially the ones who did not speak English. Whereas suburban parents evaluated their children's teachers on an individual basis, inner-city parents either gave their children's education over to the school one hundred percent, trusting all the teachers and administrators, or withdrew completely. Fortunately, St. Luke parents generally practiced the former approach.

In at least one respect, the reaction of the Harrisons (who responded to their daughter LaToya's minor insubordination with extraordinary seriousness on back-to-school night) was typical: St. Luke parents almost always sided with the teachers in conflicts with their children. Most inner-city parents, at least those who send their kids to Catholic schools, believe that the authority figures in the school know what is best for the kids and are willing to back up the teachers whenever necessary. No teacher I knew at St. Luke ever received a phone call from a parent seriously disputing a punishment or questioning a lesson, teaching style, or grade. In one sense, this is good; teachers are professionals and do not like being told how to do their job. But there is a sobering lesson here as well: inner-city teachers must always be self-motivated because a crucial check on their authority does not exist. They could get away with nearly anything and must watch themselves every day to ensure that they do not take advantage of this lack of scrutiny. This was not a problem at St. Luke because all of the teachers were there for a reason and with a mission. Anyone with a college degree working in an institution where the salary ceiling is under twenty-five thousand dollars is self-motivated—or, in the case of many of my colleagues at St. Luke, motivated by God.

In a suburban school like in Millburn, a teacher cannot have a bad day without a parent calling and complaining. Teaching in a town where almost everyone has the highest degree in his field makes for a very different dynamic than is found in an inner-city school. Good suburban parents can use their knowledge and experience to deepen and reinforce the lessons of teachers, as my parents did. But it does not always work this way. When I went to Millburn Junior High, there were three levels: Honors, Standard, and Basic. But now, because enough parents demanded that their child be put in a higher section, there is no Basic level. The Basic kids are now in Standard, and the majority of the class is in Honors. When I heard this, I could not help but think of Garrison Keillor's observation on the educational system in Lake Wobegon: all the students are above average.

This might be an ordinary irony if it did not have serious educational implications. Standard and Honors classes are now taught at a lower level to accommodate the flood of Basic kids into Standard, and Standard kids into Honors. Students who belong in a real Honors or Standard section are being denied the benefits that come from being in a section in which they are challenged. The students who are "raised" into a higher section also suffer since they are overwhelmed by those in their section who are performing at a higher academic level. Why, then, did the elimination of Basic classes pass with so little controversy?

Because it is a lot easier for parents to demand that their child be placed in the highest section than to demand that a higher section be created for their child.

Mr. Sachsel described an incident some twenty years earlier, when he was called to a meeting at a church in Millburn. He did not know what to expect but went nonetheless. He entered the church and was ushered into a room full of Millburn's men of cloth—rabbis, priests, and ministers. *What could they want?* Apparently, some of their congregants had called and complained that he had been teaching religion in his American history classes. *So?* he wondered. It is tough to teach American history without teaching religion; Americans, after all, are a religious people; the country was, in fact, formed by people who had left their homeland to obtain religious freedom. The clergymen acknowledged this, but were still concerned that teaching the world's religions might shake the faith of some of the students. Mr. Sachsel wondered out loud who was not doing his job if a Christian or Jewish kid had a crisis of faith upon learning about Zoroastrianism. The meeting broke up shortly thereafter.

All stories about public education do not have such a happy ending, as is evidenced by an event involving a student organization. In the spring, Mr. Sachsel told me, there was an election for the presidency of a particular club, just as there had been every year in the past. The adviser to the club, a teacher with whom Mr. Sachsel was close, was a woman of the utmost integrity. It was she who counted the ballots and declared the winner. The next day the mother of the losing candidate called the supervising administrator to demand a new election. She was convinced that the adviser had thrown the election to the winner, and she demanded that the administrator conduct a new election with someone else to count the ballots. The administrator had several choices, the obvious one being to tell the mother that he had the utmost confidence in his teacher and that her daughter should simply accept losing the election. But no.

What do you think happened? Mr. Sachsel asked me.

The administrator probably held a new election, where he counted the ballots himself.

Nope.

My second guess: He probably used the reasoning of the old Vietnam-era aphorism—"We must destroy this village in order to save it"—and dissolved the club. That was right. The principal dissolved the club just as summer vacation was starting (when the students and their parents would be thinking about beach houses and summer jobs rather than club activities). To avoid the spectacle of even an obviously deluded parent complaining, this administrator followed his principle: Avoid controversy at all costs.

At the end of one school year Mr. Sachsel announced to a class that if they lost their (college-level) textbooks, the fine would be only three dollars.

"What?" they asked.

"I just wanted to tell you," he informed them, "that if you should happen to lose your textbook, you will only be fined three dollars."

After a couple of minutes the students caught on: Mr. Sachsel was telling them to keep their textbooks, which they recognized would be very useful in college the next year. Sure enough, most of the students "lost" their textbooks, and the sixty dollars or so collected was used to buy additional movies for the "film and society" class.

What was Mr. Sachsel up to? The school district was planning to buy new textbooks for the class, which meant the old ones would be thrown away as garbage.

"This is crazy!" I said to Mr. Sachsel. "Don't they know how many poor schools like St. Luke could use their textbooks and not even notice that they are old?"

"They might know, but that is beside the point. The point is that the school district does not want some irate taxpayer to call up and say, 'Why are my tax dollars going to pay for new books when the old ones are still fine?' Throwing them away avoids that problem. Anyone calls, and those books were so bad that they were only fit for the dump. Of course, I could never bring myself to throw away books. There are too many poor schools that could really use them. You remember Mrs. Peterson, who used to be a principal of Stevens Elementary School until last year? She had a friend who taught in Appalachia, so this is what we did when I was at the middle school. I collected all of the books to be thrown away, and we put them in boxes. We prominently displayed these boxes near the garbage cans in our respective schools for a couple of days so that everyone who cared to think about it figured that they were being tossed. But after the building was clear on the third day or so, we would write the name and address of this man in Appalachia on the boxes, go to a post office, and send them. We were never caught. But because I just came to the high school this year, I was not ready to do that quite yet. So I encouraged the students to 'lose' their books."

This incident was striking to me, partly because I knew what St. Luke did with old books. All St. Luke's books were old and were replaced only when they were completely unusable. But if in a set of such a few were salvageable, Sister Theresa would get on the phone and find another Catholic school that could use them. "There is," she once told me, "always someone in greater need than even the very poor." Wealthy Millburn taxpayers might call and complain if this were done in their town, but it is inconceivable that poor tuition-paying St. Luke parents would do the same.

This tendency for public schools to placate their worst elements has even begun to dominate curriculum decisions. For example, the school board of Brookline, a wealthy suburb of Boston, voted to abolish the high school's advanced placement European history course because it "was not compatible with multicultural education and did not fit in with the unified set of values the [school's] department of [social studies] wanted to promote." It is hard to imagine that a majority of parents, administrators, or teachers—or, for that matter, a majority of any group of sane people—would go along with that. But the school board's resolution passed, and it is not hard to figure out why.

Most educational administrators are not like Mr. Sachsel; controversy is to be avoided at all costs, and principle can be costly.

One of my former teachers at Millburn told me that the idea of pandering to the basest instincts is more far-reaching in public education than even the dramatic publicized examples suggest. In the last few years public school teachers and schools (including Millburn) have been strongly encouraged by administrators and department chairmen to develop nearly homogeneous lessons, all specifying a particular purpose, goal, beginning, middle, and end. This has nothing to do with classroom excellence, considering that good teachers will often leave one idea hanging at the end of the class so that students will have something to think about in the lunchroom or at home. Few things in life have a distinct purpose, goal, beginning, middle, and end—and lesson plans should be no different. Catholic schools realize this. The only teachers who had to submit lesson plans at St. Luke were the new ones, and we were only required to do so for the first semester (so that we could receive help if we went astray). We were given guidelines to establish a curriculum but were told to adapt our teaching method, materials, and interests to each class. That way, if a history teacher was an expert on, say, the First Amendment and had a special way of enticing kids to love Constitutional law, he could spend more time on that and breeze over, say, the rechartering of the Second Bank of the United States.

Why have public schools become so rule oriented? It is because strict legalism makes it easy to avoid controversy by playing to the lowest common denominator. If schools invest trust in their teachers and allow them the freedom to practice their craft, some teachers will be recognized as much better than others. Take any subject that Mr. Sachsel teaches: Western Hemisphere, for example. The gap between the number of students who want to enroll in Mr. Sachsel's section and those who want to take the class from another teacher will always be enormous.

Two undesirable consequences follow. First, the less popular teacher will feel bad. Second, the school will be put in the uncomfortable position of explaining to disappointed students and furious parents that Mr. Sachsel is one person, incapable of teaching fifteen classes a day, meaning that not every student can have Mr. Sachsel for Western Hemisphere. If the difference between Mr. Sachsel and another teacher could be lessened, perhaps by rigidly prescribing the curriculum, this problem would diminish significantly. The trade-off is between equality and excellence; equality makes things a lot easier, but excellence makes them a lot better. In their desire to serve a variety of conflicting constituencies and to avoid controversy, public schools often choose the former; urban Catholic schools, which have the trust of parents and are backed by a revered institution, usually choose the latter.

Unlike public schools, Catholic schools do not have to dive lower and lower to reach their lowest common denominator. Why is this? One reason is the sense of shared purpose and common struggle that pervades many Catholic schools. This is manifested in a number of ways, for example, in the area of school funding. In 1995, Jersey City public schools failed thirteen out of forty-nine tests the state administered, including deficit spending.

The public schools ran a deficit of $15,656,943 owing in part to an "unfunded improvement authorization." From the vantage point of St. Luke this is inconceivable, and not just because St. Luke is a small school that runs on under $1 million a year. Simply, St. Luke has a very tight budget and could not spend any money it did not have. Even if the St. Luke administration were so inclined, there is no way it could make an "unfunded improvement authorization."

Toward the middle of the year it became clear at St. Luke that we needed a new van. For months the students who rode in the old van came back with near-horror stories: the door had to be held shut, the transmission went, again, in the middle of traffic, and so on. Maura's father, a mechanic, came to school to look at it. He concluded that no amount of tinkering could fix the thing.

Even getting a good deal for being a Catholic school, a new van would cost upwards of twenty thousand dollars. A formidable sum, indeed. "How will we manage?" I asked Nathan Siderville.

"Don't worry about it. Our annual card party is coming up."

"What's that?"

"We have a bunch of raffles and raise money for something new every year. This year, obviously, the object of the night will be a van."

"Nathan, I know about raffles. We had them all the way through when I went to school. They raised maybe a couple of hundred dollars. That won't buy the radio for a van."

He laughed. "I bet we'll do better than a couple of hundred dollars."

Soon thereafter, the preparation for the card party began. It would be held in the cafeteria, a very large room in a small building twenty or so feet away from the school. One group of student volunteers would handle the decorating, another would set up the places and the raffle tables, and another would serve the chicken dinners. Every student in the school would be asked to bring in something to be raffled—a toaster, a costume, whatever. Raffles of these items would go on through the night. People could not enter a raffle for, say, the toaster but only for any of the hundreds of items to be raffled in a batch, but there would be a dozen or so big items for which guests could enter separate raffles.

Sister Theresa asked all of the teachers to come, and we were given assignments for the evening. Mine was to run the raffle for one of the big items—the baby basket. The job was very easy: just standing in front of the basket and perhaps doing a bit of salesmanship, collecting money, and dispensing tickets. The largest raffles would be for a 486 computer with a CD-ROM drive and a "fifty-fifty," where half of the cash donated to that particular contest would be won by a lucky contestant. "Are there any other ideas?" Sister Theresa wanted to know. I volunteered to run a poker game or a blackjack table. "Stick to the baby basket," I was politely informed.

Several teachers and I arrived early for the card party. My table had been set up by a student. There was the basket, overflowing with diapers, dolls, stuffed animals, pacifiers, and a lot more. With a half hour before the start of the party, people started coming in. Some had bought the ten-dollar entry ticket from a student beforehand; others purchased their tickets at the door. Before I knew it, I was very busy. People were lined up in front of me, and everyone was chatting and waiting amiably. Some of my customers wore what were obviously thrift shop sweaters, others donned shirts with their name written on the front, and others sported pinstripe suits with wing tip shoes. From where did all of these people come? As the night went on, I learned that many were relatives of students, friends of relatives of students, parishioners at St. Luke Church, and people from the community and neighboring communities who just wanted an evening of socializing. All of the St. Luke clergy were there, as were priests and nuns I did not recognize; they had come from churches all over the region. All of the lay teachers and administrators were there as well, having brought their spouses, children, siblings, nephews, and nieces.

I don't know if there were any firemen there, but I doubt it because the cafeteria would have certainly qualified as a fire hazard. It was simply packed. People were eating, drinking, raffling, talking, meeting the teachers of their children, or simply having a great time and spending a good amount of money. The raffles for the hundreds of items that no one really wanted started right away, and almost everybody ended up winning something. A sister from a nearby parish won my baby basket; I don't know what she did with it. A student won the computer, and she was ecstatic. Before spinning the wheel to determine the winner of the fifty-fifty, Sister Theresa announced how much money there was to be won: $2335, half of what had been donated. All were silent as the wheel turned and turned. Finally, Sister Theresa took the winning ticket and read the name of the winner: Stephanie O'Malley. No one rose to claim the prize. Then Jenny Smith, the religion teacher, indicated that Stephanie was a friend of hers and that she had left early. I'll bet that Stephanie was never so glad to hear from Jenny as she was that night.

We stayed and cleaned up after the party ended. Sister Theresa emerged from a backroom after about an hour to announce the profit on the evening: $13,420. We had more than enough for a down payment on the van and several payments after that. It was a smashing success, I thought. Veteran teachers agreed but added that it was no better or worse than most years.

I was shocked by the amount of money we raised; I did not know how we were going to raise a fraction of what was necessary for just the down payment on the van. But I underestimated the power of the St. Luke community. Teachers, administrators, parishioners, students, their parents, and other interested people worked together for a cause in which all believed and to which all were willing to give their money and time. We needed the van and had to get it ourselves; no combination of campaigning, pleading, or complaining would have done anything. There was an important goal to be met, an expensive goal to be sure, but this financially poor community had absolutely no trouble raising the money. A strong and inarticulate sense of community funded this St. Luke improvement authorization.

This sense of community, solidified by events like the card party, was St. Luke's greatest asset, as important as any of the tangible amenities of which Millburn or a Jersey City public school—each of which spends $10,000 per pupil—can boast. At some level, everyone—parents, students, school personnel—knew that a vibrant community revolves around a strong moral consensus and that membership means sacrifice. Parents gave everything they had to St. Luke in the form of tuition, the sisters gave their whole lives to serving the students, and the teachers worked for minimal pay and advised after-school activities for free. Because the community was consecrated by a shared purpose and consistent sacrifice, it was able to hold high standards and enforce them effectively. There was an ethic of sacrifice, an ethic diametrically opposed to the individualistic ethos where anyone—by virtue of paying taxes or residing in a certain area—

can throw demands at some authority whose real function is to satisfy the people by executing those demands—regardless of their merits.

Infused with an ethos of sacrifice, St. Luke was able to apply a central rule for all genuine communities: Those who do not share the aims of the community and are not willing to give of themselves to further those aims are no longer welcome. This rarely needed to be discussed and even less frequently needed to be applied. It was common sense. If a parent had called St. Luke to complain about textbooks being discarded, he would have been gently but firmly told not to worry about it. And if the parent persisted, Sister Theresa or Mr. Murphy would have reminded them that it is a privilege to be a member of the St. Luke community and that there are plenty of other schools his child could go to if he did not like St. Luke. In other words, respect it or leave it. Knowing what the latter entailed, the parents would have invariably shut up.

But it is entirely different when people have a "right" to be a member of a "community" by virtue of residing in a particular location or sending a check to the proper authority. It is impossible for such a group to rally around a principle when it cannot exclude those who reject the principle or those who pay it lip service but refuse to make the attendant sacrifices. This "community" must resort to its lowest common denominator to ensure that the demands of the most selfish—often those asserting their "rights"—are satisfied, regardless of the cost those demands exact on the community. This has nothing to do with wealth or social status; Millburn parents in a parent–teacher association, United Way affiliate, or soccer club will quickly silence obstreperous, selfish boors. Such voluntary communities are composed of busy people sacrificing their valuable time for a cause they find worthy, and they will not tolerate someone whose interests do not coincide with those of the group. But when a selfish boor has a "right" to be an "equal" member of a "community," what can be said to him?

Just as Millburn students refrain from publicly proclaiming

their love for their parents, they rarely discuss the impact of God in their lives, or even the impact of religion in the moral structure of their society. As one senior told me, "The only time you hear of religion at Millburn is at Christmas time and in the narrow context of 'What are you doing for the holiday?'" Many students at Millburn are observant Jews or devout Christians, but all keep their faith to themselves. For Millburn kids, faith is treated like sex: it is okay for others to know that you have it, but the details remain private.

On the first day I visited Millburn, Mr. Sachsel told his Western Hemisphere classes about the Catholic shrine at Lourdes and the role of religious pilgrimages. He spoke of visiting a shrine in Canada and seeing thousands of crutches and wheelchairs left behind. Mr. Sachsel offered no opinion on the veracity or possibility of such experiences. Instead, he asked his students what they thought. Few had anything to say about this, but the consensus of the first class was summarized in the words of one junior: "It must be mind over matter. People think they will be cured if they go to the shrine, and it happens to work out that way."

Mr. Sachsel's second Western Hemisphere class generally agreed; there was only one dissenter. After one student offered the mind-over-matter explanation, a senior in the back of the room, Joe, volunteered, "Possibly that is not all there is to it."

Mr. Sachsel responded, "Could you deepen that? What else could it be?"

The rest of the class looked at Joe, who took a moment to ponder Mr. Sachsel's question. "Well," Joe suggested, "perhaps it is just luck."

"Luck?" Mr. Sachsel asked.

"Yes, luck. Maybe the crippled people are suddenly cured the moment they step up to the shrine."

Another student chirped in: "At that very moment? Thousands of people, crippled for their entire lives, are luckily cured the moment they step to the shrine?"

"Luck, you know," explained the senior, "works in strange ways, and we can't understand it. That's why it is luck."

Joe might have found luck more believable than faith, and doubtless most of his classmates did, too. Since Millburn High School was such a secular environment, no one had ever thought to form a Bible study group there before 1994. Originally, the students who formed the group were told by the administration that meeting in the school would violate the First Amendment. So they met at 6 A.M. in the home of one of the club members. Eventually, the club members made a deal with the school administration: they could meet in the high school after school but could never post a notice on the bulletin board or announce anything over the loudspeaker. This was a real coup. A representative of the Bible study group wrote an article in the *Miller* praising the administration's commitment to religious freedom. I do not know whether it occurred to these students that the environmentalist groups, the feminist group, the baseball team, and the yearbook staff were all able to make full use of the resources that were off-limits to them. Nor do I know if the students in the Bible study group knew that they had a clearly established constitutional right to meet in the building and probably also a right to advertise like any other group. But they seemed quite satisfied with their treatment.

Why are Millburn High School students so unwilling to go outside their rational world to explain the unexplainable? Why would they not understand St. Luke students who thank God for their good fortune, "catch the Holy Ghost" in church, and sometimes even spin into a religious frenzy for hours on end? I am not positive of the answer, but I think a large part of it has to do with the fact that Millburn kids see their entire world as being under almost perfect human control. From cradle to grave, they live with greater wealth and greater security than have most kings throughout history. Never will Millburn students worry about food, clothing, shelter, education, or even a career. Even the students who, for one reason or another, are overwhelmed by the pressure of such high standards end up graduating from college with good jobs awaiting them.

In Millburn, there is never a doubt that academic success continually rewards itself until it culminates in a prosperous career. There has probably never been a more pacific place than contemporary American suburbs, where the violence that has felled young men throughout the ages and continues to do so in the nearby inner cities is nonexistent. In working-class and poor communities people are forced to fight to maintain their respect; in bourgeois society, people are respected for walking away. Bourgeois society is internally rationalized; everything makes sense as a duty or a responsibility, and the reasons are as clear as can be. It is sometimes easy to think of suburban teenagers as a myopic breed, forever doing shortsighted things and aggravating their parents. What is noteworthy, though, is that they generally know when to stop. Relatively few kids go over the edge; even the bad kids usually straighten out in due time. It is a remarkable accomplishment of bourgeois society that its youth see the future almost as concretely as they do the present.

This is not the case for inner-city kids. A couple of weeks after school ended I returned home one evening to a message on my answering machine from Charles: "Mr. Gerson, it's me, Charles. I have a question about the law, a very important question about the law, but don't worry, it doesn't involve me. I mean I'm not in trouble or nothing. Please, please beep me at 439-4893. Thank you, Mr. Gerson."[1]

I beeped Charles, and he returned the call immediately. "Mr. Gerson, thank you very much for calling me back. I am at a pay phone now. I am with my cousin, a woman from Seattle who gave her kids up for adoption there, but the kids are here now

---

[1]Before I arrived at St. Luke, I thought that beepers were used only by doctors and drug dealers. I was mistaken; most of my students carried beepers and for perfectly legitimate reasons. City kids move around a lot, and it is very difficult for parents to know where their children are at all times. So if a mother wants to contact her child, the easiest way is to beep him or her.

and she wants to see them but doesn't know where they are. What can she do?"

"Charles, I don't know anything about family law."

"But you are going to law school, and you know all about the Constitution."

"Charles, I am sorry to say, but there is nothing in the Constitution about family law, and I haven't started law school yet. I wish I could be of more help myself, but I simply do not have the necessary knowledge. But I can point you in the right direction."

"What can she do, Mr. Gerson?" The pay phone clicked; his time was rapidly expiring.

"Here, Charles. Call the Hudson County Bar Association at 798-2727. They do lawyer referrals. If you explain the problem to them, they will be able to find just the attorney who can do the job that your cousin needs."

"Okay, thank you, Mr. Gerson. I'll call them."

Would a Millburn student ever call his history teacher at home over the summer about his cousin's problem with a matter concerning family law? No, he would probably directly contact a specialist in the field, perhaps a friend of a parent or the parent of a friend, who would take the call immediately and provide detailed advice free of charge. What other alternatives are there in a world that is so properly ordered and easy to negotiate? That world is under human control, and a Millburn youngster will invariably know many of the people controlling it. Inner-city kids, however, grasp whatever help they can as they search for assistance in navigating their often senseless world. If they think their world is under human control, they must think the humans controlling it are not doing a very good job with it.

In the fall of 1994 I opened the *Williams College Alumni Review* to find the secretary of the class of 1991 reporting some proud news: "Our class has its first child!" Two married alumni, both at Yale Law School, were the proud parents. I thought, *Well, Williams Class of 1991, the St. Luke High School class of 1997 beat you guys by a year.* The week before, I had collected an assignment where I asked my students to tell me about themselves, including where they would like to be in the future. I was inspired to do this by a student in 10E, Simon, who told me one day that he dreamed of becoming a broadcaster on the news. Sure enough, he knew the names of the news anchor and reporters on every station. I heartily encouraged him, telling him that his dignified comportment would resonate well with the viewing public, who were always in need of a reassuring figure to bring them the evening news. Simon said that no one had ever taken him seriously before—and he was even skeptical that I did until I taped several evening news programs for him on a night when he had to be in church. On a spring day he asked if he could interview me in homeroom. "Mr. Gerson, do you think that the Clinton tax cut will have a profound effect on the revaluation of the dollar?"

"Well, Simon. Interesting you should ask that. I think that the Clinton 'tax cut'—if (and that is a big *if*) there is a tax cut at all—will likely be too small to have any effect on the dollar."

"Jermeine!" Simon exclaimed, turning to the student next to him, "Mr. Gerson does not believe that Clinton's tax cut will have a profound effect on the value of the dollar. As a matter of fact, he does not believe the tax cut is meaningful at all."

Jermeine was unimpressed. "Who gives a shit?"

"Mr. Gerson," Simon responded immediately, "does Jermeine get a Frank?"

Simon had a vision for his future, and many others did as well. A great many (maybe 25 percent) wanted to be pediatricians. I don't know why this is, but I suppose a pediatrician is the most respected figure in the life of an inner-city youngster. Many other students wanted to be lawyers; one girl even wrote that she wanted to be a "corprite [sic] lawyer." Clearly, she had no idea what a corporate lawyer is, but she probably knew that corporate lawyers make a lot of money legally. Whether or not she achieves her goal, it was surely encouraging to me that she wanted that kind of lifestyle. Some students had plans based more directly on their experience and interests. Shaneka, who came in every week with a new and interesting hair arrangement, wanted to own a beauty salon. I have no doubt that she will be successful in that endeavor, as I tried to make clear to her by reading her favorite magazine, *Hyp Hair* (so I would know what to discuss with her).

The one constant that almost all the students wrote of—from the would-be doctors to the would-be beauticians—was the kind of lifestyle they wanted after work. They all wanted to be married and to live in a house with several children. In that regard, and to a large extent with their careers as well, St. Luke students had the same dreams and aspirations as their affluent age-mates. Enrique in 10L, for instance, wrote that he wanted to be a doctor and live in Jersey City with a wife and five children. "I already have one of those children," he wrote. "My daughter Tamara is the most precious person in my life." Enrique was far from the only St. Luke student to become a parent at age fifteen or younger. On Valentine's Day, Laura, an excellent student in my top class, received an astounding array of flowers and balloons from her boyfriend. I had never seen anything like it. The footprint of this package covered the surface of a large table in the office, and the flowers sprouted to the ceiling and intermingled with balloons cascading to the same height. I have never seen anyone happier than Laura was that day—not even three months later when she proudly showed a photograph to other students in the class. I figured it was a picture of her and her boyfriend, and I asked to look. Excitedly, she came to the front of the room and showed me a photograph that was primarily a black background with some large white markings on it. "Mr. Gerson, look, there is no penis. I am going to have a girl!" It was from her ultrasound. Laura's pregnancy became more obvious during the next month, when she abandoned her school-issue polyester pants for cotton sweats with an elastic waistband.

Laura was hardly alone; by the next fall, there were at least six more known pregnancies in her class. By the end of their junior year, at least a quarter of the female students had become pregnant. There is no way to know how many of the boys are fathers or fathers to be.

The high rate of pregnancy at St. Luke stood in contrast to the attitude these students maintained about teenage pregnancy. In class and out, I discussed this issue with my students— as I discussed any issue that was important in their lives. Every student opposed it. No girl said she hoped she was pregnant, and no boy bragged about impregnating a girl. They all saw teenage pregnancy as something they should avoid because it is a hindrance to their future and because it is wrong.

In April I was filling in for a senior health class whose topic of discussion that day was teenage pregnancy. After the students all agreed that pregnancy should wait until marriage, I asked, "Why, then, do teenagers get pregnant?"

One girl raised her hand. "It is simple," she said. "Some girls get pregnant because they want to keep their men. They think that if a man gets her pregnant, he won't leave."

Another girl raised her hand. "Right, and other girls get pregnant to make someone to love."

No one disagreed. These two explanations seemed to constitute a consensus. So I asked next, "But single women still get pregnant, anyway. You know that men are not going to stay around because they get their girlfriends pregnant, and you also know that one should not get pregnant in order to make someone to love. Right?"

Both girls who had spoken agreed with me, and the others indicated their assent.

"So what can be done about it?" I asked.

The first girl raised her hand again. "More education and better birth control."

"Education?" I asked. "But don't you know what causes pregnancy?"

"Booty calls."

"Late at night, maybe 2 A.M., a guy calls a girl and says, 'You want to fuck me now?' He ain't have to know her well or nothing. That is the booty call. Sometimes the answer is yes, sometimes no."

"Booty calls or no booty calls, what about birth control?"

"Everyone knows about birth control," another girl said, explaining the good and bad points of every conceivable method in detail that surpassed my knowledge. Another student indicated where the means for each method could be obtained at little or no cost.

Millburn students (and Williams students, too, for that matter) did not worry much, or even think a lot, about getting pregnant. Not, of course, that they didn't have sex. They did. But they were experts at birth control; the means were cheap, available, and effectively used. Why did they use birth control? It goes without saying. They all felt that illegitimacy automatically derails completely one's well laid-out plans for the future and is a great embarrassment to oneself and one's family. When middle-class people—from Millburn, Williams, and elsewhere—are asked how to curb teenage pregnancy, they invariably offer the same solution as their peers in the inner city: More Education. Why this answer? Perhaps those in the middle class assume that if inner-city kids had the same information they did, the inner-city kids would make the same correct decisions.

But it turns out that with the big issues—drugs, hard work, and pregnancy—kids at Millburn and St. Luke had the same information. St. Luke and Millburn kids agreed completely on which forms of behavior are acceptable and which are not. St. Luke students could recite, as well as anyone in the suburbs, the cliches of why they should work hard and behave themselves. They could give an antidrug speech that would make Bill Bennett blush, and any of them could deliver a tribute to family values worthy of a Republican Convention keynote address.

But as Lord Byron wrote, the tree of knowledge is not the tree of life. In the beginning of the year, for instance, the students in 10Y often condemned teenage pregnancy. The fathers always leave, they said. Children cannot support children. Children should come after marriage. And so on. But when Laura became pregnant, these condemnations stopped immediately and never picked up again. Why? Simply, their friend had become pregnant, and they did not want to offend her. So social pressure against teenage pregnancy evaporated immediately.

At Millburn, where students do not become pregnant, there is no way anyone would consider it acceptable for a child to have a child. But Millburn students are better able to avoid the abyss into which their peers in Jersey City fall for another reason as well. Good behavior is taught to inner-city kids; it is ingrained in suburban kids. A St. Luke kid steps outside, and who does he see? Peers with children, people out of jail and others on parole, menacing bums on the street corners, rampant crime, and much of the community on welfare. He sees no fathers. A Millburn kid steps outside, and what does he see? Fathers coaching their children in Little League, teenagers rushing to the post office to see if the acceptance or rejection letter from Yale has arrived, a father of a friend receiving an award from the American Medical Association, construction workers arriving to build an addition on the house next door. A St. Luke student and a Millburn student might indicate that they have the same goals and agree on the means to get there, but what does it mean? For one, such ideas constitute a vague conception; for the other a way of life.

"*Two nations . . . as if they were different zones.*" I proctored the midterm for 10Y. After the exam, Shanquilla came to see me. "Mr. Gerson, I didn't do so well," she said.

"Shanquilla," I responded, "I am sure you did just fine. You have been doing well all year, and it is unlikely that you forgot that much, even if you didn't study as hard as you should have."

"Mr. Gerson, I studied. I just could not think straight." This was out of character for Shanquilla, and I nodded that she should keep talking. "It is my mother. She died two days ago, on Sunday night, and I didn't find out about it until yesterday. My brother is in jail, and I had to tell him—"

"Oh, God, Shanquilla, I'm sorry. Is there anything I can do?"

"She died of AIDS. I don't—or I didn't—see her that much because I live with my grandma and they don't get along too good. I found out yesterday that I have to go to the funeral this afternoon. Mr. Gerson, I should have known. She looked so sick when I saw her last. Mr. Gerson, I didn't do well on that test."

"Shanquilla, you can take it again whenever you feel comfortable doing so. I won't even look at this test if you don't want. You just take care of yourself, and call me if you ever want to talk."

Shanquilla retook the exam two weeks later and earned a B+. She did not recover that year from the shock of her mother's death, but she had support. Many of her classmates also had intimate contact with the plague. Another student told me that her aunt had just died of AIDS. This woman's husband had been fooling around, but his wife did not feel right about asking any questions until she was doomed.

St. Luke made a concerted effort to educate kids about AIDS and how the plague is acquired. There was no need to teach them to have compassion for AIDS victims; that came naturally, given that so many were in contact with those suffering from the disease. Likewise, no one had any fear of acquiring AIDS from casual contact; if AIDS was contracted that way, many of them would have tested positive long ago. AIDS education at St. Luke was a part of sex education; the health teachers stressed over and over again that there is no protection from AIDS except for abstinence, that the allowable holes in a condom are smaller than sperm but larger than the virus that causes AIDS. The balance of the sex education curriculum consisted of pointing out how easy it is to acquire other devastating venereal diseases. Vividly describing and showing pictures of patients with gonorrhea, herpes, and syphilis has a way of concentrating the mind. How long these lessons will remain with the students after they leave school, I do not know. But if they deter just one kid from engaging in irresponsible behavior, they are worth it.

The week I visited Millburn High School was AIDS Education Week. The program was kicked off with a speech—a tender, moving address by a woman who had acquired the disease from her ex-boyfriend, a drug addict. Despite crippling sickness and excruciating pain, she spoke about AIDS to groups of high school students all over northern New Jersey. She was accompanied by a psychotherapist who dealt with AIDS patients. Most of the questions were directed at the woman with AIDS and were gentle and not very probing, but one student asked the psychotherapist (apropos of nothing), "Are you gay?" He was clearly shocked, as was just about everyone else in the audience. Teachers and students talked about this incident all day. For me, it was just a casual venture into the shock-the-bourgeois game, a pastime with which I had become very familiar.

Most of the discussion in Millburn's classes following the speech by the woman who had AIDS centered around how one should respond to someone suffering from AIDS. Outspoken students and teachers exhorted others to treat AIDS patients with respect rather than fear. All this was obvious to St. Luke teenagers. Parts of the national AIDS quilt, which consists of patches sewn to commemorate victims of AIDS, found its way to the Millburn gymnasium that day, and the students talked about it in hushed tones. But then the AIDS quilt disappeared, as did the program. There was no attempt to frighten the kids into behaving in a certain way, because it would have been unnecessary. Straight Millburn students know that they will not, except in an extraordinary circumstance, acquire AIDS. And unless a rare tragedy strikes or they volunteer in a hospice, they might very well go through life never knowing anyone afflicted with the plague that was decimating communities only ten miles from their home.

The difference between Millburn and St. Luke students in their reaction to tragedy became even more strikingly clear when we discussed the Holocaust. Aside from religion, the one topic—whatever academic or grade level of the class—that would immediately generate a reverential silence among St. Luke students was the Holocaust. My students knew about the Holocaust because their English teachers assigned them *The Diary of Anne Frank* and showed the film *Schindler's List*. I was the only Jew most of my students knew, and they did not learn about the Holocaust at home. Nonetheless, they felt almost instinctive deep appreciation for the tragedy of Jewish history. For instance, I read them the *New York Times* obituary of Franciszek Gajownicek. On August 3, 1941, a man from Gajownicek's section at Auschwitz successfully escaped. In response, the Nazis chose ten men at random to die of starvation. Gajownicek was one of the men. He cried out that he had a wife and children, and begged to be saved. Father Maximilian Kolbe volunteered to die in his stead. The Nazis granted the priest's request. Kolbe survived for ten days, leading his nine compatriots in prayer for nine days until they all died. After ten days Father Kolbe was still alive, and the Nazis gave him a lethal injection of carbolic acid. Father Kolbe, canonized in 1973, gave a Jewish stranger, a man who had been chosen randomly for death, a gift of more than a half-century of life.

I planned to give my students a brief account of this story, to read them an interesting obituary from that morning's paper, and to get on with a lesson about the Constitution, but no more than a half dozen lessons all year captivated them as much as this one. Without planning to, I discussed the Holocaust and Jewish history in several classes that day. Never before or after were the students in my classes so polite, inquisitive, and respectful as they were on that day.

St. Luke students were immune to what Alvin Rosenfeld calls "the Americanization of the Holocaust," which he characterized as the tendency to "metamorphose the Nazi Holocaust into that empty and all but meaningless abstraction 'man's inhumanity to man.'" With such a mind-set, the Holocaust becomes a symbol with which victimized groups compare their oppression. As an example of this phenomenon, Rosenfeld cited the Simon Wiesenthal Center's Museum of Tolerance in Los Angeles, which places the Holocaust into a framework that includes the Rodney King riots. This is part of what Rosenfeld terms "radical relativization" of the Holocaust, a phenomenon that has made significant inroads into suburban communities. In April 1995, Roger Rosenblatt published a cover story in the *New York Times Magazine* about how a Long Island, New York, school teaches character. The teacher in the article taught the Holocaust by writing four words across the chalkboard: *stereotypes, prejudice, cliques, Holocaust.* "What are the connections?" the teacher asked. One girl responded, "The Nazis didn't like the Jews because they thought only they were the best. They had their own special group." The teacher, evidently pleased, followed up. "So a clique is an excluding group of people. How would stereotypes fit into what a clique is?"

St. Luke students would never consider the Nazis one big clique gone awry. Kids who live constantly under the threat of drive-by shootings, rape, robbery, and domestic violence have no trouble distinguishing between childish customs and genuine evil. My students did not compare the Holocaust to anything in their own lives because they knew that the Holocaust is an embodiment of a special kind of evil utterly foreign to America. Knowing evil well and being all too aware of gradations of pathological behavior, St. Luke students were not relativists, and never would be. They had to distinguish between gradations of unpleasant behavior all the time, and it came as no surprise that they could apply this skill to their understanding of history.

Lacking any real contact with evil, suburban kids tend to see anything exclusionary as a slippery slope leading to Hitler. Suburban parents, and especially suburban Jewish parents, raise their children with an extensive knowledge of the Holocaust. Many suburban kids, raised in comfort and affected by the politics of victimization, approach the Holocaust with knowledge but little understanding. Their urban counterparts, reared in an atmosphere where genuine evil is common, approach the Holocaust with understanding but little knowledge. And it is a lot easier to impart knowledge than understanding.

"Two nations . . . as if they were inhabitants of different planets"
Though drug use is common in both Americas, there are qualitative differences. Send a Martian to the twentieth reunion at any of the top colleges in America after the year 2000. Will he be able to detect who was decadent and who was not; who smoked

pot and who studied; who spent Sundays in the infirmary, hungover, and who spent them in the library? Not likely. How many addicts will he find at the reunion? How many unmarried single mothers? How many ex-cons? How many classmates will have been killed in gang warfare? Very few. No matter what these people say about "liberation," "finding oneself," or "experimentation" in college or a couple of years out, they will all end up living like bourgeois squares.

Of course, there are the rare cases of those in bourgeois America who do not stop their self-destructive behavior. What happens to them? When they fall, there is a complex array of mechanisms designed to protect them from the consequences of their misguided behavior. First there is an internalized mechanism that prevents middle-class kids from going too far. This mechanism is subtle; it cannot be explained, taught, or imitated. As a result of living among so many successful people, most affluent youth are able to mature almost immediately, as if on command. Half or so of the students at any top college will go through the same routine: Spend freshman and sophomore year drinking and carousing; spend junior year easing up a bit; spend senior year in interview clothes, as sober as the designated driver in a beer commercial. The second safety net is parents. Parents can provide several things: Military school is one option: drug rehabilitation is another; psychological counseling is a third. These all have a chance of working and can be purchased for a moderate amount of money. Should these fail, there is always the legal system. The prospect, or even the suggestion, of spending a night in jail—especially among the most violent residents of the already strange other America—will make most middle-class youth reconsider their behavior. The threat of incarceration has a way of concentrating the bourgeois mind.

While bourgeois students are often shielded from the consequences of their misbehavior the same cannot be said about their inner-city age-mates. The latter have none of the safety nets of the former. Having very few successful adults in their midst, inner-city kids do not possess that inexplicable sense of when and how to mature. Marijuana use in the city quickly escalates to crack, a drug as real to the suburbs as are polo fields to the cities, and inner-city parents rarely have the resources or the wherewithal to obtain the professional help that is readily available to suburban kids.

The same dichotomy between suburban and urban kids applies to teenage sex. Suburban teenagers engage in it all the time, with few noticeably negative consequences. But it yields the most destructive pathologies in the inner city. A handsome, charming, but immature young man in the suburbs is a delight, a legend, even if he's a rogue. But when I saw such qualities among one of my students in Jersey City, I could only dread the inevitable. Girls swooned over him, and he took advantage of the delicious opportunities. Nine months later his life was irrevocably changed, although he was still getting Frank Sinatra detentions.

Young people in both the cities and the suburbs violate the rules—often in the same ways—but experience drastically different consequences. If we are going to stop accepting the unacceptable in the cities, we must do so in the suburbs as well. The exquisite sense of fairness among inner-city kids demands no less. The fact that different consequences are attached to the same kind of behavior is irrelevant. Behavior standards seek their own level across the two Americas. In order to realize the dream of inner-city transformation, the youth outside of our urban areas will have to start behaving responsibly, even if the consequences of their wayward actions are not so obvious, even if there are no negative consequences at all.

For two generations, suburban Americans have been exhorted to discharge their social responsibility to other Americans by paying high taxes to support expensive government programs. But it is too easy just to write a check. And as the ancient principle of the civil law makes clear, if a contract seems too good to be true, it is probably just that. Solving complex human problems with money is an idea that is too good to be true. The two Americas could never be connected with a bridge of green.

As we enter the new century, it seems as though there are two ways to connect the two Americas. First, it is important to realize that behavior across the Americas seeks its own level. Young people everywhere are promiscuous, but only those in one America become pregnant. Young people everywhere use drugs, but only those in one America are felled by crack and crime. Young people everywhere listen to rap, but those in one America act on it. And so on. If the youth of middle-class America act more consistently bourgeois, it will not take long for inner-city youth to follow.

What form would this behavioral reformation take? It would require a thousand small compromises—and some big ones. Take drugs, the root cause of many of the ills afflicting the cities. Most people intuitively realize that drug use is deeply wrong. It is simply wrong for people to risk their safety, dull their brains, disappoint loved ones, and surrender their rationality for a cheap physical thrill. But how do we stop drugs, which are prevalent in both the cities and the suburbs? Forget education. The students of both Millburn High School and St. Luke have so much drug education that the students ought to get a degree for it when they graduate.

The solution is to punish drug use harshly, everywhere. If someone uses a car to buy drugs, the government should take the car and sell it. A school like St. Luke could use the money. If someone is caught with marijuana, he should have to perform one thousand hours of community service, doable over five years. That punishment would deter drug use and would have the happy consequence of providing our public places—parks, schools, roads, nursing homes, and bridges—with the upkeep that thousands of hours of community service would provide. It would also provide those who obviously have too much time on their hands with a constructive outlet for their energies. Seeing the fruits of their physical labor, they will come to appreciate abilities and gifts they may never have noticed before. This kind of punishment would entail a lot of sacrifice: it is a lot harder for a parent to see his child punished with a thousand hours of community service than to pay an extra one thousand dollars in taxes. But if we are serious about inner-city problems, this kind of sacrifice will be needed.

Bourgeois America can also help poor children in the inner city by providing role models, properly understood. I say "properly understood" because the idea of role models is so often grossly misconstrued. Take, for instance, the June 26, 1995, issue of the New Republic. In it the astute and insightful columnist Robert Wright, the author of a wonderfully learned book of psychology, comments on Bob Dole's now famous speech about Hollywood: "Bob Dole can't much change inner-city music tastes (that's a job for Michael Jordan)." No, it's not. Inner-city kids, like everyone else, think Michael Jordan is terrific, but the affection someone feels for such a figure is inherently shallow. Michael Jordan could spend every hour of the off-season preaching to kids the virtues of hard work, discipline, and abstinence from drugs and sex, but he would probably not change the behavior of one inner-city kid. It would be nice if Michael Jordan had such powers, but he simply does not. The great Boston Celtics center Bill Russell knew better: during his career, he refused to grant autographs, telling kids to ask their teachers for autographs instead because teachers are far more important figures in their lives.

Why is Russell right and Wright wrong? Because it is only possible to help someone you know. Inner-city kids will behave like famous role models only when they regard the bourgeois virtues not as an idea but as a code, a code followed every day by lots of people they know. It is not enough for kids to know that they should stay away from drugs and irresponsible sex and that they should work hard and go to church. They need to know, love, and be loved by people who do all of these things—and more. This idea is taken for granted in the suburbs; no one ever suggested to me or any of my friends when we were growing up that we ought to look up to Larry Bird as our role model. If Bird were busted for cocaine, we would not have traded in our schoolbooks for crack pipes. Our parents would have told us that Bird's misfortune was too bad for him but that we still had homework due for Mr. Sachsel tomorrow morning and that it better be done— and done well.

Just as absurd as the role model example is the notion advanced by Helen Straka of the United States Department of Education in defending her agency's $14 billion budget: "By having a Department of Education you're saying the kids are number one, and there's someone in Washington who's their friend, who's pulling for them." Not one of the kids I knew at St. Luke was aware that the Department of Education exists, and they do not need friends in Washington any more than they do on the Chicago Bulls. Far more important than strangers in Washington who think that kids are "number one" are teachers who give a lot of homework and parents who see that it gets done.

There can be no substitute—not Michael Jordan or friends in Washington—for close, personal daily contact with successful people who live according to bourgeois virtues. I have never heard a student reject the temptations of the street on account of an inspiring speech by a famous athlete. But I have heard lots of students talk of honoring their parents, teachers, ministers, and God.

So the bourgeois should adopt the maxim of Glenn Loury and realize that the problems of the inner city can only be ameliorated "one by one from the inside out." A great tragedy of the modern welfare state has been in inculcating the belief that one can discharge his social responsibility by sending a big check to the tax man every April 15. That is a delusion, a cop-out, an easy way out of a very difficult situation. It is much simpler to send money than to spend time; it is much easier to debate government spending than it is to curb self-indulgence. What is needed is not monetary gifts but social intercourse.

How is such social intercourse achieved—in fact, how is it being achieved right now? There are an infinite number of ways. People with a thousand dollars to spare can sponsor an inner-city student at a Catholic school, not only paying half of his tuition but also supervising his grades and conduct. Others can give their time, perhaps coaching a team or teaching a trade to inner-city kids. Just as there are future doctors and lawyers among inner-city kids, so are there future carpenters, plumbers, soldiers, and craftsmen. Our society may glorify the former, but there is enormous potential among students who could succeed in the latter occupations. And there are other, less obvious, avenues that could be taken by interested individuals. It would be wonderful if a private group could set up an 800 number that interested and qualified college seniors looking for social service work could call, and—if qualified—be guaranteed a job. That way, promising graduates would not have to spend months frantically searching for a $20,000-a-year teaching job when their peers have lined up employment for several times that salary on Wall Street.

There is also an important role for an active, energetic government. A year of mandatory national service for young men and women between the ages of eighteen and twenty-four would be ideal. As William Buckley points out in his book *Gratitude*, we hear a lot about the debt that criminals owe to society, but how about the rest of us? Buckley's debt metaphor is a useful one—properly understood. We can owe a gambling debt to a bookie or a mortgage debt to a bank. The first is something we have to pay or else, and we receive no benefit for doing so. The second is something we want to pay; indeed, having such a debt is connected to the American dream. The debt young men and women would repay through national service is of the second kind. For national service would, after all, most certainly help those who "serve" far more than those who are "served." Indeed, it would break down this dichotomy. From Walt, Cynthia, Maura, Celeste, Charles, Mr. Harrison, Paul Murphy, Father Peter, Sister Peter and so many others, I learned more in my one year of teaching than in any five as a student.

What about the conservative objection to national service on the grounds that true community service must be voluntary? Sure, it would be better if all kids wanted to go to school, but we don't take that chance. As a society of mature adults, we have no problem asserting our authority and requiring that kids go to school. Whether they want to or not is of no consequence, nor is it controversial that we spend large amounts of money on educating our children. Why not apply this logic to mandatory national service? It is the best education we can give young people between the ages of eighteen and twenty-four, and it can help them to begin to discharge a debt to America, as they develop a sense of service and sacrifice that may last a lifetime. It is probably no coincidence that the best generation of students this country has ever known—and the best generation of Americans as well—were those who fought together in World War II and went to college as mature veterans on the GI Bill. It is impossible to replicate that experience, of course, but war is not the only way to elicit the values of national service and patriotic commitment.

The recent efforts of many of the most important American institutions—the federal government, elite universities, and some corporations—to channel our natural communitarian instinct have often been grotesque and destructive. High schools, colleges, and even corporations sponsor "sensitivity sessions," "diversity training," and "prejudice reduction seminars." All are manifestations of the idea that people of different races and backgrounds need the assistance of experts to help them get along. Instead of all of this nihilistic victimization and solipsistic feel-goodism, which conveniently ignore the real problems of society, national service would bring all kinds of people together to serve real, valuable, identifiable, tangible goals. Whether by working together to introduce a class of youngsters to the wonders of science, to build a home for a low-income family, to replace the roof of a church in need of repair, to fix the potholes in a highway, to ameliorate the loneliness of the homebound elderly, to reclaim a park from drug dealers or a street from muggers, national service would lead young people from different backgrounds to see beyond their parochial identities as they work together to serve a noble goal of which all can be proud. As such people work together and live together—as their lives become inextricably intertwined—they will learn about each other in ways they can articulate and in other ways they cannot. And the communities they serve will be better off for it.

If a full-blown plan for national service is not possible, an extensive expansion of Americorps is second best. Conservatives complain that Americorps spends too much and supports some useless projects, but what is a conservative if not someone who realizes that every good idea has costs? And what are the costs of national service? It does not contribute to single parenthood, family breakup, or a culture of entitlement where something can be had for nothing—the real costs of the welfare state as we know it today. The interesting question is not whether national service is always helpful and perfectly efficient but whether the inevitable waste is offset by something more valuable. For anyone who has participated in anything like it, the answer is obvious.

In *The Other America*, Michael Harrington wrote, "That the poor are invisible is one of the most important things about them. They are not simply neglected and forgotten as in the old rhetoric of reform; what is much worse, they are not seen." When the two Americas see each other, they will invariably discover great similarities and great differences. They will find that they have a lot to teach each other and a lot to learn from one another as well. And once that meeting begins—person to person, face to face, as equals and as partners—those in both Americas will be delighted to see suspicion, fear, and despair transform into hope and regeneration.

Acknowledgments

I did not plan to write *In the Classroom* when I began teaching. It happened quite by chance, and there are a number of people who deserve my deepest appreciation for their efforts in making this book possible.

First is James Q. Wilson. I met Professor Wilson when I was a senior at Williams College and involved in researching my first book, *The Neoconservative Vision: From the Cold War to the Culture Wars*. He asked me what I was doing the following year, and I responded that I was hoping to teach high school in a northern New Jersey city. Professor Wilson heartily encouraged me, adding that I must write to him about my experiences in the classroom. I began doing just that in September, and Professor Wilson wrote detailed letters back, providing me with invaluable insights into many of the larger issues and problems with which I was coming into contact. At one point in the fall he mentioned that my letters would constitute the basis of a book. I did not believe him. In any event, our exchanges continued throughout the year, and at an even brisker pace as we switched from letters to e-mail. Suffice it to say that without Professor Wilson this book would never have been conceived, let alone written. Aside from all the monumental help that he provided in my teaching and writing, the idea that one of America's greatest political scientists would take such an active interest in the workings of a single high school classroom three thousand miles away was a great inspiration to me.

In December, the editor of *Commentary*, Neal Kozodoy, sent me a note asking how I was doing. In response, I combined several of my letters to Professor Wilson and sent a letter to Neal. Two days later he called to say that he wanted to publish my letter to him as an article in *Commentary*. I was delighted. "In the Classroom" ran in the January issue. David Brooks, then the op-ed page editor of the *Wall Street Journal*, called to ask if he could condense my letter for his newspaper. It ran the following day.

On the same day that David Brooks asked for permission to condense "In the Classroom," I received a call from Chris Calhoun, an agent with Sterling Lord Literistic in New York. He had read the *Commentary* article and wanted to know if I would be interested in turning it into a book. Remembering that was what Professor Wilson said would happen, I replied, "Sure." We met the following afternoon after school, and we hit it off immediately. Chris put me in contact with Mitch Horowitz of The Free Press, which, Chris reminded me, had recently published *The Moral Sense* by James Q. Wilson. Now I am proud to count Chris among my closest friends. As good an agent as he is a friend, Chris manages to combine an excellent business sense with intellectual incisiveness and deep loyalty.

Chris did many, many things right by me, but nothing could possibly equal his introducing me to Mitch Horowitz, who edited this book at The Free Press. My first meeting with Mitch lasted nearly four hours, and I walked away not only with an armful of Free Press books but with the confidence that a very special person believed deeply in what would now surely become a book. Mitch worked with me in devising an outline for the book and a proposal, which he presented to his colleagues at The Free Press. Three weeks later a phone call from Mitch verified that what I once considered a flattering suggestion from James Q. Wilson would become a reality. If I were only casually acquainted with a man with the deep compassion, warm kindness, and exquisite professional gifts of Mitch Horowitz, I would consider myself very lucky. To be able to work with and be a friend of such a man is nothing short of a blessing. My affection for Mitch and my appreciation for all that he has done is beyond articulation.

I am also grateful to Andrew Sullivan, the editor of the *New Republic*, for soliciting and publishing "Race, O.J. and My Kids," which forms the bulk of chapter 6 of this book.

I owe much to two extraordinary teachers and mentors: Mr. Gerard Sachsel of Millburn High School and Professor Jeff Weintraub of Williams College. It was Mr. Sachsel who ignited my interest in history over a decade ago as I sat enraptured in a seventh-grade classroom at Millburn Junior High School listening to his lectures. We have stayed close over the years, and I relied on him completely when I taught at St. Luke and wrote this book. He not only gave me recaps of his best lectures to deliver to my students but provided me with invaluable insights based on his thirty years of teaching United States history. Without his influence, teaching would not have been nearly as much fun for me or as productive and this book would have been radically different—or nonexistent.

Jeff Weintraub is the most eclectic man I know. Fortunately for me, his generosity of spirit is as boundless as his knowledge. I would often call him to describe an incident that happened in my classroom that day; he would immediately connect it to a historical event or a social trend in a way that made seemingly random events seem perfectly correlated. I learned many, many lessons from Jeff; among the most lasting are that everyday actions are pregnant with social significance, that people do things for moral reasons, and that the gateway to understanding others is to figure out those reasons. Those lessons were with me every time I stepped in front of a class.

There are a number of friends, colleagues, and teachers who read the manuscript or parts of it and provided me with valuable advice, encouragement, and suggestions. I cannot possibly name all of them, but the following people in particular deserve special recognition: Adam Bellow, Don Carlson, Richard Carlson, Tucker Carlson, Kathy Cooperman, Kristin Daley, Jon Fielder, Gertrude Himmelfarb, David Klinghoffer, Eugene Kopacz, Irving Kristol, Cassie Motz, Michael Novak, Jorge Pedraza, Julie Ruder, Adam Scheer, Arthur Shay, Elena Vega, and Karl Zinmeister.

I owe much appreciation to the students and the faculty of St. Luke. I could not have asked to work among a more interesting, dedicated, and supportive group of people. They made my first job out of college one I will always treasure with the fondest of memories.

Most of all, many thanks go out to my parents, Susan and Michael Gerson, for providing me with the most wonderful home and family that anyone could dream of.

About the Author

A 1994 summa cum laude graduate of Williams College, Mark Gerson is a student at Yale Law School. He is the author of *The Neoconservative Vision: From the Cold War to the Culture Wars* (Madison Books), the editor of *The Essential Neoconservative Reader* (Addison-Wesley), and a contributor to *The Neoconservative Imagination: Essays in Honor of Irving Kristol* (American Enterprise Institute Press). Gerson's essays and reviews have appeared in *Beckett Basketball Monthly*, *Commentary*, *First Things*, *The New Republic*, *Reader's Digest*, the *Wall Street Journal*, and other publications. He has also served as the editor-in-chief of *Steve Hawes Fantasy Basketball* and *Fantasy Hoops*. He lives in Short Hills, New Jersey, and New Haven, Connecticut.